multi layered

engineered variety

multi layered

engineered variety

Birkhäuser
Basel

sbp
schlaich
bergermann partner

multilayered—engineered variety

The title of our book may seem puzzling at first glance and some readers might wonder why we have chosen to call it *multiple layers—engineered variety.* Two years ago, we began thinking about a follow-up to *The Art of Structural Engineering, Light Structures,* and the volume in the *DETAIL engineering* series. It didn't take long to identify a number of key aspects of our work that seemed important to us and deserved publication.

Before choosing the actual content, we considered the questions of whether the book as such is still a viable medium in our digitized world, and whether it is adequate for presenting our way of working. Nowadays, doesn't a publication have to appear online in order to be continually updated? This led to a passionate debate among us. In the end, we agreed that a book about schlaich bergermann partner would also serve as a personal record of recent years, which would be indispensable because of the topics that it covers, and which would give pleasure not only to others but also to ourselves. So really, a book just for ourselves? No, because that would not do justice to its contents. We are sure that the issues, as we have experienced and addressed them in the book, will also arouse the interest of others—not least because they give insights into the design culture at schlaich bergermann partner.

Once this decision had been made, we were faced with a wide variety of possible content to choose from, ranging from the many projects on which we had worked since our last book in 2012 to innovations in geometry optimization and in form finding, as well as rapid development in the solar energy sector, and unbuilt ideas. We also considered topics such as our sketch-based working method, and the locations and circumstances in which our projects are built all over the world. In short, we wanted to show the full diversity both of our work and of the team at schlaich bergermann partner.

We believe that the complexity of planning tasks that exists today can only be tackled and managed by well-coordinated designers in a partnership of mutual understanding, which is how our own team functions. In this respect, what schlaich bergermann partner has achieved in recent years is the sum of the contributions made by each employee. We, the partners, see ourselves as the initiators of these feats, as sources of ideas and inspiration, but only by working together as a unified team are we able to turn our ideas and visions into reality.

We want this book to reflect the versatility of our team and the many facets of our work, which is why it is built up in layers. These are experienced as separate parts, visually and tangibly, while their contents remain interlinked. Additionally, the analog content is supplemented with digital content (for more details see front cover flap), which can be viewed in parallel or separately You can, of course, read the book in the traditional way, starting at the front and finishing at the back. Alternatively, you can jump from layer to layer, following a thread of thought or an internal connection, and pause to delve more deeply into a particular topic or browse a *set of pictures*. This book is meant not as a textbook but as a window onto the world of our work in all its breadth and creative energy. We hope it will give you an idea of what we are passionate about and will encourage you to contact us in person with your own thoughts, because what makes schlaich bergermann partner special is best experienced when you work directly with us.

↘ 52

Perhaps this book will be the first step on a shared journey. On behalf of all the partners and staff, you are very welcome to join us.

Sven Plieninger

Layer 01

Working Methods

by Clementine Hegner-van Rooden

I have been allowed the opportunity of shadowing, questioning, and looking over the shoulders of the people who make up the consulting engineers schlaich bergermann partner (sbp). For over a year I have been at their sides in meetings, workshops, and discussions, and chatted with them during lunch and coffee breaks. Gradually, I have been able to peel away the layers one by one and discover what lies behind that well-known name.

The result is a progress report, a snapshot of an engineering consultancy's dynamic history that is far from being over. From its offices in Stuttgart, Berlin, New York, Paris, São Paulo, and Shanghai stems a continuous flow of buildings, bridges, and other impressive structures. Some are dynamic, elegant machines, while others are first and foremost virtuous, slender structures—always precise and cleverly thought out, right down to the details. The projects appear just as dependably in the industry's specialist literature as they do among the prizewinners of major design competitions. Looking at the list of almost 3,000 projects and recognizing many notable building works by their name or their picture, I found myself questioning in more than one case how that happens. While walking through the modern offices and looking over the shoulders of the staff, I wondered how they arrived at such a productive and creative method of working.

After many hours of observation, I had the answer and it was so obvious, even in how their projects themselves come across: sbp strives for balance—not only in the design for each project but also in the design team. Therefore, the structures are based on a balanced interplay of forces and the team on a balanced interaction of members. This aspiration is the most important prerequisite for good structures. Only in this way can projects emerge that accord with the values and guiding principles applied from the time sbp was founded in 1980. Building culture is indivisible. Appropriate design and ecological efficiency are on an equal footing with functionality and architectural quality. Form and load-bearing structure convince the beholder when they merge into a single, self-explanatory whole that can be understood as part of a comprehensive "Baukultur".

The values sbp live by at work are an important part of the corporate culture. That became especially clear to me during an inspiring presentation by Mike Schlaich in front of all his employees: ***"I want everyone who works in our office to understand where we come from and what makes us who we are. I want to communicate the passion and pioneering spirit embodied in so many of our projects—and ideally I would like to infect the younger generation with it."***

A working climate characterized by team spirit and lateral organization prevails in the company with the aim of enabling everyone to identify with the values and projects. The free expression of opinion is paramount here. Andreas Keil believes everyone should be encouraged to play an active part right from the beginning, when they join the company as young engineers. He goes on to stress: ***"Strictly hierarchical practices are simply out of date in the modern world. Participative leadership is a much more common approach today—as it was already under Jörg Schlaich and Rudolf Bergermann, when we, today's partners, were the newcomers to the company."*** Sven Plieninger adds: ***"You have to trust people. Jörg Schlaich and Rudolf Bergermann let me handle my first project directly by myself—naturally accompanying me with constructive criticism."*** This way of influencing the future generations of the company is axiomatic and actively promoted. Without asking questions and trying things out, people cannot learn. Everyone must pull together. Thus, fresh views get to mix with decades of project experience and specialist knowledge; the one gains equally from the other. The individual pieces of knowledge are collated within the company and communicated as a consistent and authoritative body of knowledge to the outside. This gives rise to added value for employers, architects, and clients because the whole is more than the sum of all the individual parts. Underlining this thought, Knut Göppert adds: ***"It's just as in sport: the team that leaves the pitch as the winner is not the team with the best individual players but the team that plays the best together."***

The objective of teamwork is to make the right use of every ounce of talent and bring together individual strengths in the right projects. The stronger the team spirit and the cohesion within the group, the easier it is to achieve the set goals. This is also confirmed by Knut Stockhusen: ***"If we are all helpful and considerate to our colleagues and all our individual capabilities are used to best effect, then success is also easier to achieve."*** That is an important aspect because projects are often only achievable by working together as a group.

So far, so good. But how is this team spirit to be promoted amid all the pressures and urgency of the everyday work? Sven Plieninger answers the question in this way: ***"Working together within a team can only happen not only by knowing the individual team members but also by interacting with them."*** Not quite so simple if the team is spread all over the world and has grown to more than 180 members. By giving employees the space and time to enter, maintain, and strengthen the required communication, the partners build the link between each individual's knowledge and a genuine collaborative work effort. Individuals and teams that are committed to networking on a personal and a business level minimize errors that often arise from poor communication or lack of knowledge. Knut Göppert believes that the projects themselves also benefit: ***"The more we know and the more we are able to interlink this knowledge, the more flexibly and inventively we can react to complex requirements and the more confidently we can explore what is feasible and get to grips with what we do not yet know."***

Everyone is involved in this integrated process. Mike Schlaich puts it metaphorically: ***"We pick up the employees and take them with us on the journey."*** And naturally this includes all new employees—as it has been over generations. Jörg Schlaich and Rudolf Bergermann achieved milestones in engineering and passed their way of building and designing on to their successors. The current partners also allow their employees to play a significant part in the development of the project. Consequently, it is sometimes not at all easy to find potential candidates for the team. ***"We recognize from a very early stage of the application process whether the person sitting in front of us is a match for sbp, someone who has a passion for structures, someone who can think unconventionally and has an affinity for architecture,"*** says Knut Göppert. Every new member of staff adds strength to the team. ***"Because we are all involved in the work process, we create a fruitful basis for discussing solutions in a can-do atmosphere. Together we have the courage to make reality what may have been thought impossible,"*** explains Knut Stockhusen.

The five partners give their employees an early opportunity for continuing professional development. Everyone who is willing may and should develop their professional skills in a personal or project-specific context. Those who are willing and able to take on a leadership role are given the opportunity. And others who wish to remain out of the limelight are allowed to contribute in the background. This is the way skills are built up and passed on to others. It is also the way to remain successful over the long term.

Exchanging views and opinions internally is also interdisciplinary: not only in the field of solar energy must structural engineers work with mechanical engineers, energy specialists with physicists, and aeronautical engineers with electrical engineers. With sbp, you will find no siloing of skills. The employees think across disciplines, thus creating added value for present and future projects. After all, collaboration is the foundation of good structures. Cooperation with different disciplines is enriching and stimulating, and generates new ideas. Buildings that arise from real cooperation between the disciplines are the best examples of how synergies can be used across projects and new insights advanced. So we see an increasing number of moveable structures emerging with the development of solar energy solutions, and *the question of form finding* comes up in projects time and time again. With each new cross-connection, sbp extends its horizons and the body of knowledge. ***"That also means,"*** says Mike Schlaich, ***"that we engage with the industry's current challenges. We concern ourselves with questions of energy efficiency, conservation of natural resources, cost effectiveness, and retention of value."*** As Jörg Schlaich wrote in sbp's book *leicht weit—Light Structures* in 2003: ***"Baukultur is the only adequate means of partly making good our destruction of nature."***

28 ↙

Communication tools developed in-house for sbp support this dialogue in and between individual offices. Similarly, the design of the offices contributes to spontaneous meetings and informal discussions. All offices have a common coffee break, which is used regularly for short project presentations. In addition, they also hold monthly events where information is transferred between different offices, where project-specific and internal-office innovations are discussed, attention is drawn to conferences or articles, and lessons learned from completed planning or design processes are shared.

After one of these coffee break presentations about a successful competition for a bridge in China, Sven Plieninger said: ***"The exchange of detailed information and knowledge can function effectively or be improved only if we are actively interested, open, and ready to assist in other areas of work, offices, and countries. This creates the fertile ground for our office culture to thrive."***

The same applies in the workshops, where knowledge transfer and collegial relationships are fostered through projects carried out jointly by different offices—capabilities from Berlin are brought to Stuttgart or knowledge is transplanted from Stuttgart to São Paulo. In addition, there are regular Lunch-and-Learn events with external speakers, and the sbp Academy. These professional development sessions are internally organized and specifically focused on the requirements of sbp projects. Internal know-how on topics such as cables or membrane behavior, dynamic aspects of lightweight construction, or structural details in bridge construction is disseminated at these events. This format enables employees to satisfy their curiosity on different subjects. Special events for entry-level engineers ensure that everyone is supported in their early professional life and that nobody has to rely solely on the skills and knowledge they already had before joining sbp.

To hold the horizontal tubes at here position.
Use catwalk to get more stability.

All partners and project managers with whom I have spoken also emphasize that they themselves want to continue to learn and develop professionally. They are always looking for new information and opportunities to learn something new. They work in an environment of continual change, because when the principle of "old solutions for new problems" does not apply, people must *develop their own solutions.* 251 ↙ This echoes what Albert Einstein once said of his success: "I have no special talent, I am only passionately curious." The basis of innovative activity at sbp is therefore its openness to new experiences—curiosity is one of its core competences. Andreas Keil puts it this way: ***"The creativity embodied in many projects is ultimately a product of our curiosity. That is the basis of our good reputation. And we cultivate this reputation prudently, because it is not carved in stone."***

This wish or desire of sbp to try out and learn from new things as a natural mindset is one thing that marks them as different from other offices. Another is the typical sbp philosophy of storytelling. Stories are an instrument, as old as they are effective, to start a thinking process. A lively story gains the attention of other people much more easily than a sober speech. Stories fascinate people, engage and motivate them to form an opinion. The engineers at sbp know a story about a design, about a structure—from the initial idea through the planning to the implementation. Listeners remember these subjectively cast messages for many years, because they are reinforced by the personal connection with the messenger. Authentically delivered, they also increase identification if the storytellers project themselves as other than infallible—and that is a personality trait approved and encouraged at sbp. Together with their message, it generates the fascination, perhaps even the charisma, that the office radiates. They also drew me in and made me feel a connection to the work and the people.

The stories are part of the history and tradition of the office. They help sbp retain and emphasize its heritage, even with the constant growth of the company and in spite of changing organizational structures, technologies, and media landscapes. They add excitement to the projects, an emotional commitment that flows into the designs. They whet the employees' appetite to work on a project, contribute to it, and cooperate with others. ***"Because,"*** says Mike Schlaich, ***"the effect is better when the design is told as a story. Therefore communication is very important to us. My father was a master at this. With his stories of the Olympic Stadium, the Hooghly Bridge in India, and the solar updraft tower, he inspired and carried us all away."*** Knut Stockhusen added from his own recollection: ***"Jörg Schlaich saw this as a way to infuse vitality, emotion, and color into the world of engineering, which was technocratic and perhaps a little aloof. He always accompanied his theoretical rationalizations and highly technical explanations with impressive examples."*** In easy-to-understand, straightforward language accompanied by illustrative sketches, he rendered the sometimes complex or abstract structures accessible to all—including the lay public. Regardless of whether the listener understood every last detail, they would pick up the main points and, in the ideal situation, be inspired. This approach is very beneficial in discussions with clients, architects, or other project stakeholders. When people communicate effectively, they are able to discuss and evaluate different, sometimes contradictory requirements and have the opportunity to react appropriately to them.

sbp works together with many people on a wide range of project types over both longer and shorter periods of time. The engineers see countless designs with an abundance of climatic, technical, contextual, or local boundary conditions. There are competitions, alternative proposals, conceptual designs, detailed designs … The breadth of ideas—including many that are never built—is large. This multifarious world of thought is a resource for new designs, and each engineer at sbp can contribute to this as an equal partner in the design process. Clients who become involved in this creative discussion and know how to benefit from it can gain great information to advance their projects. Andreas Keil reemphasizes the point in this context: ***"Engineers are frequently seen as number-crunchers for architects, following the architect's proposals without adding ideas of their own. We, on the other hand, always look for other options with the intention of entering into a dialogue with the architect. This is appreciated by many of them, because this interactive and interdisciplinary process leads to fully developed and convincing buildings."*** According to Knut Stockhusen, sbp remains credible ***"because during the design we represent the interests and objectives of our clients and design partners, and with our know-how and all our passion we stand fully behind our projects all the way up to their completion."*** The

↘ 327

numerous *long-term partnerships* of the office are the best testament to this strength, which finds its expression in the complex process of structural design. For the engineer, structural design often means performing a balancing act between safety, cost efficiency, rational functionality, and high levels of innovation and aesthetics. The result turns out well if the designers strive to react sensitively to all these requirements. This inner drive becomes obvious in Mike Schlaich's assertion: ***"We don't allow ourselves to rest until the best solution has been found."*** Then again, for Sven Plieninger, ***"the finished building is the motivation to keep on going. Naturally, there are always projects that never make it beyond the competition design stage. But after putting so much thought into often complex ideas, I would rather like to see them constructed eventually."***

Andreas Keil adds that engineers must develop an acceptance of this design process: ***"It is demanding because it needs effort to design something that appears to be effortless."*** It sometimes seems challenging in that respect to keep the project development perfectly on track, and Knut Stockhusen's observation rings true: ***"We may drift well off course from time to time, making a detour. But this detour has never done us any harm. On the contrary, we find interesting approaches that may fit, if not in this project, then perhaps in another."***

An internal design competition exposed the intrinsic motivation for this design process and put the focus on a deliberate form-finding procedure on display: As part of the Remstal Garden Show 2019, a platform was to be constructed at the **Sieben Linden viewpoint** near the village where Jörg Schlaich was born. There was a lively interest in this competition within the office; 34 employees decided to respond to the challenge. They would do it in their free time and continue with their ongoing projects at work. Following a detailed examination of the proposals, a jury made up of internal and external members chose the winning project. Andreas Keil puts it succinctly: ***"We considered every project individually and arrived at the most technically and aesthetically apt solution for the specified requirements. What was perceived as a fairly restrictive brief concealed an enormous design potential."***

"Creativity in design and contextually appropriate structures contribute to the art of Baukultur" is the guiding principle of the office. Special solutions are designed with this as the theoretical basis. In addition, sbp takes advantage of its many years of experience, the use of innovative technologies, and a coherent choice of materials.

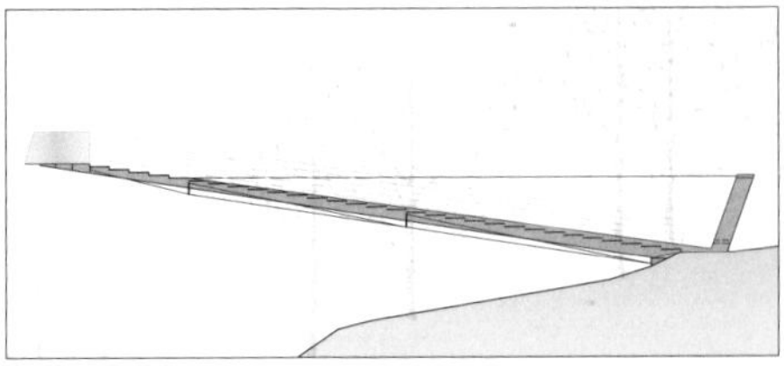

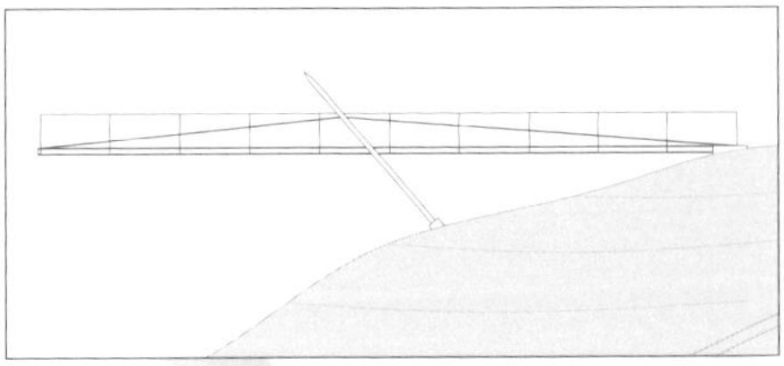

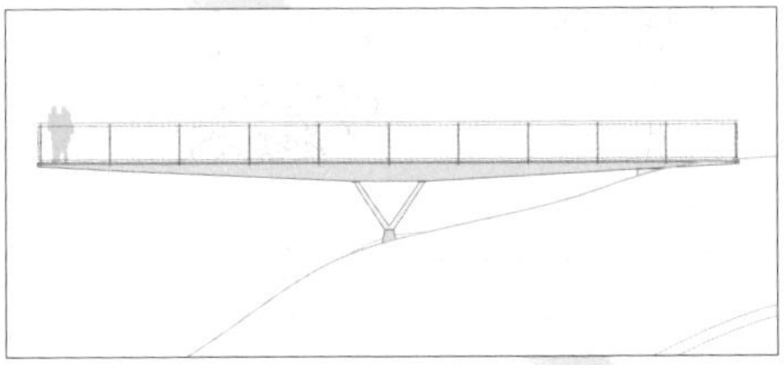

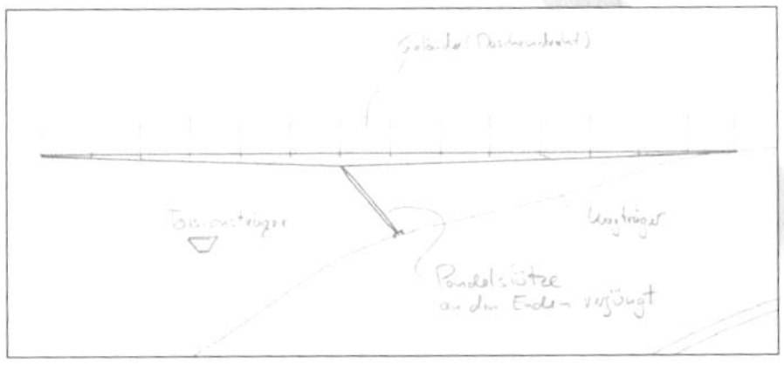

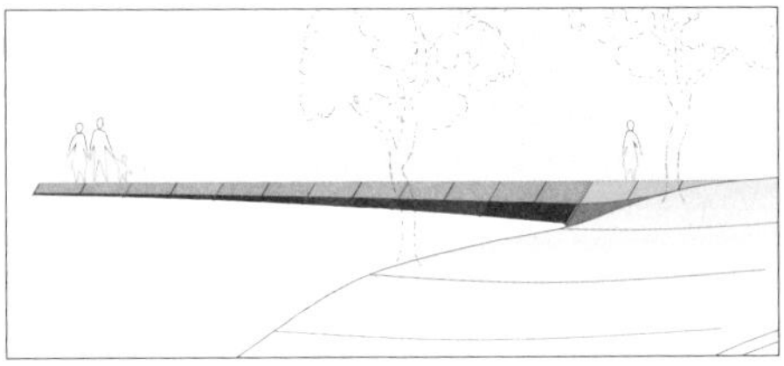

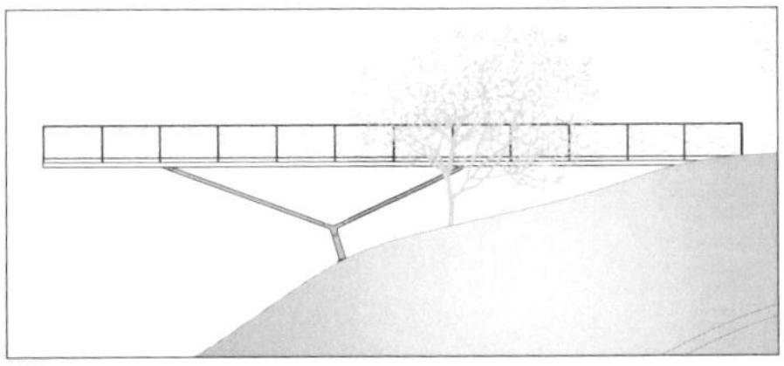

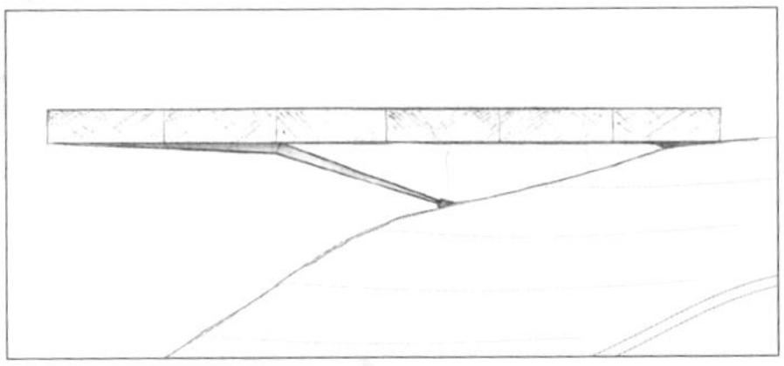

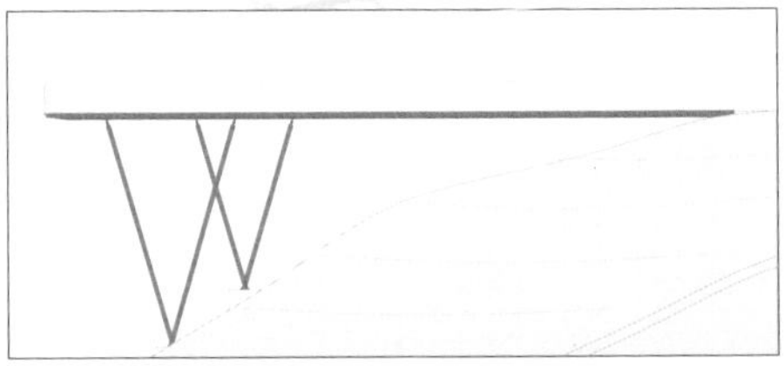

The characteristic traits of the partners vary in as many different forms as there are different sbp projects. However, despite their individual personalities and their different interests and emphases, they show the same passion. They are curious, hungry for knowledge, empathetic, and dynamic. They do not turn their backs on any culture—be that a regional or *international social culture,* or any particular design or architectural culture. This characteristic provides the foundation for sbp's capabilities and performance. Knut Göppert summarizes it like this: ***"The core of our creative work lies in the fact that we have learned to be courageous. And we would like to pass this trait of curious courageousness on to others."*** And Sven Plieninger expands on this: ***"Thanks to our many successful activities abroad, we also contribute to maintaining the good reputation of German engineering."***

↘ 45

It is the shared pride in the projects that motivates the whole team, drives them forward, and is celebrated throughout sbp. Every employee is thoroughly trusted by the partners, which prompts them to identify much more strongly with their projects. Young engineers receive a unique opportunity to build up experience and—with a guiding hand—to bring their own projects to fruition by their own efforts. This process is also interlaced with pain, which is not surprising for something driven by passion. Passion holds potential. And from the released potential comes enthusiasm for more completed projects. As Newton's third law says: Action and reaction are equal. An action gives rise to a reaction.

The result is the balance mentioned at the start of this chapter: schlaich bergermann partner believes in achieving a balance of forces. A balance in which creativity and careful design keep the scales level; in which passion and obligation complement one another. The balance of the collegial interplay of forces, consisting of a creative team of people with various capabilities, is reflected in the resulting multifaceted structures. And from this ultimately arises the creative power of sbp, which has existed at home and all over the world for decades.

I am impressed and doff my cap to the self-composure, patience, and calm of the partners. Because without doubt, during my interviews and visits, all of their construction sites throughout the world have been buzzing with activity. This presence makes clear how trust allows them to spread the responsibility among many different shoulders. This eases the burden on each individual and enables them to bring their abilities to bear. It is smart and farsighted. And it deserves every respect.

Building Construction

Cultural Buildings

Glass

It is the responsibility of the architect to use our knowledge and experience. I often want to tell architects: "Don't shy away from talking to us. We offer added value."

Sven Plieninger

Living the values established by our founders and upholding them in every project often requires an almost unconditional, even idealistic attitude to work. These values, which assume that structural engineers, too, assign importance to architecture as an art, lie at the heart of our practice; they are communicated to—and are instilled in—every new member of staff.

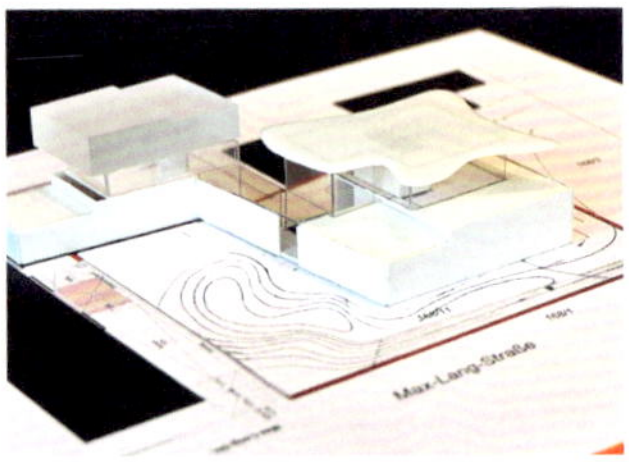

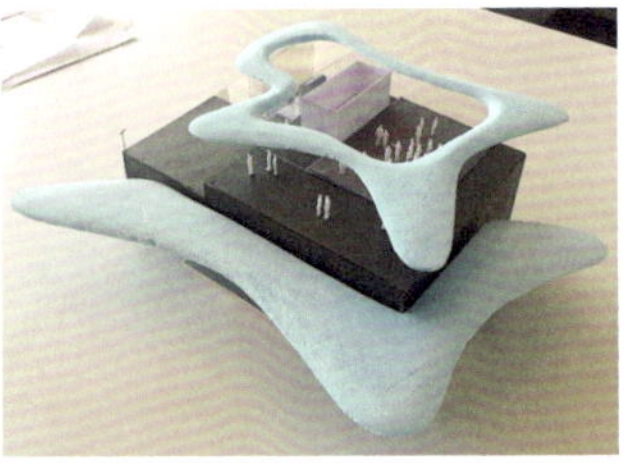

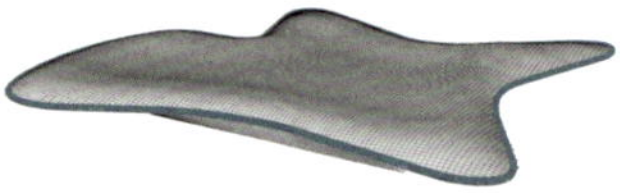

Among other things, we see our engineering work as a contribution to culture. Ideally, the creative and inspiring interplay between architectural and structural design is reflected in an unforced manner in the buildings themselves, as with the **Froehlich Foundation show depot.** The Froehlich commission was preceded by a project for the German National Library in Leipzig, on which we collaborated with the architect Gabriele Glöckler. Collaboration works best on an equal

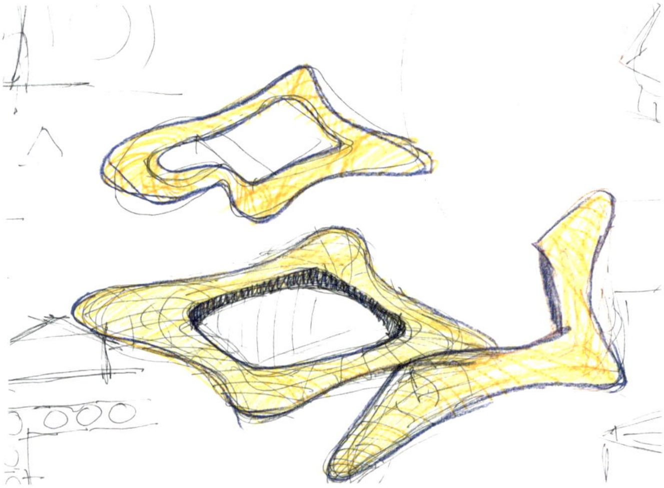

footing. The independent, professional viewpoint of each individual results in a creative whole that is more than the sum of the contributions made by the two disciplines. Bit by bit, the architectural and engineering aspects become ever more closely interwoven, at both the conceptual and constructive levels.

Taking the initial idea of a cloud floating over the building and working it up to arrive at a supporting structure in monocoque construction is a feat that requires a process of abstraction in which the actual load-bearing behavior is broken down into the elements of a structural concept. A complex entity is reduced to a simple, clear, and ultimately calculable static system, whereby the pattern of forces should remain comprehensible.

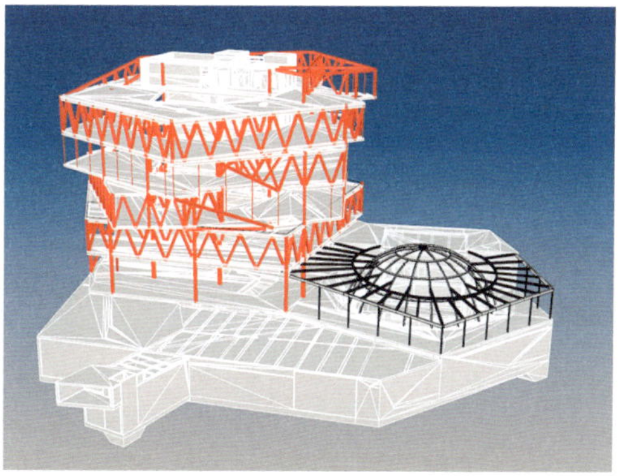

This approach is not based on a rigidly inflexible system. The process is rather governed by complex and sometimes contradictory constraints and by experience. The solution is approached iteratively, but may be guided by intuition.

The **Experimenta** stands on the banks of the Alt-Neckar in Heilbronn and was completed in 2019. The Science Center introduces visitors of all ages to the world of science and technology using an innovative, interactive exhibition concept. The new building is the result of collaboration with Sauerbruch Hutton architects and Drees & Sommer (General Construction Management). It forms an ensemble with the existing building, an old warehouse with an extension dating from 2009. The exhibition space of 7,500 m² is thus boosted by an additional 13,500 m².

The new space is spread over five levels with pentagonal floor plans in a sophisticated geometrical arrangement. Each floor is offset at an angle to the next, creating a twisting effect. The exhibition is accordingly divided into sections, the "theme worlds." These are linked by circulation and recreational spaces arranged in sequence as a spiral. The area of the building's footprint that is common to every floor contains the reinforced concrete core, nearly 7 m wide and 22.5 m tall, which braces the steel composite structure

Owing to the design's geometric complexity, 3-D modeling was used to develop the structure from the start, with parametric modeling, calculation, material selection, optimization, and exploration of alternatives. This was later integrated into BIM software and prepared three-dimensionally for the production process.

AR

of the rest of the building. From the spacious foyer, an atrium rises through all of the floors, and inserted into this volume are heptagonal steel modules housing the "studios." Here visitors can try out the practical applications of what they have learned in the exhibition. These rooms are linked to the exhibition spaces on the respective floor by short steel bridges. The exhibition spaces—organized in four themes from the worlds of natural science and technology—are arranged in a rising helix. They are constructed as Holorib-composite decks supported at the perimeters by floor-to-ceiling steel trussed girders. The glass facade, which is transparent in the circulation spaces, frames views of the neighborhood as a counterpart to the exhibits, some of which are of a microscopic scale. In the exhibition areas, the building envelope is opaque but is articulated in triangular elements that express the underlying structure on the outside. The interdisciplinary work that gave rise to this building can thus be experienced directly in the architectural design, reflecting the dialogue between technology and people that Experimenta represents.

Accordingly, we want our projects—built or not (yet) built—to appear uncontrived and thus, at best, to outlast their time and passing fashions. This is especially the case with cultural buildings, which, owing to the spotlight of public attention, are treated as flagship projects for the construction sector as a whole, in terms of both architecture and structural engineering. Buildings for cultural use ought to create an identity and a sense of place as well as, ideally, serving society as a mirror of its cultural values. This can be achieved not least through high-quality architecture and an efficient, well-designed, robust structure that embodies and complements the architectural concept. This kind of project therefore tends to succeed best when there is genuine dialogue between all of the parties involved.

One such productive dialogue was the one that developed with BIG (Bjarke Ingels Group, New York). We worked with them on a competition entry for the headquarters of the **beverage manufacturer San Pellegrino.** This **flagship factory** project involved creating new buildings, refurbishing existing buildings, and constructing a road bridge. The design was inspired by the brand, translating "purity, transparency, and naturalness" into architecture. The jury was impressed by the architecturally simple and clear vocabulary of the load-bearing structure, consisting of uniform arches constructed completely of concrete, which exemplified a successful cooperation between the architect and the structural engineer.

The concept for the **Art Mill** in Doha owes its memorable quality to a bold, creative intervention. We won the four-stage competition as part of a team with ELEMENTAL, Transsolar, and Stantec. The gallery is to be built near the port of Doha, on the site of a former flour mill. Important goals of the art gallery concept were to integrate the existing grain silos into the design and to condition the interiors in the most natural and resource-saving way. The distinctive cylindrical shapes of the silos defined the character of the location and were to be retained as industrial heritage.

The design by ELEMENTAL, the Chilean architectural practice of Pritzker Prize–winner Alejandro Aravena, proposes interrupting the strict geometry of the rows of silos. This is achieved by adding further silo-shaped structures and connecting the existing grain silos by cutting large openings of varying sizes in their walls. This allows air to circulate through the buildings and facilitates their conversion into

art gallery spaces. The resulting interiors combine old and new and, despite their immense size, form a built work of art that fulfills all of the requirements.

On occasion, the visible structure—most impressively in its purest form—truly expresses the complexity of the engineer's contribution. The **Shanghai Library East** is a particularly striking example of this. Situated in an earthquake zone, the distinctive building, designed by Schmidt Hammer Lassen Architects, represents the efficient solution of a classic problem.

Quite different, but characterized by its structure to an equal extent, is the **Black Forest National Park visitor and information center** at Ruhestein. Designed jointly with Sturm + Wartzeck, EWT engineers, and [f]landschaftsarchitektur, it won an international, interdisciplinary design competition in 2015. The site lies among wooded slopes at more than 900 m above mean sea level (AMSL). The initial inspiration came from seeing fallen tree trunks lying on top of each other, which found architectural expression as a complex of multiple buildings in the form of long, thin bars. Measuring up to 65 m in length, they provide exhibition space totaling 3,000 m². The natural environment of the Black Forest is reflected in the facades as well, which are clad in wooden shingles. The unconventional architectural concept allows the complex to blend harmoniously into its surroundings, despite its considerable size. The highlight of the visitor center is the open-air skywalk at treetop height, 35 m above the ground, which leads to a tower and lookout platform.

The long buildings overlap each other and some are gently inclined at a slope of 3.5 percent. Some of them have point supports, while others are connected off-centre or cantilever out. Their main structural elements are trussed girders made of beechwood, which as a hardwood can withstand significantly higher forces than softwood. The girders form the longitudinal walls of each building, and the wooden roof and floor elements are hung between them. This construction of trussed walls and decks functions statically as a box with point supports, either horizontal or (in the case of the tower) vertical. In addition, some of the buildings have been constructed as "mega-tubes" of construction-size panels consisting of cross-laminated timber. At the truss nodes, the flanges and the diagonal struts have multi-shear connections with slotted plates and bolts. Concrete has been used only for parts of the building that touch the ground, or are subjected to bending or high stress. In certain places, wood had to be replaced by steel. Thus the supporting structure in some sections of wall is a hybrid wood-steel truss. The timber construction method with flexible shear connectors makes the visitor center better able to withstand earth tremors, while the choice of materials is consistent with the design concept of affinity with nature.

AR

Our "art" lies in contributing to an architectural design in the early stages, which in the best case allows the opportunities for a good structure to arise in harmony with it. Andreas Keil

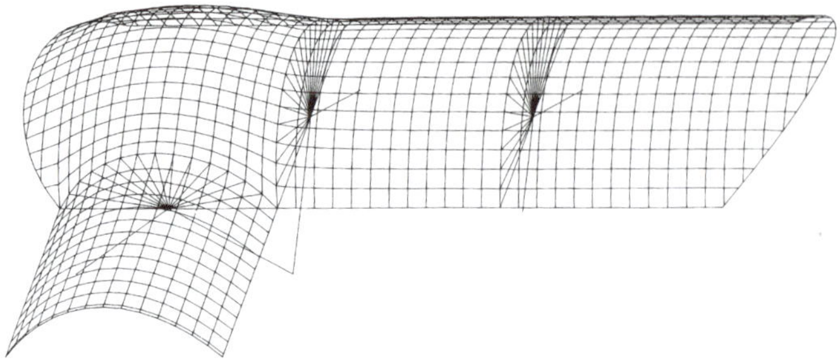

Adding value

211 ↙

The motivation for building glass structures is clear for all to see. It results in highly transparent, lightweight structures that offer protection from the weather yet allow views in and out as well as merging indoor and outdoor space. The building envelope also allows a *degree of climate control that extends the temperate season of the year.* These intentions are perfectly illustrated with the **glazed roof over the courtyard of the Hamburg Museum,** which we developed in 1989 with gmp · von Gerkan, Marg and Partners Architects. A delicate, lightweight lattice shell spans the L-shaped museum courtyard. Sophisticated and elegant, the roof structure is also a groundbreaking innovation, which attracted international attention at the time and since then has often featured in publications and inspired other designs. It was needed so that the outdoor space could function as a continuation of the interior rooms. However, a conventional glazed structure, with a hierarchical geometry of regularly arranged arches and purlins, proved to be unfeasible. It was inappropriate from an architectural point of view, owing to the irregular rhythm of the existing facade; and impossible in structural terms, because the historic building was inadequate for bearing additional point loads. Rather like a kitchen sieve, the glazed lattice of steel mesh, cross-braced by prestressed cables, distributes loads evenly across the existing structure without overloading any one point.

The design, calculation, and dimensioning of transparent shells are complex processes. Construction with glass requires comprehensive knowledge of structural behavior, material science, and expertise in the field of geometry, including the software skills needed for calculation. As engineers, we can achieve the greatest possible transparency and slenderness only if we optimize the supporting structure statically and geometrically, and do so in a unified, integrated way.

The roof geometry is generated by translating a transverse arc along a longitudinal rail (scale-trans surface). The gaps between the roof perimeter beams and the eaves of the building's two wings are closed with inclined panes of flat glass. This means of modeling makes it possible to surface the roof with transparent glass: rectangular panes of flat, laminated glass.

We *refine and adapt existing models* to arrive at new glazed roofs, such as the canopy over the public plaza of the **Ernst & Young headquarters** in Luxembourg, by Sauerbruch Hutton architects. Here we see an extremely shallow variant of the cable-braced lattice shell. The volume below it is trapezoidal in plan, 20 m high and 36 m in length, with considerable spans: 17 m back at the building's main entrance and 42 m where the plaza opens onto the street. In addition to the parameters of the ground plan, there were restrictions on height: the roof was not permitted to rise more than 3.8 m above the top of the last story, and the horizontal edge beam on the street facade was to be at the same level as the eaves of the building's wings so that it could appear to continue as a fine, straight line. This left very little leeway for the rise (the structural height) of the canopy shell. In the first phase of design development, we explored the potential of lattice shells, membrane structures, and cable-supported lattices in countless variations of orientation and arrangement.

↘ 249

AR

The inverted shallow lattice shell proved to be the most suitable design solution—being transparent, cost-effective, and structurally efficient under the given conditions. The requirement to rise from the same height on all four sides of the trapezoidal plaza led to a biaxial arched grid with a variable panel size of 1.7 m × 0.8 to 1.7 m. The lattice consists of standard hollow steel rods with uniform dimensions of 140 × 80 mm and wall thicknesses varying from 8 to 14.2 mm, depending on the stresses. Since the ratio between arch rise and span is only 1:15—the usual target is a ratio of 1:5, or at a minimum 1:10—additional supporting elements have been inserted to prevent problems with the structure's stability, such as warping or buckling. Every second transverse axis of the roof is therefore trussed with cables. These spiral strand cables are prestressed so that dead loads do not cause horizontal deformation at the bearings. Vertical hinged struts are installed between the roof envelope and the cables. When asymmetric loads occur, these pendulum rods activate the truss cables and stabilize them, thus making it possible for the dome-like canopy to have an unusually low rise. Thanks to their small diameter, the struts and cables are barely perceptible. Efficient load-bearing behavior thus combines with sophisticated geometry to create an aesthetically pleasing, delicate roof structure.

The projects demonstrate again and again the potential of glass-and-steel structures, and the variety of forms and applications possible when you build with glass. Sven Plieninger

The aforementioned models find their next stage of evolution in the free-form, sculptural glass roof of **Jinji Lake Mall** in Suzhou, China, completed in 2017. This project, which we planned together with Benoy Architects, combines various static systems as a unified whole, so in a way it symbolizes the wealth of experience accumulated in our office, which we continue to enlarge with each project.

The huge glazed roof covers a shopping and leisure center in the new district of Jinji Lake. As well as sheltering the courtyard from the weather, it links the four seven-story buildings of the complex to form an instantly recognizable landmark. Its shape is supposed to recall the wings of a phoenix. The roof is illuminated at night, making the mall and the skyscraper behind it (named "The Gate of the Orient") into an attraction for many tourists and visitors. The complex is located in an area where strong earthquakes can occur, so this too had to be accounted for in the calculations.

The four buildings of the shopping and leisure center are statically decoupled from each other. Since it connects them, the glass roof had to rest on them in such a way that any forces would be distributed among the individual buildings without the latter transferring stresses to the roof in the event of seismic activity, when each building would act completely independently of the others. Seismic movement joints in the roof were undesirable, as these would interrupt the continuity of the phoenix's wings. We therefore chose a lightweight structure based on the principle of the cable net. Above the large courtyard, the cable net becomes a suspended roof. This is a more efficient way of coping with the long spans of up to 60 m needed there; it reduces bending moments and allows the rods to have narrow cross sections throughout the roof. Formed without movement joints over its entire length of 600 m, the roof can withstand high stresses and large relative displacements of the buildings if they move independently in an earthquake. Instead of the nets of triangular mesh or braced square mesh that are commonly used, we created a flexible square net without diagonal bracing, because it allows change in the internal angles of the mesh and can thus absorb deformation and

The treelike supports, spaced 15 to 25 m apart, reduce the spans within the canopy, which covers 35,000 m²—one of the world's largest free-form glazed roofs. Branching them allows the supports to be slenderer at the roof and shortens the spans in an efficient way.

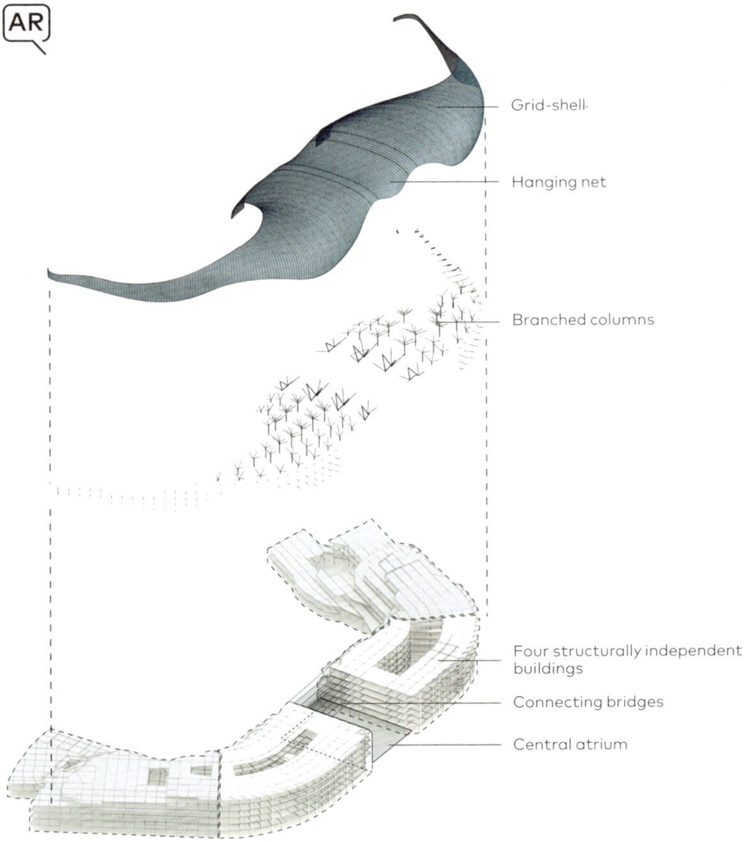

distortion. Furthermore, eliminating diagonal members makes the net more transparent, reduces the number of rods and panels, and significantly simplifies the nodes.

It is usually difficult to subdivide the area of free-form structures into identical smaller areas. Identical components simplify both the production and construction processes on-site, which is economically advantageous. Nevertheless, to standardize the mesh openings as much as possible and thus reduce the number of glass pane types, the surface geometry of this design had to be rationalized within strict boundary conditions with regard to rod length, spatial distortion of the glass panels, and consistency of the internal angles. This was done using subdivision surface modeling, a complex but unified digital workflow and automated process with which the huge geometric shape was developed and prepared for static analysis and optimization. This enabled us to process the numerous static and geometric parameters and their variation in different sections of the roof in a common digital and iterative workflow.

The rational digital process was particularly important for the joints to be formed between the glass panels. Since the internal angles of the mesh change under load, the joints must be capable of absorbing these deformations and must be dimensioned accordingly in order to prevent any contact between adjacent panels of glass. The width of the joint—acting as a buffer for panels of various dimensions—was therefore the critical boundary condition for defining glass panel categories. By making use of these joint tolerances, it was possible to lower the number of unique panels significantly. Finally, static optimization reduced the distributed steel mass of the roof structure to 60 kg/m^2.

The **basketball stadium** in Dongguan, southern China, which resulted in 2006 from a competition entry with gmp · von Gerkan, Marg and Partners Architects, represents a variation of our well-known cable-net facade (Hotel Kempinski). The hall is enclosed by a double-curved cable-net facade almost 500 m long, which varies in height from 16 to 26 m. The form of the hall follows that of the grandstands, but it also alludes to the form of a basketball hoop. With a diameter of about 160 m, it stands on a conical plinth 9 m high, part of which also forms the steps up to the hall. Embedded in the plinth is the central structure: the stadium bowl, which is constructed of in situ concrete and has a diameter of around 126 m. The "basketball hoop" rises from the plinth. Its load-bearing structure takes the form of a spoked wheel with the compression ring beam supported on 28 pairs of columns. The inner supports are hinged columns bearing on the stadium bowl at the upper edge of the grandstands. The outer supports are located in the facade plane as inclined pairs forming a V shape. The hub of the spoke wheel roof, formed as a tension ring with an opening of about 30 m in diameter above the center of the pitch, also takes the 35–40-t load of the mobile video cube.

AR

We aim to combine expertise with creativity in order not only to assist, but also to influence the conceptual development of the project positively at an early stage. Both architects and engineers benefit from the early exchange of ideas. Michael Stein

Behind the V-shaped columns, the circumferential, inclined cable-net facade spans between the compression ring beam and the upper edge of the plinth. Since the panes are double-glazed, the secondary seals are very sensitive to geometric warp, so the cable-net facade had to be designed in a way that eliminated this possibility. The mesh geometry is therefore triangular, consisting of two sets of vertical cables running at an angle to each other and a set of prestressed cables running tangentially. This allows a double-curved facade to be formed with flat panels. The double curvature lends it rigidity, so it can withstand the forces that had to be taken into consideration in the region, from winds or earthquakes, and creates an attractive foyer with benefits for passive climate control behind the transparent facade.

Extending the use of glass

Cable structures with glass and steel continue to evolve. Although glass retains its unfavorable properties when used as a building material, it is *now possible to develop constructions* that eliminate, or at least reduce, the difficulties associated with them. To this day, tensioned cable-net facades have their origins in the solution devised by Jörg Schlaich for the Hotel Kempinski in Munich (with Murphy/Jahn Architects) in 1989–90. His innovation achieved the greatest possible transparency for glass facades at the time and influenced glass architecture significantly thereafter, as it was imitated and adapted throughout the world. The load-bearing structure consists of a flat, single-layer tensioned cable net, at whose nodes the square or rectangular glass panes are point-fixed by clamping plates, which make it unnecessary to pierce the glass.

↘ 214

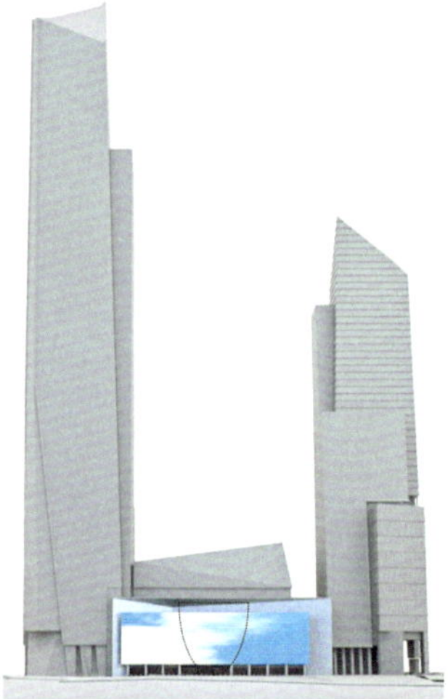

Ever more frequently, our offices are asked to devise glass structures that, in addition to load-bearing, architectural, and structural functions, serve physical and acoustic purposes. That means that for many innovative glass facades, advances also must be made in material technology. A good example of this can be found on the **Hudson Yards Art Wall** on 20 Hudson Yards in New York by James Carpenter Design Associates, for which we worked with chemically strengthened glass. This is one of the first cable-net walls in the world to incorporate individually curved glass panels. The glass panes are individually curved in an inverted J shape. Therefore, instead of mirroring the nearby sculpture and buildings as a flat facade would, they reflect the fluctuating light of the sky.

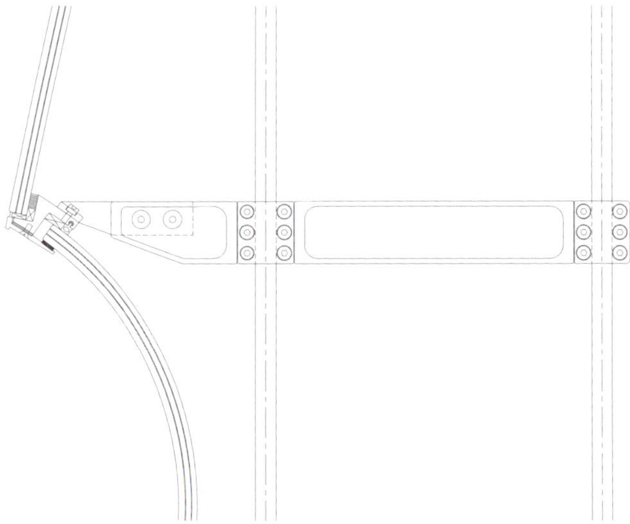

The hot-bent glass is chemically strengthened and is the first example of architectural glass printing directly on an SGP interlayer. A number of innovative details allowed the wall to span across three different primary structure support arrangements while remaining watertight.

On its completion in 2019, **30 Hudson Yards** by Kohn Pedersen Fox Associates became the tallest building of the new neighborhood on the west side of Manhattan. Especially striking features are the observation deck on the hundredth floor, and the specialty facades at the base of the tower.

Cantilevered at a height of 335 m, the 690 m² observation deck has a glass perimeter and is intended to be accessible to the public. Its unparalleled views of New York and the surrounding area are enhanced by walkable glass floors and a gently inclined structural glass parapet with a height of 2.75 m.

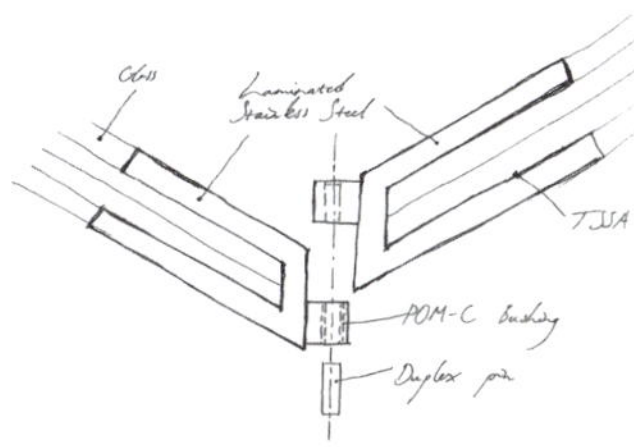

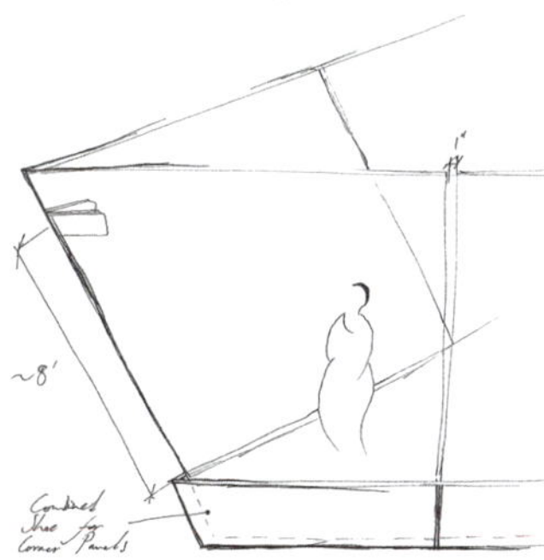

The **Nordstrom Tower,** Nordstrom's first flagship store in New York City, likewise has an undulating facade. Commissioned for the American department store and mail-order chain Nordstrom, the skyscraper rises to a height of 472 m, making it the second-tallest skyscraper in the city—for the time being. The design of the facade, by James Carpenter Design Associates, draws attention to the entrance facade. The facade gives the effect of waves of glass, and even at night it lets passersby see into the building. It looks like a giant glass curtain hanging from the topmost concrete deck of the podium. The horizontally undulating panels span vertically from floor to floor (almost 5.5 m), with no visible vertical supports. The curvature of the panels creates a geometrical stiffness that allows the glass units to span between floors without additional support structure. The challenges, in terms of technology, material, and design, lay in producing four-layer laminated insulating glass with the tight radii needed for the curves.

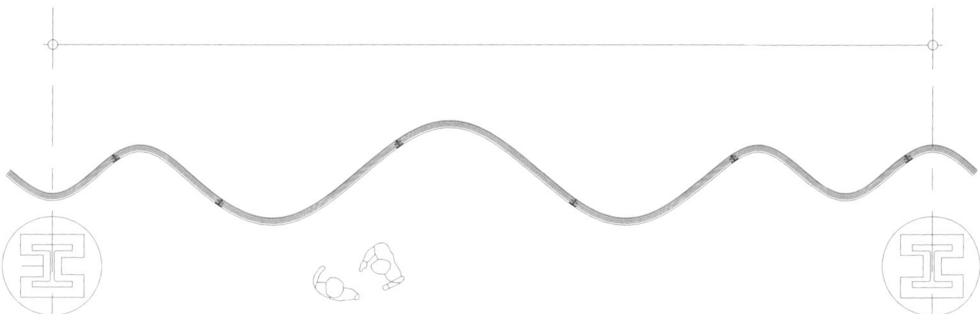

The curves result in differential solar heat absorption, which affects the panel edge stresses, while wind and seismic loads mean that the facade must tolerate a certain degree of movement. The requirement for rigidity together with flexibility was eventually satisfied by devising sophisticated design details. Once again, a construction solution has made a reality of an architectural vision, and here it delivers an eye-catching entrance for a flagship store.

Layer 02

Internationality

We believe that truly good buildings that make a valuable contribution to what in German is called Baukultur—the culture of building—can only be created if they relate to the specific, local circumstances of their surroundings. Therefore, we also base ourselves in the region when we design structures outside Germany. For each project, we immerse ourselves in the context, with different people, cultures, and social and building histories. Proximity to the site and the client is essential for a successful building project.

The international connection is motivating because it allows us to undertake interesting activities in other cultures while expanding our horizons with every project. Our international design offices and their ability to thrive are founded on people who commit themselves in those countries and, with motivation for the subject and an appetite for something new, contribute to the construction industry of these cultures. Through our colleagues who moved to a new country, and complemented by sbp's local employees, we have built up highly capable teams and offices in New York, Shanghai, São Paulo, and Paris.

The change in atmosphere that accompanies a move to a new country provides energy to our employees. We encourage this drive and have established regular sessions where interests, views, and experience are discussed between staff among our offices all over the world. The associated cross-office project work enables our localized collections of know-how to be disseminated, which then become universally available to all employees. To accelerate this process, we also hold workshops every two years in Stuttgart, where all our employees from around the world assemble.

Good ideas need space

The project that symbolically marked the beginning of our activities in the USA was the competition for *One World Trade Center* in New York.

↘ 138

The project was to be built at Ground Zero in place of the Twin Towers destroyed on September 11, 2001. As part of an international team, we participated in this renowned competition and were later involved in the implementation of the project, working with Skidmore, Owens & Merrill LLP. Participation in the competition and the realization of the project were the foundation for the formation of our office in **New York City** in 2004. The transparent cable-net facade and cable-guyed spire of One World Trade Center marked the start of our work in North America. These special lightweight structures are just the kind of construction projects that define our reputation and that we, with our international offices, are well positioned to support and realize within each respective national building and infrastructure market.

In contrast to our activities in the USA, no single, stand-alone project marked the start for our **Shanghai** office. Instead, its work developed from the ever-increasing numbers of projects throughout China; we wanted to be right where we were building to ensure that the projects developed with the quality we intended and at the same time were responsive to the local context, and that we could speak for them with our usual passion.

China's construction industry has grown continuously since the end of the 1990s. This enduring construction boom has led to interesting projects largely because whole city districts or even cities are being created. In the beginning, we worked mainly on public buildings in conjunction with gmp · von Gerkan, Marg and Partners Architects, trade fair centers in Nanning and Shenzhen, and a swimming pool in Foshan, making many new contacts there thanks to our local presence. These new business relationships allow us to make the most of our capabilities and intensify our work with local and international designers, colleagues, and employers. We have designed projects across our full range of activities, such as high-rises in Foshan and Zhengzhou, *the West Bund bridges*, the Shanghai Library, and the glass roof in

↘ 162

Suzhou. These projects confirmed our conviction that a presence in the region, giving us proximity to employers and our design

Stuttgart

Berlin

New York

Shanghai

São Paulo

Paris

partners, has a positive influence on the quality of the structures being built.

The story is similar for our **São Paulo** office, which was set up at the same time as the market for sports venues for the FIFA World Cup 2014 and the Olympic Games 2016 in Brazil was taking off. The design of the stadiums in Rio de Janeiro, Brasília, São Paulo, and Manaus for the World Cup required us to have a continuous presence near the sites. Our Brazil office is now part of our established network and has the objective of building projects all over South America in accordance with our office philosophy. As is the case with all of our smaller offices, in addition to their own skills they can always draw on the experience of all our employees. Thus, they form cross-office project teams that make use of specialist knowledge to suit the specific design task at hand.

Currently, we are working in mixed teams formed from staff in Stuttgart and São Paulo on the Instituto do Futuro in Brasilia, and on a feasibility study for a road bridge to link Brazil's most important harbor at Santos with the city of Guaruja.

Our latest sbp location—the office in **Paris**—was set up at the beginning of 2015. Here as well, the decisive factor was proximity. The teamwork arising from this arrangement is the basis for developing intelligent and efficient structures in cooperation with architects. Making the step to set up an office in Paris—and being locally present—showed our French planning partners our affinity and understanding for the projects in France and laid the foundations for a deeper and successful working relationship. The office has seen strong growth from small beginnings. There have been, for example, projects like the long walkway for the tourist development at *Bastia on Corsica* and the lightweight, transparent, protective glass wall required for security purposes on the concourse of the Eiffel Tower, both designed in cooperation with Dietmar Feichtinger Architectes. Other important milestones included winning the design competitions for Hall 2 at the Bordeaux-Lac trade fair center in 2016 and for the new terminal building at Nice Airport in 2018. All these projects sit comfortably in our portfolio of lightweight, long-span structures.

↘ 187

Our motivation is our passion for quality, engineering, and architecture. Our aim is to bring this passion into every project, so that we achieve the best possible solution in each case. We make our expertise available to do this across linguistic and national boundaries. Andreas Keil

Tradition and history of a structure

Our corporate values are strongly linked with our history. Three projects from the early years of our office spring to mind as having a fundamental influence on how we perceive ourselves: the **Olympic Stadium** in Munich, to which Jörg Schlaich and Rudolf Bergermann made important contributions as engineers with consultants Leonhardt und Andrä; the concept for 222 ↙ the ***Solar Updraft Tower,*** which formed the basis for our specialty in the field of renewable energies; and the **Second Hooghly River Bridge** in Kolkata, India, which was not only a milestone for us internally in terms of major bridge design but also a defining experience of working abroad.

All three projects illustrate the values for which we stand: lightweight construction, individuality, sustainability, efficiency, and, last but not least, a holistic consideration of every design commission. These values give us the wherewithal to arrive at unique solutions. Every one of our projects has its own history, a history that also symbolizes our approach to our work and gives a project its completely individual character.

The Second Hooghly River Bridge in Kolkata was the first of our major overseas projects. The two-masted cable-stayed bridge with two H pylons from which parallel wire cable bundles fan downwards is the result of an intensive, sometimes grueling 22-year design-and-construction process. When it opened in 1992, it was India's first and Asia's longest cable-stayed bridge. It was also one of the first bridges of its type in the world to have a dead load composite deck. What still makes it a special project today is that its design was based on indigenous construction practices. It therefore reflects the immediate economic, cultural, and social environment—and therefore also our attitudes and values. Jörg Schlaich and Rudolf Bergermann conceived and designed the bridge so that it was adapted to local conditions and could be built using exclusively local labor and materials. The methods used were complex but based on current construction practice in India at that time: the steelwork is riveted, not welded, and was done manually. Local tradesmen supplied the necessary skills, and work progressed largely unaffected by daily power cuts on the site and despite strikes, as well as coordination and financial problems.

The composite deck design was further developed and used in 1998 for the **Ting Kau Bridge,** which has main spans of 448 m and 475 m. Here, an even lighter, bolted steel beam grid acts compositely with a concrete deck, in this case consisting of precast concrete units. Their principal advantage is that, compared with in situ concrete, precast concrete units older than six months exhibit much less shrinkage and creep deformation as a result of compression stresses in the superstructure arising from the large cable forces that must be transferred by the concrete slab into the longitudinal steel girders.

Second Hooghly River Bridge (above), Ting Kau Bridge (right)

Further developed over generations

In our recently completed major bridge project, the **Yamuna Bridge** in New Delhi, the composite deck system finds further use in a more refined version. The system originally designed by Jörg Schlaich and refined by Mike Schlaich has thus been further developed through a generation.

The Yamuna Bridge has a total length of 675 m and is a single-masted cable-stayed crossing with a sharply bent, 151-m-high, inclined steel pylon. The pylon legs, which are each supported on a spherical bearing, are fabricated out of rectangular box cross sections stiffened with ribs and come together halfway up the pylon. Above this height, the pylon cross section is V-shaped, with the V opening in the direction of the main span. The four backstay cables and two 15-cable, harp-shaped fans supporting

the 251-m-long main span are attached to the upper part of the pylon, which was fabricated in large segments. The pylon pinnacle directly above the final cable anchorage is a 30-m-high, steel-glass structure that is illuminated at night, allowing the bridge to serve as a landmark. The inclined pylon relieves the load on the backstay cables. Because the pylon's center of gravity is on one side of the pylon foot, it counteracts some of the weight of the superstructure on the other side. This three-dimensional consideration of the stabilizing moment about the pivot point at the pylon foot leads to an efficient structural system. The pylon legs stand eccentrically on the bearings under the bridge deck so that the bending moment created by the bend in the pylon greatly reduces the moment in the opposite direction at the pylon foot.

The bridge is part of a major traffic route designed to relieve existing high-speed roads. The route connects Wazirabad and the Shahdara district in the New Delhi conurbation and carries four lanes of traffic in each direction. The client, Delhi Tourism and Transportation Development Corporation (DTTDC), in the first instance asked only for a concept and feasibility study for the bridge, but in the end commissioned us with the detailed design. The client wished the structure to be a "signature bridge"; in other words, a bridge that would by its size and design become an important and immediately recognizable icon for the megacity.

Like that of the Second Hooghly River Bridge, the composite superstructure of the Yamuna Bridge consists of two edge girders and a central girder, each 2 m deep with cross-beams at 4.5-m centers. Low-shrinkage pre-cast concrete units act compositely with the steelwork. The steel components were not riveted together as in the Second Hooghly River Bridge but instead are connected using high-strength, friction-grip bolts at splice plate and end plate joints. The result is a lighter composite superstructure, which was temporarily supported during construction. The concrete carriageway slab acts like a strut to resist the horizontal force components from the cables. The composite superstructure of the Yamuna Bridge is therefore automatically prestressed or, more accurately, "precompressed."

In this way the equilibrium of forces in the structural system is maintained and the usual complex arrangements for transferring the horizontal forces into the foundations are not necessary.

The client required a landmark that would lend special significance to the location and its surroundings. On the basis of our values, we have created a bridge that achieves an appropriate balance between a well-designed, ingenious structure and this specific wish of the client.

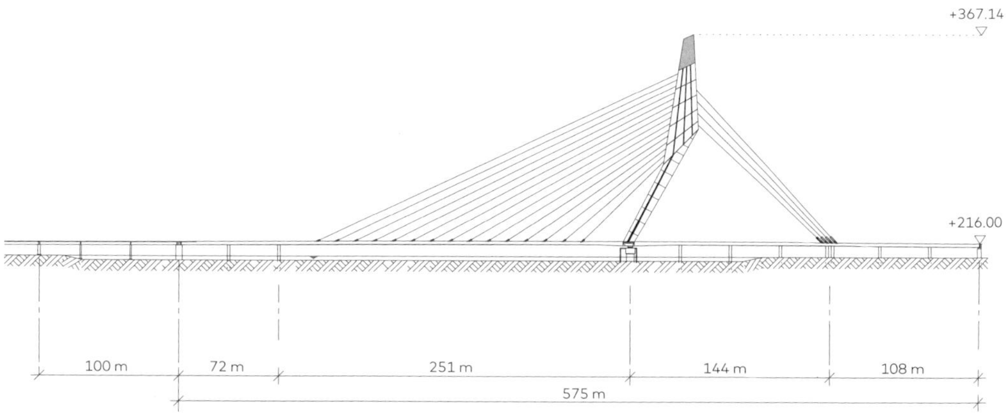

We draw on a vast reservoir of knowledge and experience—including know-how of our own. We learn from that resource, gaining in confidence and reputation. Mike Schlaich

An ornamental graphic making reference to a peacock feather dominates the upper part of the pylon. It embodies in its symbolic nature the image of a modern, striving India.

Building Construction

Infrastructure

Special Purpose Structures

Our strength is that we can design a special and efficient structure that is unique but based on solid and proven technologies and principles.

Sven Plieninger

Public buildings reflect the value that a society places on the art of building. They reveal how we deal with the quality of the built environment and how important society considers this task to be. Our projects show how successful structures can bestow an identity on a place, give a purpose to a particular area, or enhance an entire neighborhood.

40 ↙

In September 2015, the 34th Street—Hudson Yards subway station opened in Manhattan. It was the first new station in the city in 25 years. It forms part of the extension of the No. 7 line through western Manhattan, to the *Hudson Park and Boulevard* redevelopment area. The station is intended to serve the area as a gateway and therefore has to satisfy both functional and aesthetic criteria. The design of two glazed steel canopies, the **Hudson Park Subway Canopies,** as entrances to the subway station, together with a matching steel structure for a small café, was developed from a winning competition entry that we produced in collaboration with Toshiko Mori Architects. These roofs are among the largest subway entrances in the Metropolitan Transportation Authority's network. The steel structure consists of high-performance stainless steel and is therefore corrosion resistant, valuable, and durable. The differently sized, double-curved grid shells with free-formed edge beams each rest on three V-pillars. The rectangular glass panes lie linearly on the grid shell and are point-fixed by clamping plates at their corners to resist uplift forces. Diagonal bracing cables span the rhomboid apertures and are positioned close to the underside of the glass to prevent birds from roosting. Some members of the grid shell have been reinforced to take the load of suspended lighting and signage. The stainless steel members are corrosion resistant and durable.

An equally strong identity is created by **Hamburg Elbbrücken** (Elbe Bridges) metro and local railway station (U and S-Bahn). The former opened in the winter of 2018. Its load-bearing structure is likewise efficient, lightweight, and expressive. It shows that infrastructure buildings can be more than profane functional buildings, and that they can fulfill their purpose at least as well if constructed with an eye to their aesthetic value.

Together with the S-Bahn station yet to be built, the U-Bahn station forms an important infrastructure hub connecting the eastern part of Hamburg's HafenCity (harbor redevelopment area) to the city center. The roofs of both are glazed steel frames forming semicircular vaults—the one more or less circular in cross section, the other shallower. A skywalk takes passengers changing trains from one station to the other; this too is a steel structure, prefabricated in the workshop and lifted into place in several segments.

The supporting structure of the station roofs, which we designed together with gmp · von Gerkan, Marg and Partners Architects, consists of steel arches at 8-m intervals, in two different orientations. The arches cross each other to produce the rhomboid pattern that is a significant characteristic of the design. The maximum dimensions of the U-Bahn roof are 135 × 33 m. In cross section, the system corresponds to a two-hinged arch with a rise of around 15.5 m. At both ends of the semicircular vault, the forces resulting from the interruption of the arch girders are absorbed by stronger edge beams. At the apex of the vault, the edge beams come

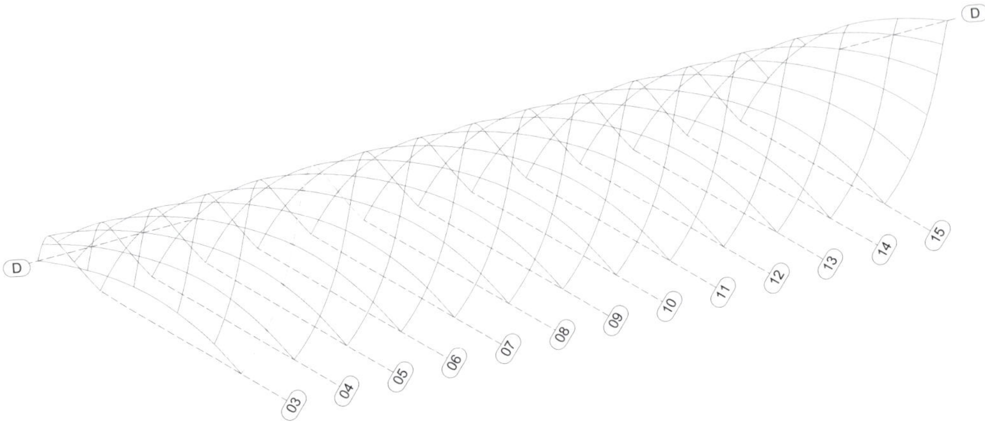

together at an acute angle, as if they were being pulled into the slipstream of outgoing trains. The edge beams consist of box sections; the other primary members are sheet metal girders with efficient I-sections. To maintain a uniform appearance, the flange width of the girders is kept constant at 350 mm. The height of the sections, however, varies along the arch according to the load, from a minimum of 350 mm to a maximum of 600 mm. The structure may appear complex, but it is based on a rational system. The flange plates of the diagonal girders lie on a developable, cylindrical surface that is spanned by a basket arch construction. In this case, the flange plates can be made from straight flat steel with a single curvature. The slightly twisted girder webs, too, can be produced from flat sheets. The inner edge of the web plate is defined by the corresponding radius of curvature of the arch as part of a spiral curve.

The 26 footings of the roof girders and edge beams are connected to the foundation pad via a bolted joint that allows longitudinal displacement. There are 13 footings on each side, of which only the middle is fixed, allowing the roof to expand almost without constraint as the temperature rises. At the northern and southern ends, the roof bears directly on a massive substructure. Above the street that runs beneath the station, however, it rests either on pedestrian bridges or on the platforms.

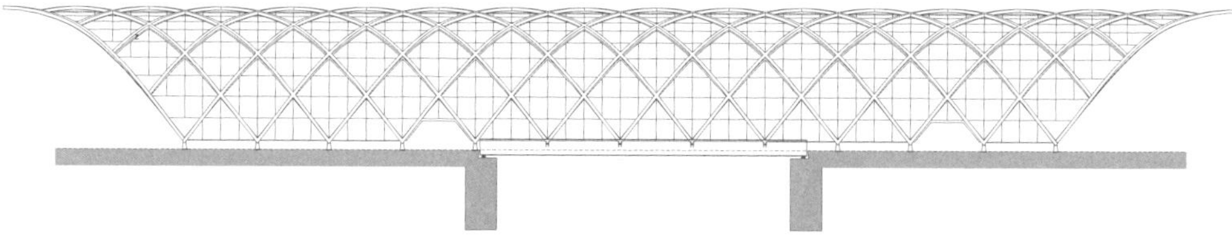

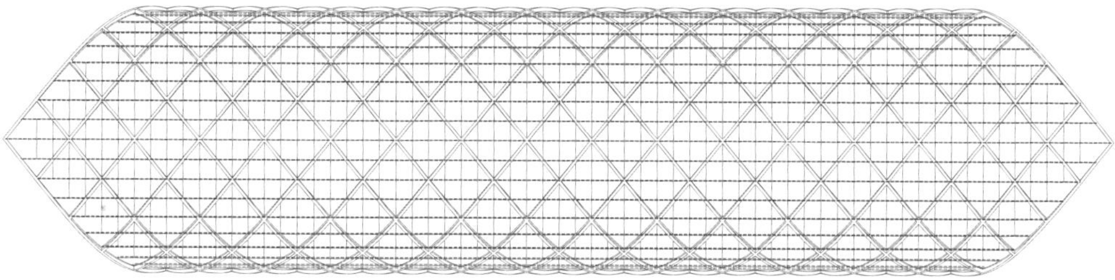

Mounted on the inner face of the girders is an envelope of laminated safety glass with spans of 2.5 m. To preserve the residual strength of these glass panes, two thin stainless steel cables are attached in parallel below each one. If a pane of safety glass gets damaged, it is supposed to stay in one piece and can therefore be stopped from falling by the cables. The glass panels are primarily supported on longitudinal purlins, fixed 20 cm from the inner face of the main structure. This subtle separation keeps the primary structure legible and strengthens the visual analogy to the historic supporting structure of the Elbe bridges in the immediate vicinity. On the skyline of HafenCity, the buildings are modern reinterpretations of their historic neighbors.

In the northern part of the U-Bahn station, a steel footbridge, which is supported by two branched columns situated between the tracks, connects the platforms. This makes it possible to cross the tracks on two separate levels, with the higher platform ensuring additional, barrier-free circulation via elevator. In the future, passengers will be able to access the planned S-Bahn station via a skywalk.

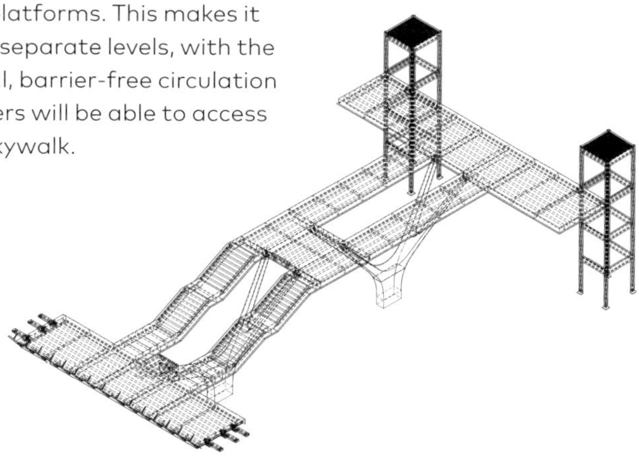

Elbbrücken

Elbbrücken

Another contemporary infrastructure project is **Moynihan Train Hall,** a redevelopment that will significantly improve the capacity and dignity of Penn Station in New York City. Constructed in 1963, today's Penn Station replaced a magnificent Beaux-Arts style train hall designed by McKim, Mead, and White in 1910. The demolition made way for Madison Square Garden, an indoor sports arena, and simultaneously turned a grand gateway to the city into an underground station that is now one of the busiest and most overcrowded in the Western Hemisphere. The redevelopment includes designs by several major architectural practices: James Carpenter Design Associates; Hellmuth, Obata + Kassabaum; and Skidmore, Owings and Merrill.

One component of the phased project is the conversion and integration of the James Farley Post Office from 1912–13, also designed by McKim, Mead & White, and located across the street from Penn Station. Not only will this increase the capacity of the existing station, it will also restore a sense of historical importance to the site.

Inside the former post office, now a protected landmark, two impressive glass grid shell roofs are being installed. These free-form, steel-and-glass structures, the most spectacular part of an extensive engineering project, are the responsibility of our office in New York. One of the roofs will cover the old atrium, where postal workers once sorted countless letters and parcels, and will become the Train Hall. Surrounding the boarding concourse will be a variety of shops, restaurants, and cafés for more than 500,000 travelers and commuters every day. The roof over the Train Hall consists of four double-curved barrel vaults with graceful lattice structures.

The vaults rest on three trusses that were part of the original building. The four vaults span a floor area totaling around 70 m × 50 m. They create a light and airy atmosphere for the hall that provides access to the subway and to the underground platforms for intercity trains.

The second, smaller roof is being constructed in the southern part of the former post office where local trains will leave for suburban New Jersey. A single lattice vault spans this hall and is parabolic in cross section with a rise of 23 m and a span of 21 m.

Both roofs comprise a rectangular grid that is cross-braced by thin diagonal cables and stiffened against unilateral loads by prestressed cable trusses. The steel structures are covered by a total of 2,936 insulating glass panels, which slightly overlap each other like wooden shingles.

This remarkable project achieves a synthesis of the old and the new. It creates an impressive public space for modern rail transport, gives the Farley Building a new lease of life, and stands as a reminder of the hall of the historic Pennsylvania Station.

Investing in lasting projects

Infrastructure projects are often expansive in scope. Their scale is significant; they are complex "machines" for traffic; they are subject to lengthy approval and participation processes; and they often overshoot deadlines or exceed budgets. Moreover, since they are always in the public eye, politics and public relations influence the outcome, adding to the potential risks. If progress milestones or cost targets are not met, the fallout is felt at every level. Professional planning is therefore especially important, with experienced and well-coordinated teams working in close collaboration and on equal footing with the client. Well-organized work processes and clever ideas are influential in every phase of the project and therefore make large projects an attractive and challenging task for us.

Munich Central Station is one such major project. Every day, around 450,000 people pass through it. After a variety of conversions and additions at different times, the current railway station is beginning to show its age. It is due to be replaced by 2027 with a new building designed by Auer Weber architects. Only the railway hall designed by Franz Hart

in 1960—and now a protected landmark—will be retained and, where necessary, structurally reinforced. The three existing forecourts will receive new landscaping and the traffic circulation in the vicinity will be improved.

To find a preferred solution, the City of Munich, the Bavarian Ministry of Economic Affairs, Infrastructure, Transport and Technology, and the German state railway company (Deutsche Bahn) held an architectural competition from 2003 to 2006. After the winning entry by Auer Weber Architekten had been chosen, we were brought onto the team, initially to carry out a feasibility study. Their proposal for a modern transport hub includes a new station concourse, designed as a mixed construction with a glass facade. The rail company's core service facilities are accommodated on seven floors above-ground. The station will also serve as an interchange to the second trunk line of the S-Bahn (local) rail network, with the access at a depth of 40 m. These two projects—the interchange track, or "nucleus," and the station concourse—are closely intertwined with respect to their construction. In addition, a skyscraper is to be erected as part of the redevelopment of another station, Starnberger Flügelbahnhof. It will have a crystalline form with slanting glass facades and a height of 75 m. Once an important hub for regional train traffic, the Starnberg site has lain largely vacant until recently. When the S-Bahn line was opened in 1972, the passenger flows moved underground and the Starnberg station declined in importance. The planned development will reactivate this attractive location. Complex interdependencies with subsidiary projects such as the second S-Bahn tunnel, which is part of the works for the second trunk line, continually generate changes to the schedule, as do the necessary political processes. The need to adapt constantly and quickly to an evolving situation means that individual parameters change again and again. This leads in turn to major alterations in the planning and thus in the structural design. We cope with these twists and turns by maintaining a fresh and inquisitive outlook and never losing sight of the broader picture.

Large projects and their complements

↘ 26

In addition to determination, willpower, and negotiating skills, large projects demand patience. The planning and construction of **Berlin Central Station** was no exception. Thanks to the delicate *steel-and-glass roof structure,* plenty of daylight penetrates the multistory concourse, while the station as a whole has a spacious and elegant appearance. The new building, including fourteen platforms and all the ancillary structures, was constructed in several phases from 1995 to 2006. We won the competition in 1993 together with gmp · von Gerkan, Marg and Partners Architects. The station is a junction between lines running in several directions. The lines are accessed via five circulation levels, with 25 m between the top and bottom levels. It has a throughput of 19 million passengers annually.

The complexity of this major project meant that opportunities for additional projects were always arising. For example, the streetcar line was extended to the **Berlin Central Station stop** on Europaplatz, directly in front of the station building. This new stop is marked by two long, gently curving reinforced concrete roofs. Their forms subtly express the crossing and convergence of different modes of transportation. Their design, which we developed in collaboration with GRUBER + POPP architects, was the result of a competition held in 2011. The entrances/exits of the underground and regional railway platforms belowground, like the streetcar platforms above them, are sheltered by canopies on either side of the tracks. The two symmetrical roof structures are each 58 m long and 6 m wide. They extend from the two centrally positioned shaft walls of the escalators that lead to the platforms below the surface. The canopies project on either side of these cores like pairs of spreading wings, supported only by slender columns along the roadside edge.

The contours of these lightweight structures, which offer a degree of shelter to passengers waiting on the platforms, allude to the changing speed of a tram between one stop and the next.

Each wing is a double-curved surface, with the high point at the end on the side of the tracks and the low point at the cores. The static load is transferred accordingly: towards the middle, where the curvature is greatest, the roof has a significant shell bearing effect, meaning that the loads are transferred via normal forces in the shell plane. At the canopy ends, however, the loads are mostly transferred via bending moments in the roof plate. At the edge along the tracks, the plate is only 7.5 cm thick, increasing to 30 cm along the road-side edge. It is made of lightweight concrete in order to reduce the dead load and make the structure more slender. The use of stainless steel reinforcement takes this a step further by minimizing the effective concrete coverage to 2 cm. The result is a highly efficient static cross section.

At the start of any project, we want to test the limits of what is possible, boldly and with an open mind. Step by step, certain aspects and limiting conditions become clear. Gradually, a solution emerges that can be analyzed more closely. We thus approach each design brief in small steps, up to and including the construction stage.

It was exactly this kind of design process, in which we collaborated with GRAFT Architects, that gave rise to the sweeping **canopy** on the grounds of Volkswagen's Autostadt (car delivery center) in **Wolfsburg.** The elegantly shaped, double-curved structure creates a sheltered place. After visiting the Autostadt and picking up their new car, fresh from the factory, customers can admire and inspect it here, without having to worry about the weather. In plan, the canopy covers an elliptical area of about 1,600 m² with axial diameters of 55 m and 38 m. The double-curved surface is the result of twisting a compression ring, which is supported at its two lowest points. It is spanned by a cable net composed of two orthogonally aligned sets of open spiral cables. The ring beam consists of a welded steel box section with a varying, pentagonal cross section. The roof covering is a thin, PTFE-coated, glass-fiber membrane.

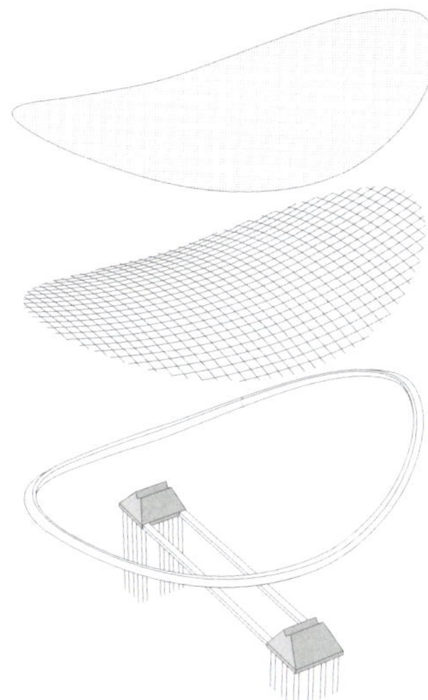

The prestressed structure has a low dead load of only 8.3 kg/m² and is statically determinate. The abutments are founded on piles and are tied together to cancel out horizontal forces. In order to achieve the desired lightness, sophisticated detailing was needed for tasks such as fixing the cable-tensioning anchors to the compression ring. The details contribute significantly to the *structure's apparent simplicity.* The resulting "Pringle," as it is jokingly called after the potato chip, is a structure that has been developed logically and consistently with respect to both statics and form.

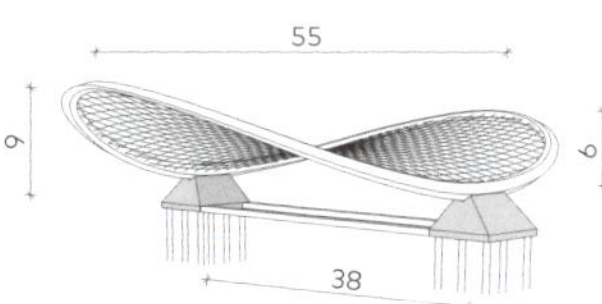

↘ 100

Two truncated, pyramidal reinforced concrete foundation pads with cladding anchor the roof structurally in the ground and visually in the landscape. Adjoining them are functional areas such as a bistro and changing rooms. The sensitive modernization of this historic site has increased the site's value to the community and strengthened its identity.

AR

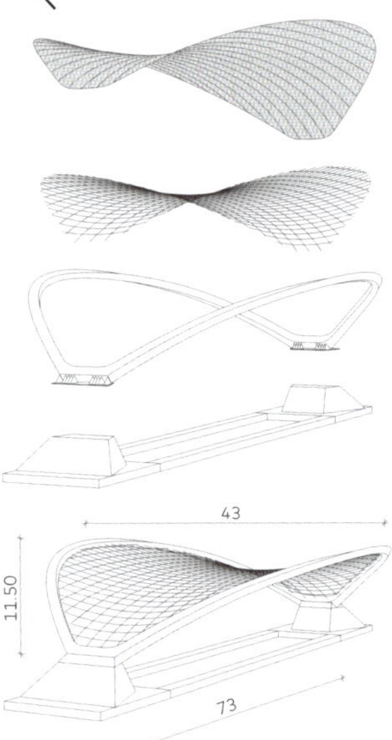

A revitalized place

We also worked with GRAFT on the design for the **Schierker Feuerstein Arena** in the Harz Mountains. Schierke lies at the foot of Brocken, the highest peak in northern Germany at 1,140 m. Its old, natural ice rink has been upgraded to a multifunctional, open-air arena, while taking care to integrate the landmarked buildings dating from 1911 and 1950. Most notable of these are the natural stone terraces for spectators and the striking wooden tower for judges or referees. The renovation was the subject of an international competition in 2013. Its main purpose was to reactivate the facility so that it could be used throughout the year for sporting and cultural events. Unlike the roof in Wolfsburg, where the low points and the bearings lie on the shorter axis, the roof in Schierke spans across the longer axis of 73 m.

The long, sweeping span over the ice rink is made possible by a steel structure with a cable-net-supported membrane. The two edge beams join at the footings to form a compression ring. The horizontal forces cancel each other out via a tie bar, so that in effect, only vertical forces are transferred into the ground. This allows for a simple, flat foundation instead of bored piles, and avoids potentially expensive collisions with large boulders naturally occurring in the subsoil. The structure is free of bending under dead load and cable prestressing. The efficient structure forms a double-curved saddle with a surface area of 2,700 m², providing shelter from the weather while preserving the outdoor ambience and continuity with the surrounding landscape.

Ongoing exploration of shell structures

Similar in concept to the roofs in Wolfsburg and Schierke, two concrete shell bridges are planned for the **Danaoke Park** in Shenzhen, in the south of China. The large natural park is being created on the eponymous mountain, which at 360 m is the highest peak of the Meilin range. A competition for the park's design was held in 2017, and our collaborative entry with LOIDL Landscape Architects was selected as the winner. Two double-curved shells reinterpret our well-known "pringle" design and take hiking trails over the highway at two separate locations. As "green bridges," they are links not merely for pedestrians but also for nature, being landscaped as a continuation of the local vegetation.

The two concrete shells represent a milestone in our own tradition of using this form, which began with the **Alsterschwimmhalle** of 1973. And so we come full circle. The impressive large shell built in the late 1960s still houses a popular indoor swimming pool. At the time of its construction, the concrete shell marked a bold new step in engineering technology. There was neither the computer-aided design technology usual today nor an established canon of experience with really large structures to refer to. This structural landmark is due to be renovated in a few years' time. Working in collaboration with gmp · von Gerkan, Marg and Partners Architects, we plan to free the shell from the facade, repair and refurbish the reinforced concrete, and install thermal glazing and roof insulation to meet today's standards. In addition, the ancillary buildings and parts of the pool basins are being renovated or rebuilt. By 2023, the roof will grace a modern swimming pool facility with a spa area.

Schierker Feuerstein
STRATIE

MEDIMAX
EISBAHNEN
STRATIE
Hasseröder

DIE LEGENDE LEBT!
Schierker Feuerstein

Herzlich Willkommen in der
SCHIERKER FEUERSTEIN ARENA
STADTWERKE
WERNIGERODE
Urlaub & Schlemmen in Schierke
UMWELTTECHNIK
& WASSERBAU
www.umwelttechnik-wasserbau.de

INTERSPORT
HANISCH
STADTWERKE
WERNIGERODE

DIE LEGENDE LEBT!

Art and Engineering

An inspiring duo

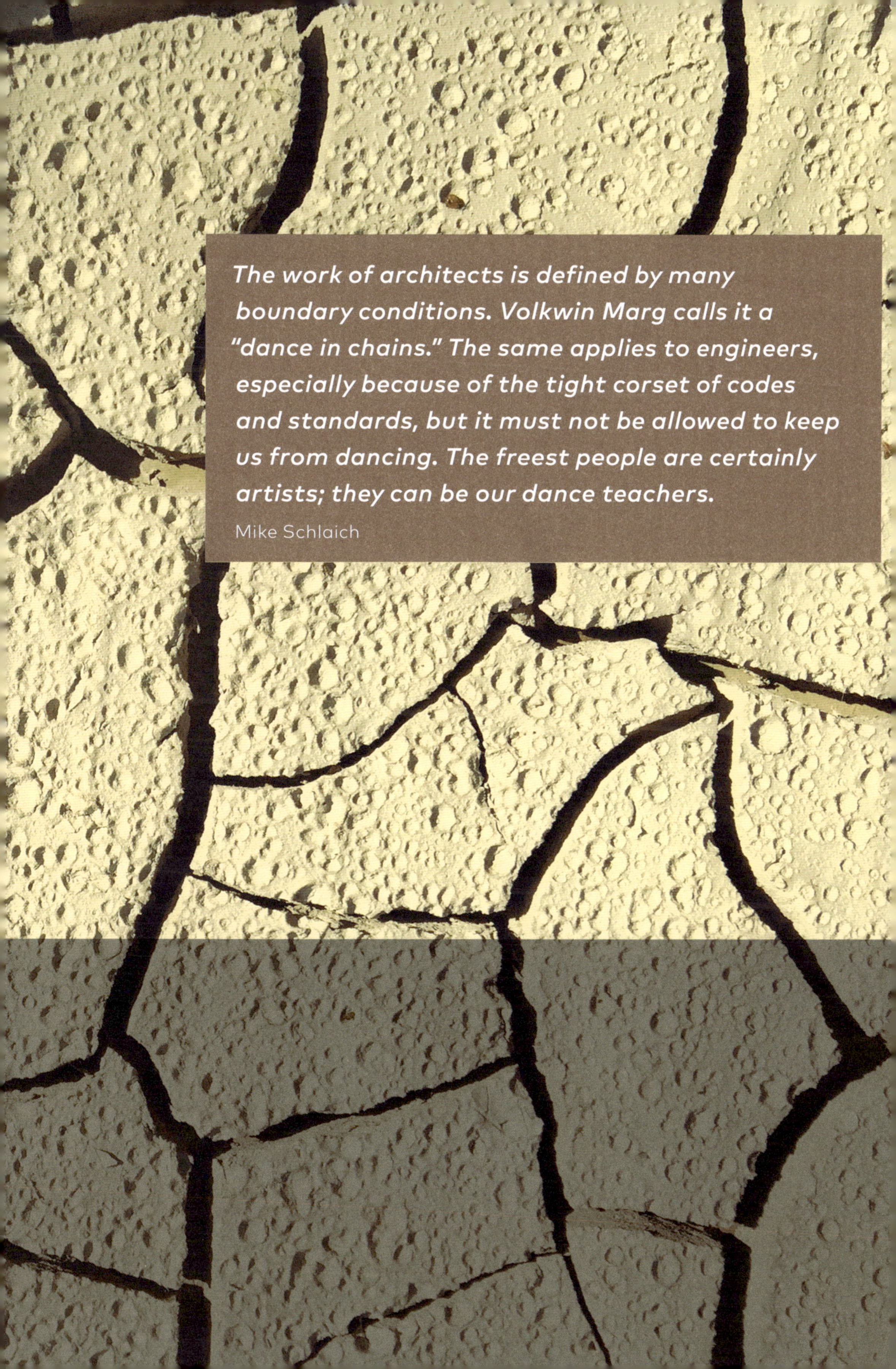

The work of architects is defined by many boundary conditions. Volkwin Marg calls it a "dance in chains." The same applies to engineers, especially because of the tight corset of codes and standards, but it must not be allowed to keep us from dancing. The freest people are certainly artists; they can be our dance teachers.

Mike Schlaich

Creators of art can devote themselves to the aesthetics of a project, free of many technical boundary conditions.

Openness to an artist's way of working can be an enriching experience for an engineer involved in such a project. Engaging with this creative process, the dance in chains, and exploring strangely defined, often age-old boundaries, shifts the spectrum of our thoughts and actions. Although the exercise may not directly benefit an engineer's structural engineering skills, this type of work—though sometimes exasperating—opens up new perspectives and widens personal horizons. The intensive interdisciplinary dialogue becomes potent food for thought. This unusual energy source brings additional stimulus to the traditional tasks of an engineering office. It also opens the door to greater project diversity. This wider spectrum of activities, together with the additionally gained experience—for example in the use of new materials—creates trust in our delivered and future contributions, both internally within the office and externally with clients, architects, and contractors.

The cooperation between artists and engineers is defined by the overlap between the specialist fields of art and engineering. On one hand, there is the intention of designing a work of art and, on the other, the will to find it a suitable supporting structure, ideally designed as an integral part of the artwork.

Getting off the ground—Horizon Field Hamburg

In an ideal case, the disciplines of engineering and art are dependent on one another. The temporary installation "Horizon Field Hamburg" in Hamburg's Deichtorhallen reflects this aspect: the installation needs the structure and the structure supports the art.

The Deichtorhallen is one of Europe's largest exhibition centers for contemporary art. As former market halls dating back to 1914, they are notable for their historic steelwork construction. At the documenta 2012 exhibition, British sculptor Antony Gormley presented a temporary installation exploring the relationship of the human body to the space around it.

In the North Hall, which has an area of 2,500 m² and a height of 19 m, his Horizon Field Hamburg consists of a 25-×-50-m platform suspended by eight cables from the roof and floating 7.5 m above the floor. Prefabricated timber panels coated with polyurethane epoxy resin were fitted onto delicately proportioned, underspanned beams. This gave the large and impressive-looking platform a deep-black, reflective surface. Visitors to the installation could access this surface shoeless via stair towers and walkways. The platform, which at 65 t was relatively light for its size, could be made to swing like a pendulum—with a long period of four to five seconds. This allowed the tremulous floor to become an elevated field for experimentation and experiences. The project got off the ground, so to speak.

↘ 139

Bridging the gap between disciplines— Slinky Springs to Fame

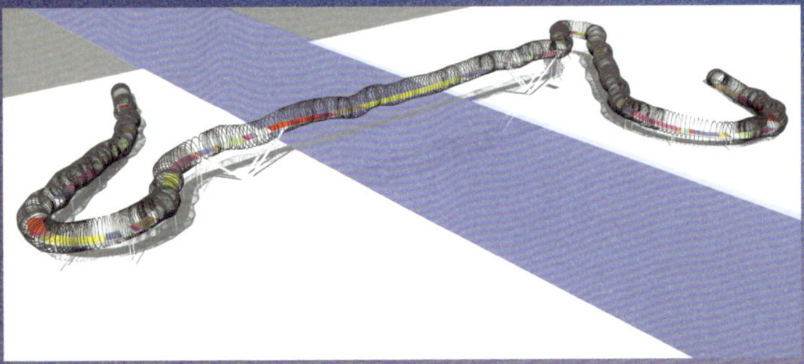

Like a casually thrown rope, Slinky Springs to Fame snakes over the canal and into the park. In addition to creating the obvious sense of playfulness, other objectives, such as functional requirements, had to be fulfilled: barrier-free access, clear headroom of 8 m above the canal, preservation of the existing trees on the site, and adequate load capacity and usability.

The structure also supports the art with the 406-m-long bridge sculpture "Slinky Springs to Fame" in Oberhausen. The highly conspicuous footbridge is part of the Emscherkunst project, which was one of the endeavors taken on by the Ruhr region as European Capital of Culture in 2010. A colorful ribbon, coiled within a spiral inspired by the eponymous children's toy, crosses the Rhine-Herne Canal at Schloss Oberhausen, connecting the Kaisergarten with the Volkspark on Emscherinsel since May 2011. In order to preserve the light, airy character of the work by German sculptor Tobias Rehberger, the structure is designed as a three-span, stressed ribbon bridge around which the nonstructural spiral winds. Making the spiral load-bearing would have increased its weight to an unfeasible level.

Two stressed ribbons fabricated from high-strength, fine-grained structural steel span 66 m over the canal with a sag of only L/50. This 1.30 m sag succeeds in creating shallow gradients for the pedestrians without generating excessive tension forces in the ribbons. The ribbons are bolted to 12-cm-thick, 2.67-m-wide precast concrete units. A pair of V columns anchor the ribbon at each bank, where two tensioned rods transfer the forces from the ribbon into the foundations. An approach ramp bridge connects to each end of the canal crossing. The ramp bridges are designed as 170-m- and 130-m-long continuous beams with a 25-cm-thick concrete superstructure supported on slender pairs of steel columns at 10-m centers. Their horizontal curvatures in plan allowed the ramp structures to be designed monolithically, because temperature deformations alter only the radii and therefore do not cause any additional reactions at the abutments. The spiral, which has a diameter of 5 m and is made of aluminum, unites all the components into one design element. In this setting, the bridge becomes an attractive place to stand and pass time. The pedestrian deck, for which the sculptor selected 16 distinct colors, is similarly attractive. The ribbon puts on a playfully relaxed display of color during the day and at night, when it is illuminated.

The spiral and the stressed ribbons oscillate when people walk over the bridge or under the effects of horizontal loads such as wind. Extensive dynamic calculations, wind tunnel tests, and additional measurements on the structure confirmed that aeroelastic instabilities such as galloping or fluttering due to wind do not occur. Bridging the gap between structural engineering and art links a creative idea with structural and functional requirements.

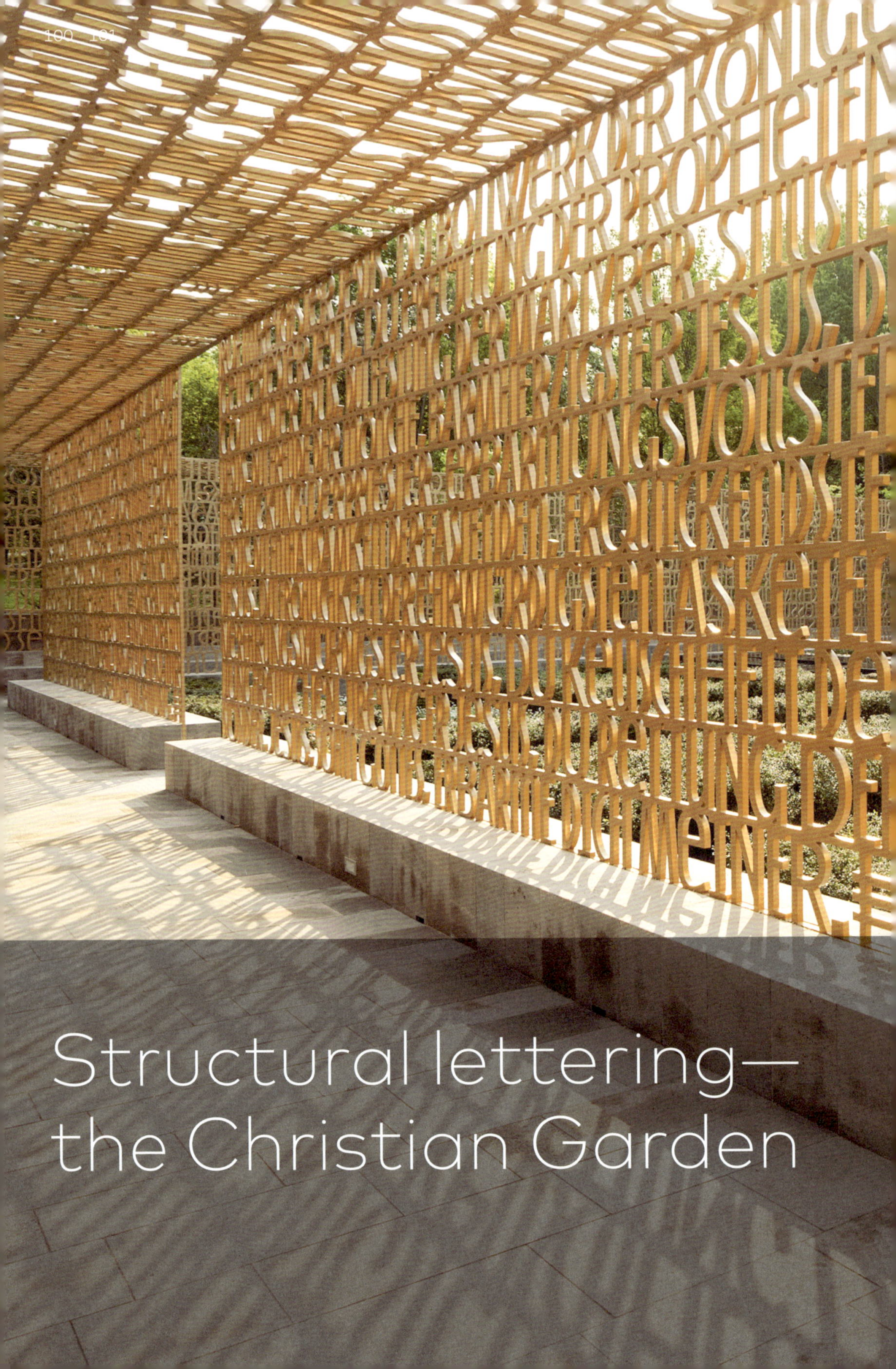

Structural lettering— the Christian Garden

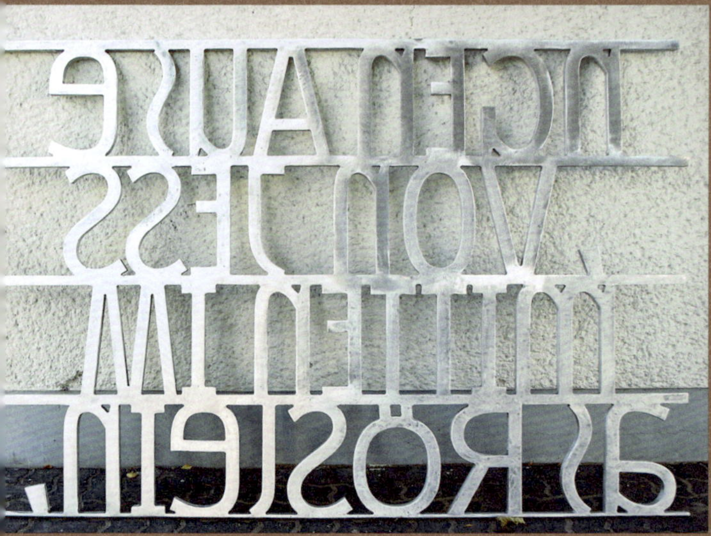

Alexander Branczyk's typographically styled letters have many points of contact for structural reasons. They ensure the applied forces flow into the foundations.

The arched walkway of the Christian Garden at the entrance to the "Garden of the World" in a recreational park in Berlin-Marzahn is an explicit example of the consensus between art and structural engineering. Here the clearly legible structure, in the truest sense of the expression, becomes the load-bearing part of a work of art.

Arising from a 2007 competition, the work of art is a modern interpretation of a medieval cloister garden with a covered walkway around a square, 20-×-20-m garden. Landscape architects relais had in mind a walkway that quoted passages of text from the Old and New Testaments, philosophy, and culture. The intense and fruitful dialogue with the landscape architects elucidated the potential of the design.

The gold-colored lines of lettering join together to form a mesh structure. Despite its delicate proportions, the structure has adequate strength and requires no further load-bearing elements. The three surfaces—two sides and a roof—join to form a 4.2-m-high, 2.9-m-wide space frame. The 1.7-m-long sections are joined by non-moment-transmitting pin joints; T- or L-shaped plates at the bottom of the walls are built into a concrete base. The frame and these built-in base details form a structure stiff enough to carry the low applied loads.

The letters are cast out of high-strength aluminum and are powder coated. The choice of material was made after a thorough analysis of the engineering, architectural, and economic restraints and conditions. Cast aluminum has a relatively high strength and a Young's modulus of at least 65,000 N/mm^2. However, it expands and contracts greatly in response to temperature. The structure's change in length is in the range of centimeters and must be accommodated by appropriate structural detailing to retain the space frame effect. The desired smooth surface can be achieved only if the melt is carefully controlled and the negative sand molds are precisely constructed. The first prototypes did not meet the standard of the reference samples because pores had formed in the aluminum during solidification.

The Christian Garden shows that even minor structures initially intended to be simple can turn out to be technically complex. Only by optimizing the process steps so that they are in harmony with one another can the unpretentious, delicate, and original structure be realized.

Giving art a frame— Cast & Place

Cast & Place, a pavilion sculpture on New York City's Governor's Island, was designed by the interdisciplinary team Aesop, consisting of engineers from our New York office, architects, sculptors, and contractors.

The aluminum for the structure was sourced from discarded soda cans collected locally.

The team first created a rectangular mold. The mold was filled with water-saturated clay from the East River and then left to air-dry for a pattern of cracks to appear in the clay. Then the molten aluminum was cast in this irregular pattern. The resulting unique and extremely filigreed infill panels were placed in series on a frame to create a small pavilion. Around 250,000 old soda cans were transformed from waste into an attractive piece of structural jewelry.

Hidden and yet visible— Monumento Madrid

Atocha Cercanias

The structure for the Monumento Madrid M11—a memorial to the victims of the terrorist attack on the Madrid-Atocha railway station on March 11, 2004—is hidden. Hidden because the artwork itself is the structure, which is made of glass and, as such, translucent.

Estudio FAM from Madrid proposed the design in a competition in 2007, which was intended to create a space free from the hectic activities of the surroundings, in particular car alarms. The memorial consists of a glass cylinder on a traffic island below which stands a 500-m², cobalt blue–painted contemplation room accessed via a subterranean passage from the railway station. During the day, the room is lit by the sun, while at night it shines reverentially with light from an internal spotlight. From the inside, visitors see the elongated "soap bubble," a transparent, floating ETFE film on which are printed the expressions of sorrow left by people passing the site after the terrorist incident.

The resulting free-form shape in plan of the glass cylinder is based on the architect's design requirements. At the same time, the curved shape provides the necessary structural stiffness. The 11-m-high glass structure therefore has no additional load-bearing elements in its surface and thus retains its uniform crystalline character. Despite the irregular curvature,

the 15,600 glass blocks all have identical geometry: with one concave and one convex side face, the blocks can be laid in courses to form an elliptical external outline. A meticulous form-finding process led up to this standardization, which resulted in a more efficient and economical manufacturing and building process.

The 8.4-kg borosilicate glass blocks are securely held together by transparent, UV-screening acrylate adhesive applied in a dot pattern. To protect the structure and the internal space against harsh environmental influences, all joints are sealed with clear silicone. Numerous tensile, compression, and shear tests were performed on the adhesive to ensure that the 2.5-mm-thick acrylate layer was adequately stiff, strong, and resistant to aging and temperature.

To reduce global imposed strains in the structure and prevent excessive shear stress in the adhesive, the 140-t tower is bedded on 200 elastomeric bearing pads. The elastic bearing support equalizes the differential deformations of the prestressed reinforced concrete roof slab on which the glass structure stands and the base of the glass wall.

Despite being a highly engineered solution, the memorial maintains a calm solemnity. The sculptural concept with its different elements and complex requirements was merged with engineering creativity into a single entity.

What sets us apart is our curiosity and striving for progress. We do not mass-produce our solutions. Mike Schlaich

In addition, in advance of the glass cylinder being constructed, the calculated elastic deformation was imposed on the reinforced concrete roof by applying an equivalent load, which was successively removed during the construction of the glass cylinder. The high self-weight of the glass cylinder allowed horizontal loads to be completely transferred into the supporting structure by friction, which dispensed with the need for complex and costly anchoring of the base of the glass wall.

The unrestrained top of the cylinder wall is stiffened by a number of horizontal glass panels, which also act as the roof. To ensure the structure was transparent, the individual panels were supported by five, up to 7.8-m-long glass beams shaped to suit their bending moment envelope. Acting as simply supported beams, they rest on EPDM setting blocks on the glass-wall coping. The beams consist of four individual elements because of the then-current production-related limitations on the dimensions of borosilicate flat glass. The beam elements were connected using stainless steel pins in the factory to form the beams. Twelve glass roof panels rest on the beams and on the glass wall coping. They are connected to finish flush with the glass blocks by structural silicone, an arrangement that stiffens the top edge of the glass structure as well.

The "soap bubble" membrane design demanded a great deal of engineering ingenuity. The complex geometry of the 150-μm-thick, transparent ETFE film depends on the stabilizing air pressure and precisely cut shape of the material. A form-finding exercise led to a shape that was unusual for pneumatic structures in that it has concave as well as convex areas. The geometry of the film depended on the stabilizing air pressure; the design had to ensure that no folds occurred despite the membrane being subjected to a system of different biaxial stresses. Four vertical and 18 horizontal seams connect the elements into an amorphous shape. The complex cut shapes of the 72 pieces of film that were subsequently welded together not only allowed for the elastic change in length of the material in two directions, but also considered the legibility of the messages of condolence. The fan unit in the contemplation room creates a pressure of approximately 100 Pa, which is imperceptible but sufficient to stabilize the extremely light film in its designed shape. To keep the pressure at the right value, visitors must first pass through an airlock before they enter the contemplation room.

Tradition combined with modern structural engineering—Qwalala

With temporary installations, the boundary conditions are often less constricting because the focus is on the experimental nature of the object. This was the case with the artwork Qwalala, which combined traditional manual glass sculpture with modern structural engineering building culture. From the knowledge of both disciplines—sculpture and structural engineering—emerged a fascinating contribution to the Venice Biennale 2017 international art exhibition. The knowledge accumulated during the design for the Monumento Madrid, in particular the jointing techniques, was further developed in connection with this project.

The work of the American visual artist Pae White is a 75-m-long and up to 2.4-m-high, curved freestanding glass wall. It consists of more than 1,700 solid, hand-cast glass blocks bonded together to form a self-supporting structure. Half of the 23-kg glass blocks are translucent. The other blocks are a mixture of 26 different colors. The colors were produced by stirring pigment into the molten glass. The artwork makes reference to the Gualala River in California. Like the course of the river, the sculpture meanders in plan. The wall is interrupted by two penetrations to allow visitors to cross sides, or "banks." The final curved geometry was arrived at using a *form-finding process* taking into account structural and sculptural aspects. Therefore, the shape of the glass wall is not only based on sculptural considerations but also stiffens the structure and gives the slender glass wall some of the properties of a shell when resisting horizontal loads, for example the effects of wind. The final shape significantly reduces shear stresses within the silicone joints and the normal stresses within the shell structure.

↘ 28

As with the Monumento Madrid, it was important in this project to ensure that the connections between the glass blocks were unobtrusive. The horizontal areas of the overlapping blocks are firmly connected to one another with a white, 7-mm-wide structural silicone bite. On the other hand, the vertical butt joints are left open, except those of the blocks in the lintels over the penetrations, which must be firmly glued to one another to act structurally. The first layer of blocks was connected using structural silicone directly to the foundation, which consisted of two 10-mm-thick steel plates on a thin layer of concrete. This allowed the foundation depth to be shallow, as required, and would permit the later planned dismantling and transfer of the artwork to another site.

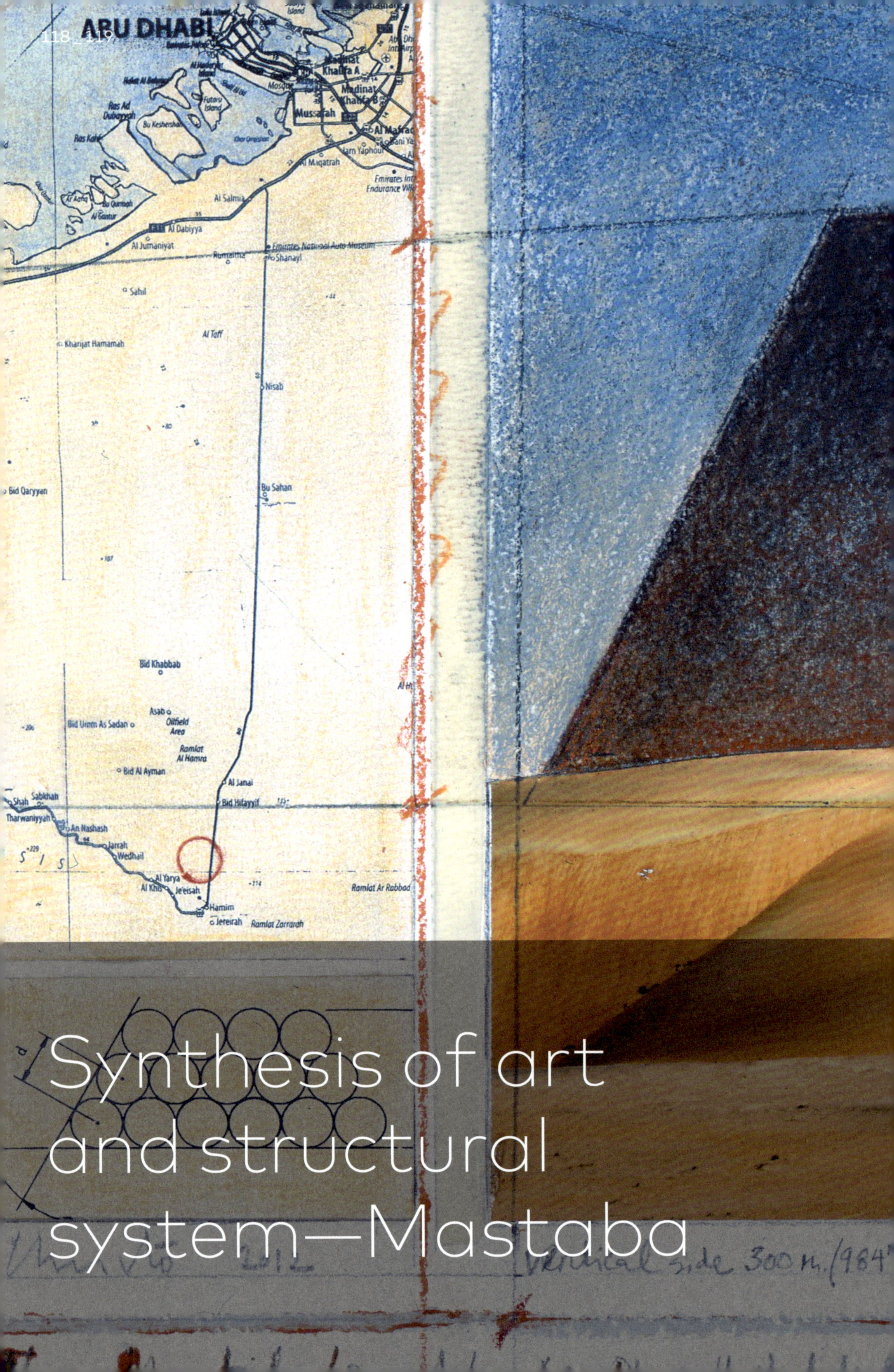

Synthesis of art and structural system—Mastaba

sloping side 60° 225 m (738'0") 229 barrels h. 150 m (492'0")

The artists Christo and Jeanne-Claude are well-known for their creations of ephemeral works of art. Their temporary textile sculptures and wrappings have made them world famous. The approach adopted for the creation of the large-scale artwork Mastaba is quite different: it is not to be a fleeting entity but a permanent work. Mastaba is to be a giant stand-alone structure made up of 440,000 stacked, colored oil barrels standing in the Abu Dhabi desert. Its stepped, truncated pyramid shape is designed to make reference to typical Egyptian tomb building, and its name is derived from the Egyptian-Arabic word for bank—Mastaba.

The original in Abu Dhabi is designed to be about 150 m high and have a plan area of approximately 300 × 225 m. An independent feasibility study, which our office prepared in close cooperation with Christo, his project manager, and photographer Wolfgang Volz, formed the basis for the concept of the structure and its assembly. The barrels are attached to a multilayered structure of primary and secondary space frames with complex node connections. A unit comprising a frame and barrels can be hinged inwards into the secondary structure on the inclined side faces so that the barrels—as the sculptor intended—can be maintained or replaced from temporary platforms inside the sculpture. Maintenance of the barrels in the vertical faces will involve movement mechanisms on cantilever arms attached to the primary structure. This arrangement dispenses with the need to have distracting auxiliary structures on the outside of the sculpture. The barrel cylinders are visible on the inclined sides and the top of the structure, while only the ends of the barrels are visible on the vertical sides.

Their installation is also part of the sculptural concept. The structure is a sophisticated mechanical system designed to be *erected in a spectacular process.* Lifting mechanisms are preinstalled and stand initially like a sewing pattern on the ground. Mastaba consists of five surfaces—four sides and one top—connected by hinges. Ten temporary scaffolding towers under the deck plate lift the sewing pattern with hydraulic presses. Like a tablecloth lifted at four points, the four side surfaces move with the cyclic lifting process on rails into their planned positions. The initial mechanism was developed into a stiffer, three-dimensionally-acting, extremely lightweight load-bearing structure. There are no longer any structural obstructions to the realization of the Mastaba, which Christo and Jeanne-Claude originally conceived in 1977.

298 ↙

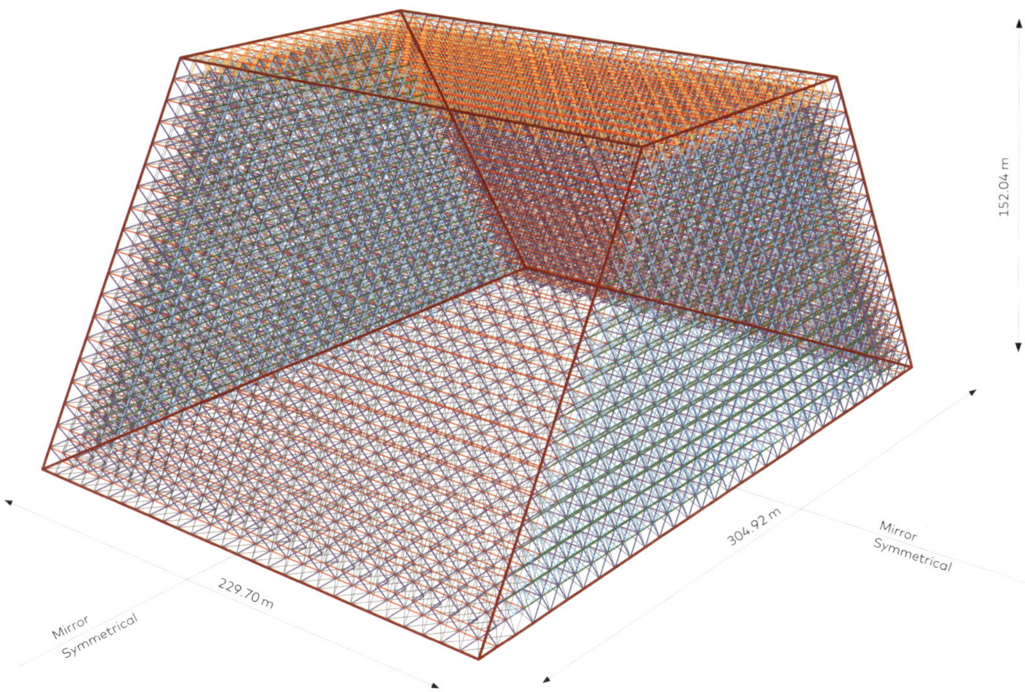

152.04 m
229.70 m
304.92 m
Mirror
Symmetrical
Mirror
Symmetrical

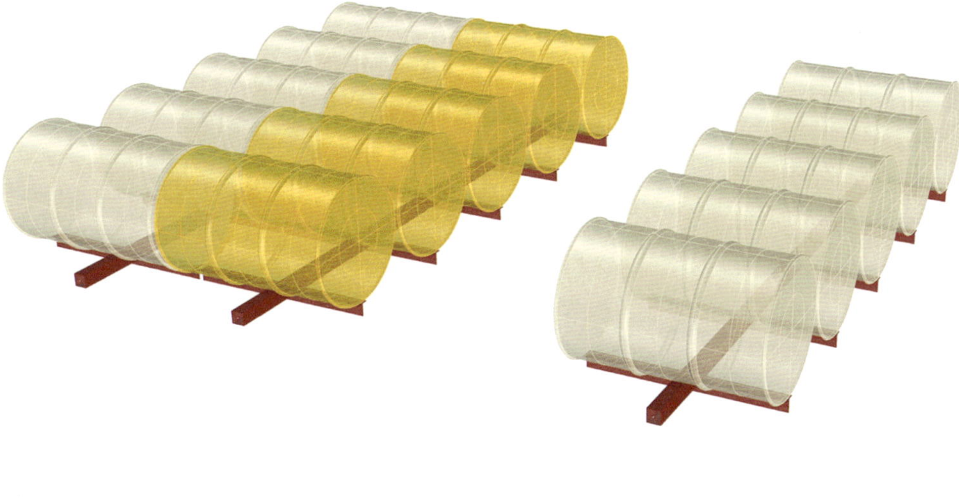

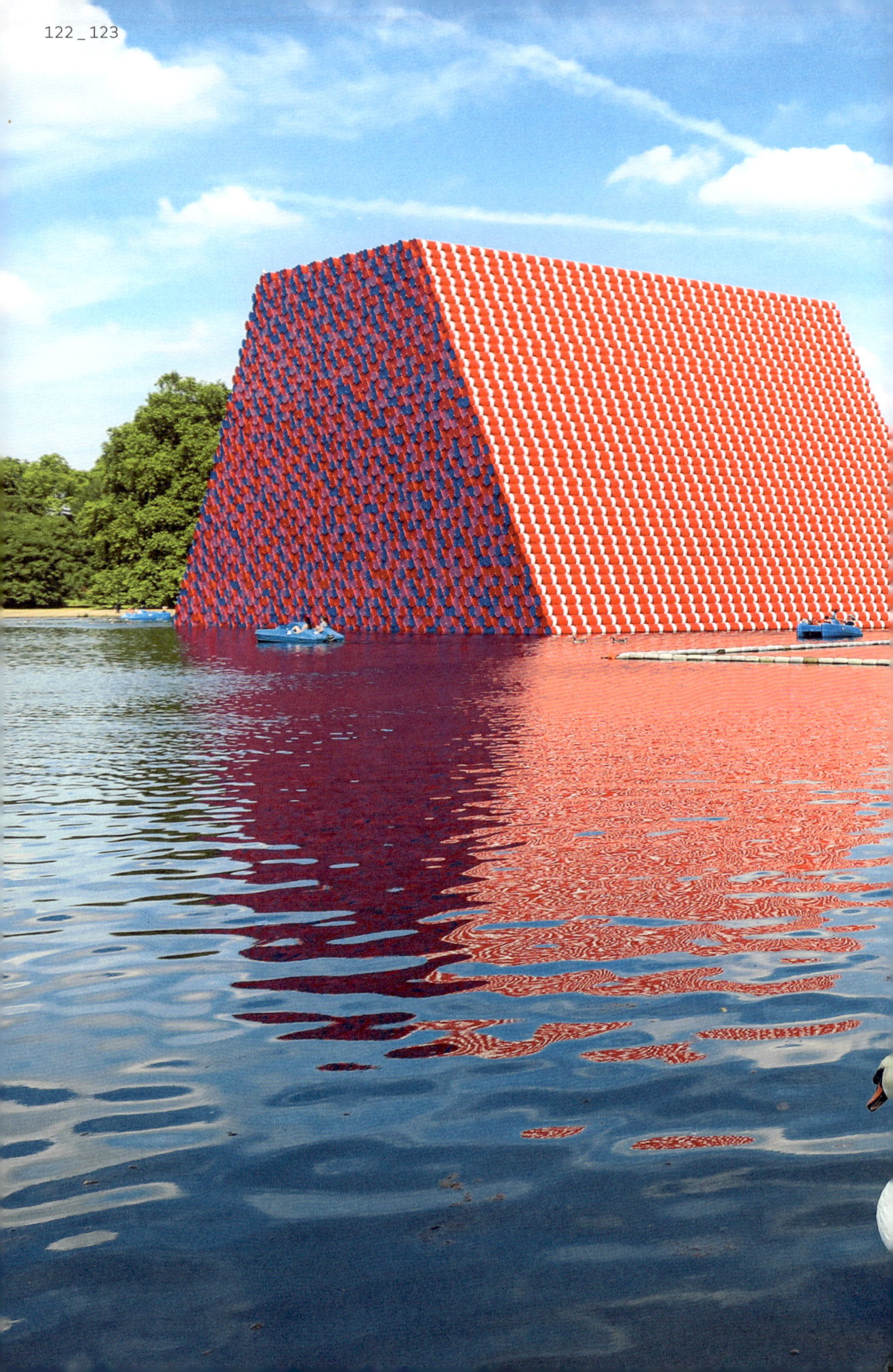

A smaller prototype of the sculpture was erected in Hyde Park, London, in the summer of 2018. Standing 20 m high and made out of 7,506 colored barrels, the sculpture floated on the Serpentine lake and drew attention to the exhibition of the works of Christo and Jeanne-Claude being held in the Serpentine Galleries until autumn 2018.

Building Structures

Towers

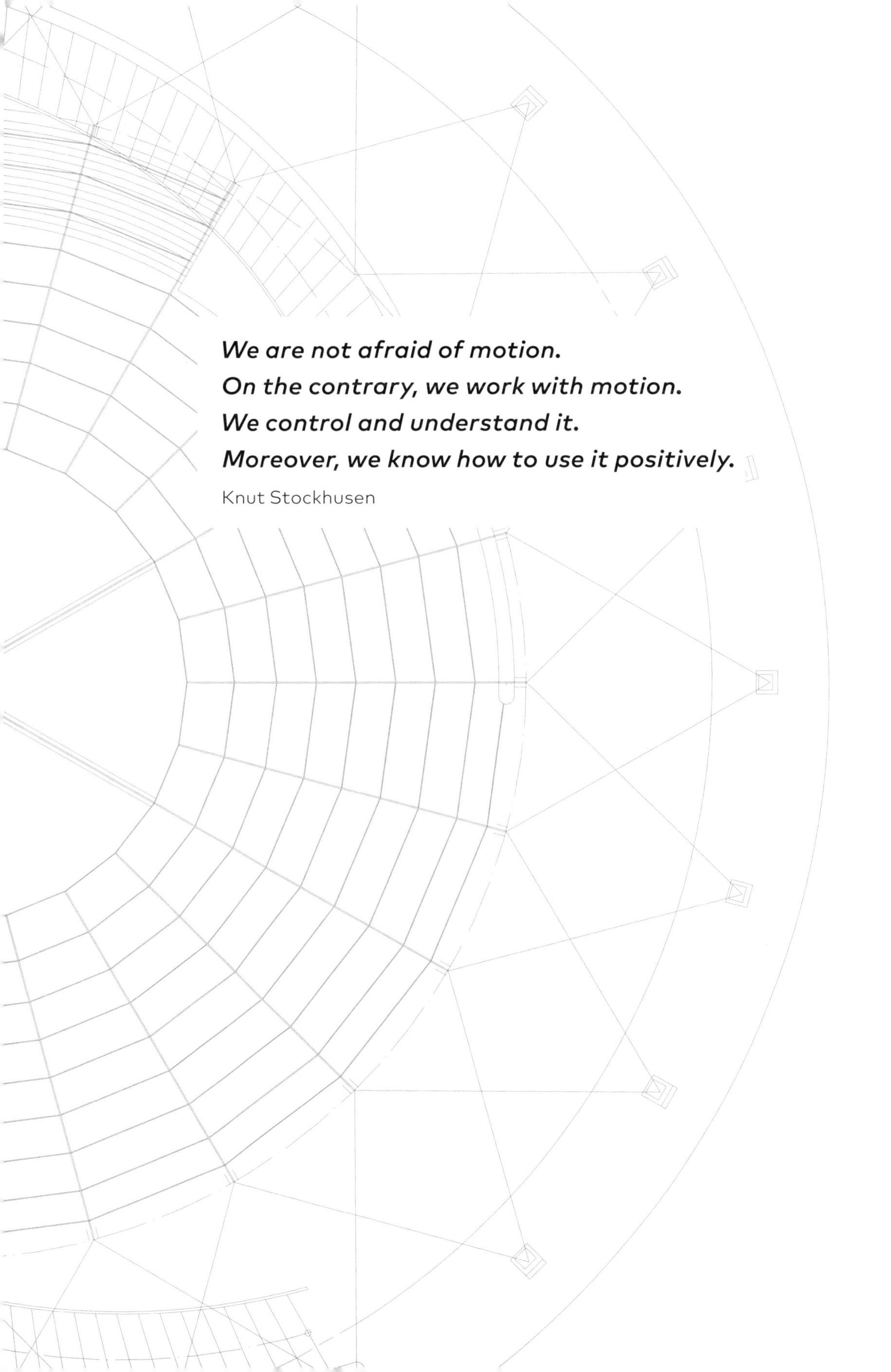

We are not afraid of motion.
On the contrary, we work with motion.
We control and understand it.
Moreover, we know how to use it positively.

Knut Stockhusen

Towers are places of freedom that allow us to see the world from a different perspective. As with all our other projects, the approach we take to designing a structure is one based on a logical, consistent thought process. We combine and give equal consideration to function, structural analysis and design, efficiency, sustainability, and aesthetics. The since-demolished **Cable Net Cooling Tower** at the power plant in Schmehausen symbolizes this approach: a triangular-mesh cable net stretches between a concrete foundation ring anchored into the ground and a steel ring forming the top of the tower. This compression ring hung like an Advent wreath from the pinnacle of a central concrete mast against which it pretensions the cable net.

The **Killesberg Tower** in Stuttgart, with its very slender and filigreed form, provides another excellent example of our holistic thought process. It has been the highest point of Killesberg Park since 2001. The 40-m-high structure allows visitors open views over Stuttgart from four platforms. During the climb to the top, it soon becomes apparent that this tower is anything but a bland, publicly accessible, vertical structure. The visitor experiences the wind and the height, because the steel structure is extraordinarily light, transparent, and gently oscillating. Essentially it consists of a central mast and a "woven" cable net made up of 48 spiral cables. Extending from the top of the mast to anchor points in the foundation soils and attached to each of the platforms, the tensioned cable net is deflected at a compression ring positioned at a height of 33 m.

The **Schönbuch Tower,** which opened in 2018 on the 580-m-high Stellberg Hill near the town of Herrenberg between Stuttgart and Tübingen, is another tower in the tradition of delicately proportioned structures reaching for the sky. Rather than narrowing in diameter toward its pinnacle, this tower widens with height. Standing on a wooded hill, the 35-m-high tower projects way above the treetops and offers impressive views over the Black Forest and onto the Swabian Alps. Two helical staircases running in opposite directions to one another spiral their way upwards via two platforms, continuously increasing their radius until they reach the third and topmost platform at a diameter of 12 m. All three steel platforms are supported on a mast of eight timber columns, which stand as a compact group on the foundation and fan out like a bouquet of flowers toward the top of the tower. The glued laminated timber columns are manufactured from larch heartwood from the Schönbuch Forest. Two cables connect each column head to the top platform, which acts as a compression ring. From there, the cables double in number, are connected to the two lower platforms, and are anchored in the foundation. The foundation is a reinforced concrete ring with an internal cross: 16 steel cables connect to the outer ring, while the cross, which is formed by tie beams, combines these cable anchorages with the mast base to form a single, integrated structural unit in mechanical equilibrium. To reduce the load on the foundation soils, the excavation was filled with lightweight, foamed-glass aggregate. This load reduction reduces the risk of settlement of the ground under the new structure on Stellberg Hill, parts of which had been used as a landfill site and therefore were likely to settle.

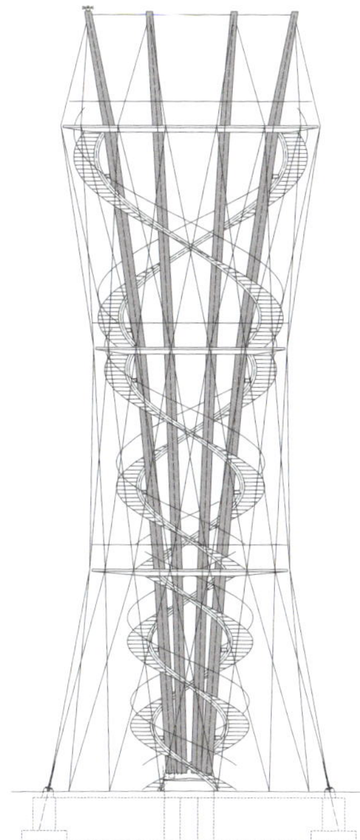

We developed a well-thought-out assembly and erection concept together with the main contractor (Stahlbau Urfer). The individual platforms including the columns and the attached spiral cables were the first segments to be assembled. Only after that were the segments placed one upon the other—first the top tower segment on the middle, then these two combined were placed on the bottom segment. This combined upper segment of the tower, which at this stage weighed 96t, was lifted by crane and placed on top of the columns of the already installed bottom segment. The hybrid timber-steel structure creates an elegant landmark in which the inverted cone is aesthetically bound inside a structurally effective, filigreed steel cable net.

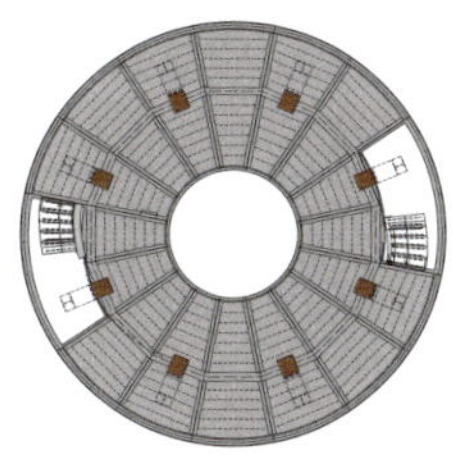

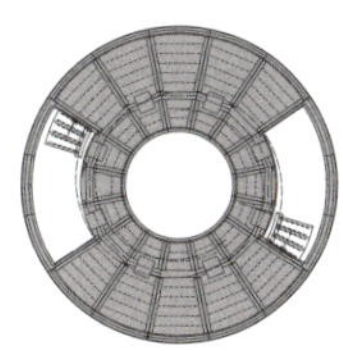

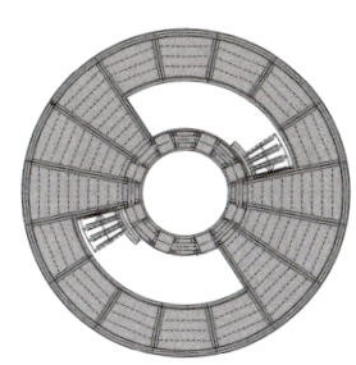

Although durable regional timber was used, the mast would have a shorter useful life than the other components of the structure. Therefore, the individual mast elements between the two platforms can be relieved of their load using jacks and replaced without additional measures being required to keep the tower stable.

A typical example of the dynamic interweaving of different aspects of one of our projects is the forward-looking energy supply tower with a pretensioned cable-net structure and an integrated spiral staircase leading to a viewing platform. This second shell not only stabilizes the tower, it also makes it accessible to the public.

Another tower defined by its cable-net construction is the **Energy and Future Storage Tower** at the Energy Park in Heidelberg, which we designed in conjunction with LAVA and the municipal utilities organization Stadtwerke Heidelberg. The pretensioned cable-net facade with its integrated helical staircase surrounds the 50-m-high, 25-m-diameter cylinder as a 56-m-high building shell. The cylindrical structure stores water for a district heating system. The two-zone accumulator operates with water temperatures of more than 100 °C and therefore is pressurized. It stores surplus heat from a wood-burning power plant as hot water and releases the heat into the district heating system on demand. The district heat accumulator is part of a new flexible energy system and a module and core component of the value-added chain of the local energy supply organization. The dynamic-looking sculpture underlines its sustainability by having multiple uses, because it also functions as a viewing platform.

The staircase to the platform is integrated in an unconventional way into the cable structure. It winds helically upwards, supporting itself in the gap between the facade of the accumulator and the cable net without any connection to the cylinder. The staircase, which rises at a constant *rate around the accumulator jacket,* acts in combination with the cable net to stiffen the whole building envelope.

↘ 96

The galfan-coated, high-strength cables in the cable-net facade form triangular meshes. The net is held by the crown at the top edge of the district heat accumulator cylinder. The cylinder with its 15 cross-braced columns forms a stiff truncated cone, which transfers the vertical and horizontal loads onto the accumulator. Thousands of small rhombic panels are suspended from the cable net. They oscillate in the wind and generate a dynamically changing surface. The result is a lively, reflective exterior. As night falls, the facade is additionally highlighted with low-energy LEDs, which make the movement of the small panels visible even in the dark. With its special facade construction and the viewing platform, the accumulator will become a tourist attraction and a technical and aesthetic landmark signaling the city's transition to renewable energy.

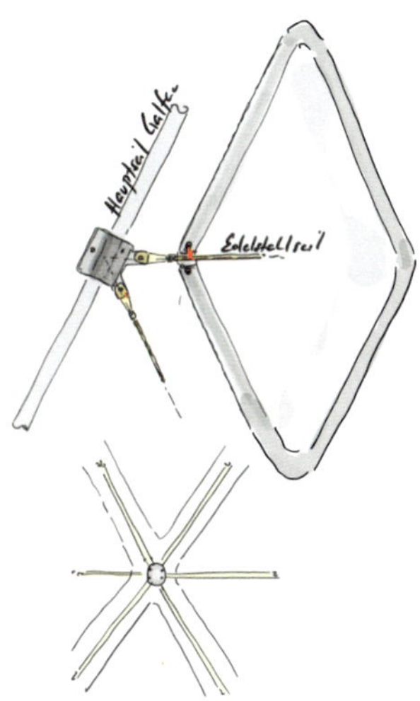

The **One World Trade Center** in New York projects out of the urban context like a lighthouse. It arose in the place of the Twin Towers of the World Trade Center destroyed on September 11, 2001. Our office in New York designed the striking spire and the 15-m-high welcoming foyer for the new building by Skidmore, Owens & Merrill LLP. Having a *structural cable facade* of prestressed, high-strength stainless steel cables, the light and filigreed-glass portal foyer contrasts with the main building, which is designed to resist terrorist attacks. Including the spire, the tower reaches a height of exactly 541.3 m. The equivalent in feet, 1776, represents the year the founding fathers of the United States of America signed the Declaration of Independence. This number, and the function of the structure as a communications mast, underlines the symbolic character the building possesses.

45 ↙

The spire with the communications ring at its base—this supports all the transmission equipment, lighting, and window-cleaning scaffolds—is meant to resemble the flame of a stylized torch. The design makes reference to the Statue of Liberty. The 135-m-high antenna mast is a steel structure with a 4.27-m-diameter base. It consists of 18 prefabricated segments each 12 m long and reduces in diameter with height. The frame segments fabricated out of round hollow sections are connected together by cast-steel joints. This very tall and slender needle at a vertigo-inducing height in an exposed position is subject to tremendous wind speeds of up to 240 km/h. To reduce the correspondingly high deformations and oscillations, the mass is stayed with aramid fiber cables tying the third-height point of the mast to the communications ring. The 40-m diameter ring is in turn supported on inclined struts, the ends of which are pin-jointed to the base of the mast. The forces in the 725-t structure cancel themselves out, with the result that mostly only vertical loads are transferred into the structure of the tower. What looks so obviously like a filigreed, lightweight structure on the top of the tower is a sophisticated and optimized structure and represents the results of a process of design, testing, and construction that lasted years, including wind tunnel tests and icing investigations.

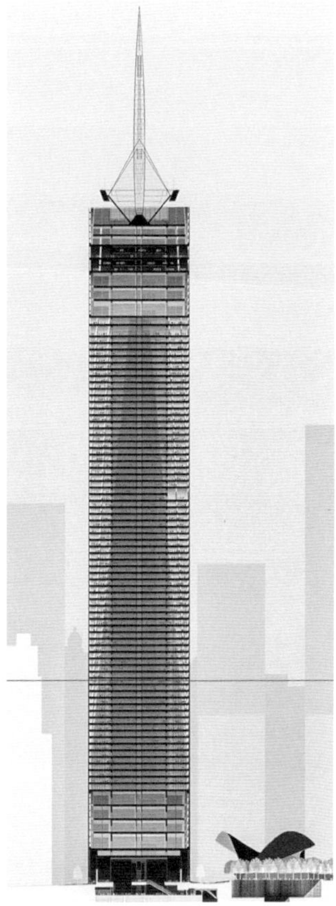

The key thoughts behind the objective

Towers—built as high-rises or viewing platforms, designed as vertical, slender cantilevers or as cable structures—oscillate. This allows them to dissipate energy in a way that users cannot fail to notice. Despite the negative connotations of the term "oscillation", we see it as positive, which is why we never exclude moving structures from our considerations at the conceptual design stage. On the contrary, we use this potential to create buildings that are lightweight, efficient, and out of the ordinary. In doing this, in some areas we go up to the currently accepted limits of possibility—and sometimes beyond them. We grow as we accumulate experience because it vindicates us in what we do. After all, limits are only established by occasionally exceeding them.

We do not consider these pioneering activities to be like tightrope walking, where no deviation to the left or right is allowed. It is much more the case that our office culture creates the freedom for us to try new things. Everyone is therefore motivated to come up with structural concepts and develop structures that perhaps initially appear to be unrealistic. We are aware that at the heart of every far-fetched idea lies a creative thought *that can lead us*
319 ↙ *eventually to our objective.*

Accumulated knowledge

In the same seemingly relaxed way in which we achieved an obvious lightness of form for the projects described above, the qualities of the extremely slender and high residential tower by Rafael Viñoly Architects at **432 Park Avenue** at the lower end of Central Park are similarly self-evident. The 85-story high-rise has a height-to-width ratio of only 1:15—its footprint measures 28.5 × 28.5 m and its height 426 m—which makes it also one of the world's slenderest residential towers. The structure is designed in accordance with the tube-in-tube principle and consists of a building core and a highly stiff outer frame in the form of a perforated square tube in high-strength concrete. The uniform facade grid with 3.6-×-3.6 m room-height window openings is interrupted and perforated in order to allow air to flow through over the height of five mechanical equipment stories to avoid dynamic acceleration under certain wind conditions.

In developing this lightweight and materially reduced load-bearing structural design, we were intensively involved in a complex and difficult work of engineering, because buildings like this are more susceptible to oscillation than their solid equivalents. The task required detailed aerodynamic investigations, which demonstrated that the installation of two complex 600-t dampers as pendulum masses was unavoidable. They allow oscillation-free and luxurious living in this residential tower, which behaves structurally like a blade of grass. The result is that only in extremely gusty winds can residents detect some slight movement.

We are a team that dares to think outside the box. Many engineers make themselves replaceable because they do not bring anything of their own to the project and the dialogue. Andreas Keil

It is precisely because we were faced with the dynamic problems in this design that such an innovation arose on Park Avenue. In our offices we have individuals or groups of experts who are particularly intensively concerned with specific topics. With the depth of technical knowledge this gives us, we can discuss and enhance projects all over the world at a high level of expertise.

Not replaceable

Another project to which we had to contribute from the whole of our experience in complex buildings and engineering structures was the ambitious reinforced concrete and steel composite structure of the 90-m-high **Ardex Tower** (with Gerhard Spangenberg, Berlin) for the headquarters of the high-performance specialist building materials manufacturer in Witten, Germany. The entire project, which includes the construction of a new 24-story office tower and the modernization of production and logistics facilities, is due to be completed by 2022. In addition to innovative energy and facade solutions, the whole design team worked together on an integrated and thoroughly sustainable overall strategy to optimally satisfy the technical and functional demands of this project.

The constructive dialogue entered into by the design team had already been put to the test on an unusual conversion project: the almost 90-m-high **Exzenterhaus** in Bochum (also with Gerhard Spangenberg, Berlin). The design for an 18-story office tower included, among other things, the conversion of a heritage-listed former air-raid bunker and placing 18 stories on top of it. This took the form of floor packages each comprising five new 3.75-m-high office stories, which equates to the 20-m height of the old reinforced concrete bunker. The asymmetric arrangement of these packages, cantilevering beyond the footprint of the tower, is a distinctive feature of the building. Each of the three packages is displaced rotationally relative to the next and separated from it by a 1.8-m-high intermediate building services story. The new 25-cm-thick floor slabs cantilever eccentrically out from the existing circular bunker and the facade columns by up to 4.5 m. To achieve these large cantilevers with a light structure, the underside of the floor slabs rises toward their edges so as to form thin shell elements. Membrane action occurs in the cantilevering slab areas as a result of vertical loads on the slabs. Circular prestressing was applied to counteract the tensile forces in the edge of the shell and prevent cracking, thus limiting the associated deformations.

The new building core and the 2-m-thick existing bunker walls carry the vertical and wind loads from the tower. The high compressive strength of the bunker concrete meant that it required only localized strengthening. However, the tower required completely new foundations consisting of a ground slab and 12 large bored piles. The renovation works and the addition of new stories to the historic bunker have created a modern office and administrative building, while ensuring that this witness to times past is retained.

A structure that allows flexibility of use and light to flood into the interior of a building brings added value to a residential development. The **building ensemble Max und Moritz** by NÖFER Architekten—two modern residential towers with approximately 400 apartments—is built in a new quarter on the site of the former eastern railway goods terminal in Berlin-Friedrichshain and is in the immediate neighborhood of the Mercedes-Benz Arena. Two six- to seven-story base buildings contain 80 retail units. The individual apartments are discernible in the facade by their irregularly offset loggias, terraces, and panoramic windows. Horizontal belts of travertine limestone forming the window breasts exercise a calming effect on the overall appearance of the facade. The belts have fewer openings in the lower stories in order to grant the occupants protection from direct visual intrusion into their homes. The loads from the two towers are transferred by a combined pile-and-slab foundation into the underlying sandy soils; the other buildings have spread foundations. Consequently, these buildings, standing as rather stocky towers on a small footprint and making very efficient use of increasingly scarce building land, also allow light to flood through transparent facades into the rooms, even those in the innermost core.

As construction projects are becoming increasingly complex, so are their load-bearing structures. The industry has seen a consequent rise in the demand for sophisticated structural and construction engineering services. These services must be correctly performed and of high quality, above all with respect to a comprehensive and error-free analysis and design of the structure and to the contract documents. This applies in particular for major projects, where the diversity of issues is correspondingly higher.

Layer 03

Checking

We place great value on such quality control. By adopting the "two-person principle," we strive to ensure nothing is omitted from consideration in our own designs. In some projects, we act as independent check engineers for reinforced concrete and steel structures. We are engaged in this role as independent consultants for and on behalf of the construction authorities or, in the private sphere, on behalf of the client.
We check the design of the structure and monitor construction on-site both in Germany and abroad.

In these activities, we do not see ourselves only in the traditional checking role, but also as a partner of architects, engineers, and contractors. We share the common obligation with them to deliver a safe structure and to recognize and rectify any problems along the way at the appropriate time. As structural engineers with decades of experience accumulated from all over the world and through our relationship with research and development, we bring all the required knowledge and necessary specialist know-how to the table.

The added value for all project stakeholders and for the project itself is best achieved if we are involved at an early stage in the design. We can focus on the success of the project if we are able to discuss the design of the structure and the route to developing the structural solution with all stakeholders before the approval design stage. This reduces the risks to quality, structural stability, and the project delivery schedule. By asking questions and rigorously examining the design approach, we can point out important aspects and, with the benefit of an outside viewpoint, discern possible sources of mistakes that are typically present in traditional construction project interfaces. In this way, a structural solution can be refined or adjusted so that unexpected problems do not occur during the approval and construction phases.

One of the projects for which we were the independent check engineers, and which provides an excellent example of this role, is the **taz Publishing House** in Friedrichshain-Kreuzberg, Berlin. The building was designed by E2A Architects Piet Eckert and Wim Eckert together with the structural engineers from Schnetzer Puskas Ingenieure. The building contains offices, conference rooms, a café, and exhibition and auxiliary rooms. The usable space is divided into seven above-ground stories, each U-shaped in plan, and two basements. The sixth and top floor has particularly high ceilings. The structure for the compact volume, which has a plan area of 33 × 34 m, consists principally of a steel-concrete composite frame of rhomboid elements, with prestressed downstand edge beams in the plane of the facades, braced with diagonal struts between similarly prestressed floor systems, the edges of which act as horizontal bracing. The 29-m-high office block makes reference in terms of its form to the 1920s Shabolowka Radio Tower in Moscow designed by Vladimir G. Shukhov; his lattice structures achieved high load capacities yet consisted of very few major structural elements. The curtain wall diagrid facade replicates the concept of the load-bearing structure but with smaller steel elements. The stiffening mesh facade structure allows 12-m-deep internal spaces with long-span, column-free floor layouts. The very few internal vertical load-bearing elements are constructed in non-prestressed reinforced concrete.

As is the normal task of independent check engineers, our involvement was to ensure compliance with technical standards and regulations and to take into account what is feasible using modern construction techniques. In accordance with the "two-person principle," we undertook an independent check of the structural engineering design. At the appropriate stages, we discussed the potential risks and interface issues with the project team and reduced or avoided potential problems that might otherwise have occurred during the construction process. The aspects we looked at in particular included the effects of the nearby subway, the poor ground conditions, and the feasibility of fabricating the complex member joints—the latter featuring cast-in steel components, precast concrete floor units, and prestressing rods running along and transversely to the plane of the facades.

S. Prinzip-UE zum
Fassadenanschl.
TAZ_AP_TRA_ST_XX_GUD_23
R4/ DV-E
R1/ DV-D
R4/ DV-D
R1/ DV-C
R4/ DV-C
R3/ DV-B
R1/ DV-B
=Tasche T1=
54 KBD
Ggf. Sonderlösung
bezüglich Balkonanschluss

Our input assisted the efforts of the authorities, client, architects, engineers, and contractors and contributed not only to achieving structural stability but also to ensuring the building would retain its value and usefulness over time.

We would like to highlight a similar contribution we made on another project, this time working with Staab Architekten and the engineers from WETZEL & VON SEHT. The designers had been commissioned with the extension of the heritage-listed **Bauhaus Archive/Museum of Design** in Berlin. This building, which was designed by Walter Gropius and opened in 1979 after his death, houses one of the world's largest collections of material on the history and influence of the Bauhaus, the 20th century's most important school of architecture, design, and art, which was founded by Gropius in Weimar in 1919. Coincident with the 100th anniversary of its founding, this important archive is to be refurbished and have an extension to the museum built over the next few years in compliance with the requirements of the heritage authorities. Particular requirements were placed on the extension relating to the respect the design should show for the existing fabric, with its high significance and value to the history of architecture.

Analysis—care—consultancy

The role of an independent check engineer is well-established in Germany. We undertake this work at our offices in Berlin through Mike Schlaich and in Stuttgart through Jochen Gugeler. As independent check engineers we get involved with the same wide range of engineering aspects as we do with our own projects. These include foundation engineering; integral bridges; complex cable structures; composite, steel-glass, and prestressed concrete construction; towers; fixed or retractable structures for long spans; right up to membrane structures, tower blocks, and stadiums. We contribute the experience gained from our links with research to activities such as geometric design and form finding, and our knowledge in the field of materials such as textile membranes, carbon, and infra-lightweight concrete to the independent check projects.

Our competence and ability to make difficult engineering decisions are greatly valued by the project planners and designers with whom we have cooperated. As a result, we frequently receive requests to act as independent check engineers, including, for example, for the 140-m-high **EDGE Tower Berlin** high-rise office, designed by architects BIG – Bjarke Ingels Group from Copenhagen. Stepped slots and small planted terraces cross and break up the appearance of the facade. Examining the designs in a close working relationship between architects and structural engineers from start to finish is enriching and inspiring to us.

taz Publishing House

Architect: E2A Piet Eckert and Wim Eckert Architekten ETH BSA SIA AG

Structural Engineer: Schnetzer Puskas International AG

Because we specialize in structurally innovative projects, we are often asked to check structures that are not covered by building standards and regulations. They involve unconventional forms of construction or incorporate products not yet granted general approval. This allows us to look into projects that use forms of construction we have not yet implemented in our designs. In Germany these projects must go through a project-specific approval process (ZiE) with the authorities. By being involved as the independent checker early in the design process, we can advise on the ZiE process. We can also contribute our specialist know-how and experience at the right time when the relevant aspects can be redesigned relatively easily and without serious consequences. By adopting this approach, it is perfectly possible to complete an innovative construction project—if the legally applicable standards are complied with or exploited to the full—without the need for a complex and, above all, time-consuming official application for a ZiE. However, should a ZiE be necessary, we can provide the input so that there is little risk of delay in granting the application.

Our advice, which is based on experience in many areas of structural engineering, will reduce risks in the construction phase and help to avoid holdups in the completion of the works. We minimize unnecessary procedural loops in the design schedule, increase cost efficiency, and reduce the amount of time required. We learn from this experience and use it for our own projects.

The **Bitzer Headquarters** in Sindelfingen is a current project that we found to be structurally interesting and instructive, largely thanks to the close working relationship we had with construction firm Stahl- und Verbundbau in the design of the composite components and connection details for the building. The new headquarters for Bitzer SE, a globally active company in the field of refrigeration and air-conditioning, stands close to a freeway and forms the focus of the Bitzer Campus. The building was designed by architects kadawittfeld-architektur. The 17-story tower has a transparent zone extending the full height of the building at its center. The zone is designed to be a multistory communication area linking all parts of the building. Built as a skeleton frame, the structure satisfies the requirements for high flexibility of use, short construction time, and a cost-effective and durable form of construction. To minimize self-weight, structural engineers Weischede, Hermann und Partner (wh-p) from Stuttgart proposed a reinforced concrete/steel composite form of construction, which allowed the floor slabs to be only 15 cm deep. Because the designer, wh-p, and sbp as the independent check engineer had already worked together on other projects and agreed on many aspects of the design at a very early stage, it was possible to avoid unnecessary duplication of activities in the design and to optimize design interfaces.

In-depth knowledge

As independent check engineers, we normally know as much about the project we have checked as the designers themselves. This applies in particular where we have already looked in detail at the site in proposals of our own during the competition phase, as was the case with the **Rheinsteg in Rheinfelden.** An earlier bridge at the site had been removed as part of the demolition of a historic hydroelectricity power plant. The connection between the two towns of Rheinfelden, one in the Swiss canton of Aargau and the other in the German state of Baden, then had to be reestablished and a competition was held in 2016 to arrive at a suitable design. We had investigated the site in detail as part of our design for an arch bridge and this helped us in the later independent check

EDGE Tower Berlin (ETB)
Architect: BIG – Bjarke Ingels Group
Structural Engineer: Arup Deutschland

of the winning project by structural engineers Frank Miebach.

The design team proposed an interesting 213-m-long, technically challenging suspension bridge with cranked mast legs. Untypically for this type of bridge, the deck was to be made of timber. The winning team of engineers has a great deal of sound experience in the design of timber bridges but less in the design of long-span cable bridges. In this situation, we were able to bring our specialist experience in this area to bear and help solve significant aspects relating to static and dynamic analysis and constructional details. The cooperative relationship between the two diversely experienced structural engineering offices ensured the high quality and structural stability of the final structure. Acting as the independent check engineer, we also supported the design team in dealing with the design and construction interfaces between structural engineering designer, foundations contractor, and the companies responsible for concreting, structural steelwork, and timber construction. The vibrational behavior of the lightweight bridge was analyzed by an external wind-loading expert and the timber deck design verified with a co-independent check engineer specializing in timber construction.

This commission proved to be an inspiring project that aroused our curiosity and provided important information for our work elsewhere. All the project participants contributed to the added value of the structure thanks to their *sustained interaction with one another.*

12 ↙

Despite not winning the competition for the **Freiburg Stadium,** we remained a participant in the project. In conjunction with architects agn, we submitted a competition design characterized by a thin forest of slender columns around the circumference of the stadium.

The winner was announced in July 2017: a design by HPP Architekten together with structural engineers Krebs+Kiefer Ingenieure and Knippers Helbig Advanced Engineering. Their design also took up the theme of columns around the circumference of the stadium: these slender, inclined columns carried a thin rectangular roof with an octagonal opening over the playing area. In this case, we did not build the project we designed, but as the second-place entrant and with our experience in stadium construction, we were able to secure the commission as the independent check engineer for the project, which was similar in concept to what we had put forward. We were able to highlight critical points at the appropriate stage and, because we knew the sequence of operations in these types of stadium projects, we agreed an efficient checking schedule with the designers and the fabricators in advance and thus saved time.

Professional development and training

Although we consider the advice we provide during the early design phase to be important and significant, the main focus is on the actual independent check of the project. Irrespective of the size of the project, we first perform some approximate calculations to check the concept, then we look at the design in more depth and detail. We consider a good approach to a structural design check of complex structures is to perform our own independent calculations and then compare the results with those of the original design. We analyze and identify the critical points, look for any fundamental problems, and determine whether the design guarantees structural stability. In addition, we also address and verify the usability

Rheinsteg in Rheinfelden

Competition Design Illustration:
schlaich bergermann partner

Winning Design: Ingenieurbüro Miebach (structural engineering); swillus architekten (architecture)

of the structure and offer helpful advice to all project participants, even in cases where this advice is not reimbursable as part of our duties under the independent check agreement. We exercise the same amount of care as we do when analyzing our own projects.

Performing independent checks in various regions of the world is also a way for us to gather specialist knowledge *and experience in construction practices globally.* 320 ↙ Therefore, we also undertake independent checks on international projects. For the **German School Madrid,** we checked the structural design of the building and supervised its construction. The fair-faced concrete project designed by Berlin architects Grüntuch Ernst won a design competition in 2009 and is notable for its striking geometric form. Three buildings, polygonal in plan, each with its own courtyard, are linked by a roofed zone to form a building complex. Like a matrix, the reinforced concrete structure brings the individual buildings together to form a single unit. Structural columns in the form of pairs of tapering walls carry the roof. In this project we acted as a partner for the participants in the project.

It was clear here that a check by us could be capable of delivering added value at all levels: for all project participants, for the project itself, and for us. The experience we have gained from so many independent check commissions has enabled us to judge ourselves against other offices, increase our efficiency, and improve our ways of working. In addition, we obtain information about new software, design tools, and materials and derive up-to-date knowledge, which we can share internally.

Because the instructions to be followed when carrying out an independent check are straightforward, well-organized, and clearly set out, and the checking engineer learns and makes discoveries from the process, we also involve our younger engineers. It is helpful for their understanding of structures and in our internal professional development program for them to work through structural calculations closely with an experienced colleague and produce results to compare with the original design. It allows newly graduated engineers to gain an overview of the design process, which they may not be familiar with at that time in their careers. In this sense, complex independent check projects and the experience checkers gain can be seen as a vehicle for professional development.

A precondition for a check carried out in accordance with good engineering practice—and for further professional training—is that we, the checkers, are always up-to-date with respect to standards and technical requirements. That turns our independent check engineers—particularly in the case of our younger colleagues—into valuable contributors to any discussions in the office. In the course of internal informative presentations, the checkers can report regularly on new aspects of the standards, interesting details, and the knowledge they have gained on-site and from the current independent check projects. Through the almost daily contact with events on-site in the course of supervising the works, they are aware of the problems and challenges that can occur when realizing structural designs on-site. This is helpful in our own designs because problems can often be prevented by anticipating them during the design.

German School Madrid
Architect: Grüntuch Ernst Architekten
Structural Engineer: GTB – Berlin Gesellschaft für Technik am Bau mbH

Bridges

BORDEAUX
ESSEN
BACKNANG
HAMBURG
STUTTGART
CLEVELAND
RATHENOW
DITZINGEN
BELGIEN
BELGIEN

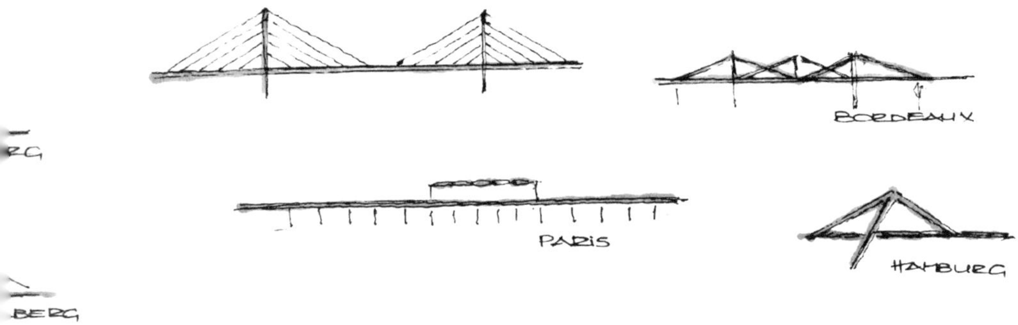

A structure is satisfactory if it cannot really be exchanged for another design. Andreas Keil

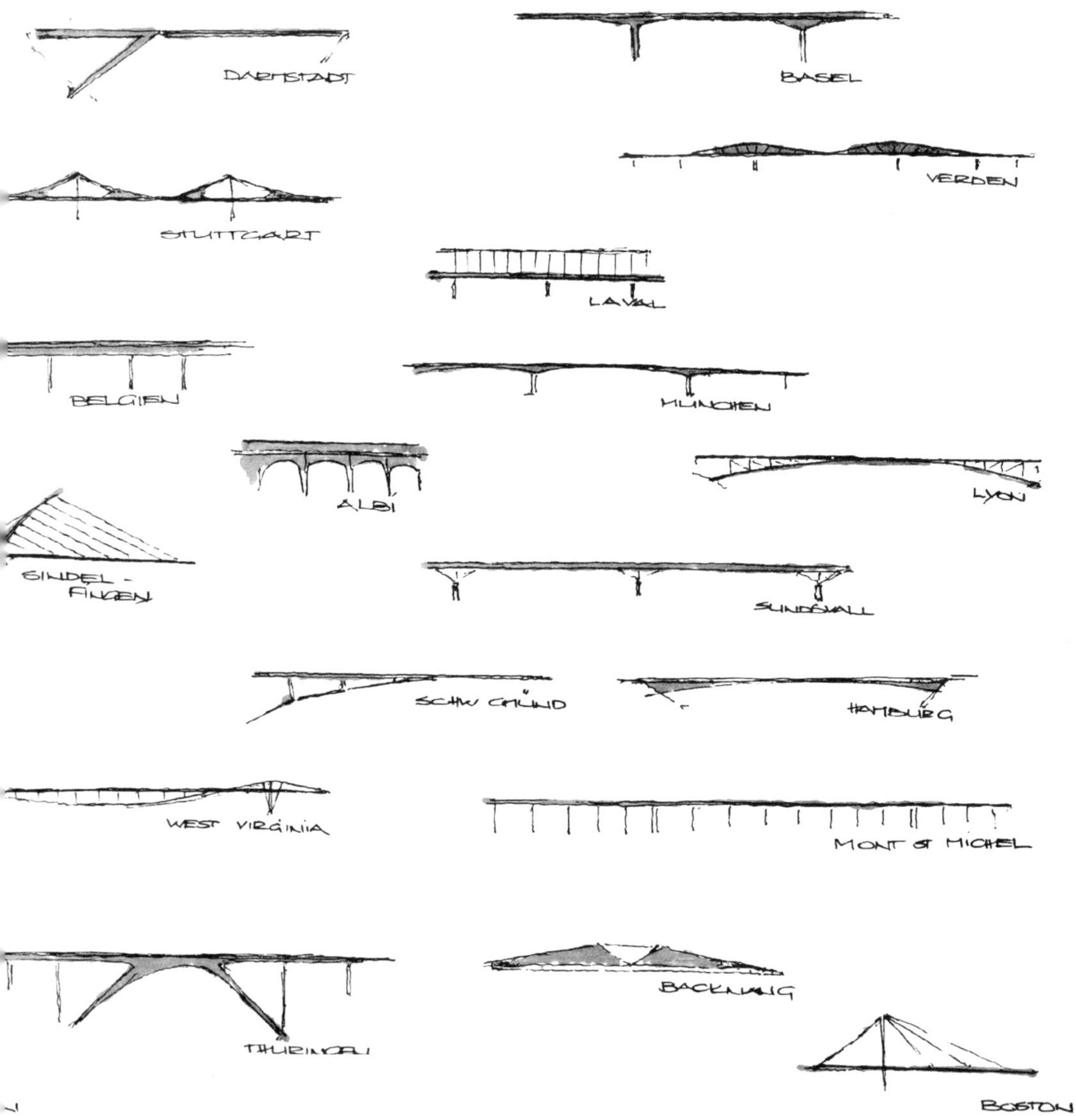

Generating diversity

Bridge construction is a field that clearly demonstrates the wealth of forms that can develop under given boundary conditions, regardless of how clearly the design brief is outlined. The most important design goals—structural stability, suitability for use, economy, and elegance—are subject to conditions set by the topography, the statics, the manufacturing and erection technologies, and the design and social parameters. At times, these goals are contradictory, or difficult to bring into harmony. This fact, however, spurs on our engineering creativity far more than it constrains us. The balancing act between requirements and resources results in a unique solution for the specific project being undertaken at a given location.

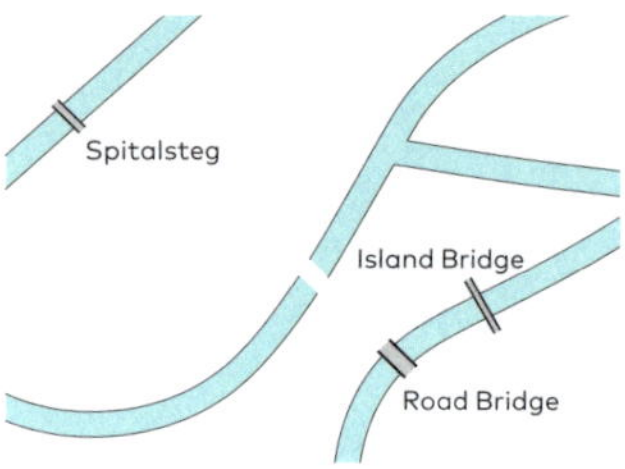

The **Riedlingen family of bridges** nicely illustrates how each bridge needs to be formulated in its very own way. Three very different bridges were built in close proximity to each other, with plans to add one more. Each of the completed bridges was designed in response to the unique parameters that exist at the three sites.

First, we were commissioned to design a **road bridge over the flood relief channel** because a trussed girder structure dating from 1901 had to be replaced after the completion of flood protection measures. Since the location is important as a gateway to the old town center conservation area, a design competition for the new bridge and its surroundings was held in 2003. sbp, in collaboration with knoll.neues.gruen landscape architects, proposed a winning entry that incorporated an integral steel composite bridge in the adjacent open spaces. The structure is placed above the deck, lending the bridge its identity: two elegant, shallow arches with a rise of 2.75 m that span more than 34 m over the channel. Viewing the bridge's cross section, the arches rise between the roadway on the one hand and the sidewalk and cycle path on the other, thus separating the different traffic zones. The monolithic connection of the components results in a slender, robust, and low-maintenance structure.

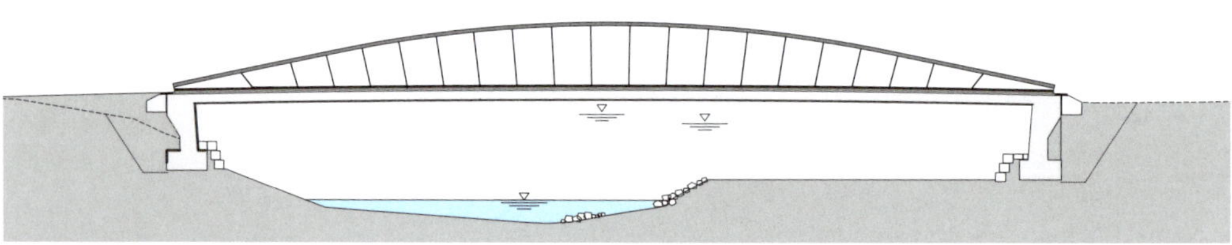

It was crucial for the project to be completed in the shortest possible time, as the bridge was located at an important traffic junction and access to the city center had to be restricted during construction. In just eight months, the main structural components, including the cantilevered sidewalk and cycle path units, were prefabricated at the factory; in parallel, the existing bridge was demolished, the civil engineering works (including pile foundations and abutments) were carried out, and the roadway slab was then concreted onto the crossbeams. All this was done without falsework, as any scaffolding would have been required to have sufficient stability to withstand a ten-year flood (i.e., a 10 percent chance of occurring in any year), increasing the labor and cost involved.

The arches consist of flat steel plate sections with flat steel hangers welded onto them radially at intervals of 1.5 m. They carry the trapezoidal longitudinal beams, which, in turn, support the cantilevered units for the sidewalk and cycle path. These taper outwards, lending the bridge a more slender horizontal profile.

The channel crossing is highlighted by a specially designed LED strip mounted along the side of each arch. In addition to the architectural effect, it provides functional lighting for cyclists and pedestrians. The *lighting design concept* makes the bridge a recognizable gateway to the historic center at night.

↘ 208

Economical and structurally rational, the walkway and railing panels consist of inexpensive gratings. LED strips are built into the flange of the upper chord on the inside so as to illuminate the walkway at night without dazzling people.

Built about 60 m upstream, the **Island Bridge** leads from a nearby car park to the Donauinsel (Danube island), from where one can walk to the central pedestrian zone. The bridge was initially conceived as a temporary structure to provide access to the town center for pedestrians and cyclists while the Channel Bridge was being constructed. At the planning stage, it was decided to opt for a permanent structure as a means of stimulating the long-term development of the Donauinsel as a recreational area.
At 37.5 m long and 2.9 m wide, the bridge is an unobtrusive truss structure in the form of a trough bridge with 1.5-m-high sidewalls. The descending diagonals follow the pattern of forces; they occur half as frequently towards the midspan and are left out completely in its middle fifth. With a form that follows the statics and using standardized modular elements, a bridge evolved that was both economical to build and aesthetically pleasing.

A structural counterpoint to this rather pragmatic solution is the delicate pedestrian bridge, **Spitalsteg,** that spans the former moat from the northwest. The graceful, arched steel bridge replaces a wooden one that had fallen into disrepair. With a width of only 2.5 m and a length of 18 m, it was completely prefabricated in the workshop and then lowered into place as a complete unit. Its structure is characterized by slender bars rising from the arches to support the deck and continuing upwards to form the railings. It makes a design statement that enhances and stages the transition to the old town.

Diversity arises from the combination of technical and scientific principles with joy in design, diligence, perseverance, attention to detail, and the particular, individual relationship to a place at a specific time. Jörg Schlaich

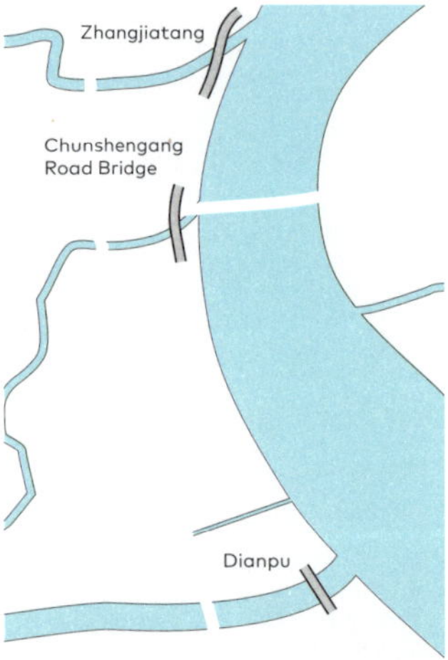

Each bridge fits into its surroundings in its own way. The same is true, on a larger scale, of the ***three bridges on the West Bund*** for the promenade along the Huangpu River in Shanghai. These bridges are part of a major plan to develop and relandscape the banks of the river in a former industrial area. The Huangpu has many tributaries, which have to be crossed by pedestrians and vehicles of all kinds, both private and public. Three of the tributaries are crossed by the Dianpu, Zhangjiatang, and Chunshengang bridges, built in 2017 and individually tailored to their respective situations.

47 ↙

AR

The **Dianpu Bridge** is a three-span girder bridge with a total length of 140 m and a main span of 75 m. It carries the West Bund's main traffic artery at a height of 6 m over the 75-m-wide river and the bankside roads. The deck accommodates two lanes in each direction, walkways, and railway tracks. The structure is essentially a continuous beam on broad V-shaped piers. The superstructure is designed with a variable-cross section along the main span over the river, which increases in a parabolic form towards the midspan. Seen in elevation, the shape of the superstructure mimics the bending moment diagram, and this curve is adapted for the walkways attached at the side.

A completely different solution can be found in the 80-m-long **Zhangjiatang Bridge,** which is designed for pedestrians and cyclists. Gently curving on plan, it spans the river of the same name at a height of 4 m. Its main span measures around 55 m and its structure adapts the principle of the Fink truss, albeit in an inverted form. Steel cables suspended from six slightly inclined masts carry a deck of around 8 m in width, which consists of a central box section with laterally projecting ribs, reminiscent of spinal vertebrae in cross section. The number of cables per mast, like the height of the masts, varies according to the load. This refinement produces a bridge structure that is even more efficient and lightweight than usual for this particular static system.

A structure with transparency; of the six masts, the primary supporting elements are the two outer ones, which rise as far as 8 m above the deck. Three cables are suspended from these mastheads on each side. The four middle masts are a little stockier, with the number of cables at each masthead reduced by one towards the midspan.

The third bridge of the trilogy is the **Chunshengang bridge,** which spans the mouth of the Chunshengang where it flows into the Huangpu. Built to relieve traffic congestion in the southern part of the city center, the bridge deck, with a width of 33.5 m, accommodates two lanes in each direction and a pedestrian walkway on each side. The bridge is characterized by its steel structure, with a static system of two trusses, each reduced to a single span. The resulting structure is strikingly simple and well-proportioned, despite its high load requirements. This design replaces the truss bridge specified in the official brief, in comparison with which it enhances the view from the nearby residential development.

Refinement and adaptation

The continual development of structures and consequently their changing appearance is evident in our projects over the decades. Thus, our style has become more sculptural—moving on from linear designs to surfaces and volumes. For smaller spans, for example, Jörg Schlaich designed bridges whose linear design makes the pattern of forces clearly legible. Each structural component shows which function it performs and what stresses it is subject to. For example, the **two bridges** from 1992 **at the Pragsattel,** north of Stuttgart city center, designed by Luz, Lohrer, Egenhofer, Schlaich consortium, both feature differentiated substructures. They are typical of the design approach that prevailed at the time. One is a continuous deck bridge over several road lanes, with steel supports that branch repeatedly, effectively creating multiple springing points. That allows the supports to be more slender and the concrete slab to be only 25 cm thick for a span of 23 m. The other is an arched bridge spanning 38 m across a road, like an inverted suspension bridge with two end masts and splayed cables.

Just how much the design language has changed can be seen by comparing them directly with the **Getwing bridge** in Zermatt, from 2017. A replacement was needed for a bridge dating from 1899 on the Gornergrat railway, not far from the valley station. We worked on the bridge in collaboration with local architects mooser.lauber.stucky and SRP Ingenieur AG. The structure was developed by playing with the volume of the classic box girder. The substructure consists of two sculpturally shaped boxes of sheet steel, which taper downwards to the one-third points of the 25-m span. Seen in elevation, this leaves a central "triangle" free. The deck was

constructed as an orthotropic plate with longitudinal stiffeners and transverse members. As space is limited in Zermatt, the bridge was prefabricated and lifted into place at night, when the road could be closed to traffic. A bifurcated tie of flat steel runs beneath the boxes from abutment to abutment. It was prestressed by jacking at what would later be the bearing stiffeners, while the bridge structure (upside down at the time) was held down at its midspan by a retaining construction. The distance between the "high" points decreased by about 6mm through elastic deformation as a result of prestressing. After the bridge had been lifted onto the abutments and as the superimposed loads were put in place, the tie stretched and the bridge acquired a level gradient as calculated.

The two lowest points of the hollow boxes define the static height of the underspanning. At these points, the tie divides into two so that the tensile force can be transferred directly to the two bearing points of each raised abutment. By reducing the structural height, the clearance below was increased to 4.6m. Thus it barely interrupts the view of the Matterhorn as well as improving the appearance of a busy traffic junction.

The **Rotes Steigle** bridge stands out for its clarity of form. Its powerful yet graceful supporting structure evolved, so to speak, from combining linear and voluminous designs, and it makes the flow of forces almost tangible. Perhaps that is why the bridge received one of the German Engineering Awards in 2018. The busy A8 highway was widened to a total of seven lanes and two hard shoulders between the Stuttgart intersection and the Leonberg East junction. The existing arched bridge had an insufficient structure gauge (minimum clearance outline), so it had to be demolished and replaced. The new bridge, spanning around 75m, is a composite structure consisting of a steel arch with a varying cross section, outwardly inclined oblique steel struts, and a reinforced concrete deck. It spans the highway without intermediate supports.

In response to its location in a cutting 11m below the surrounding terrain, it is designed as a two-hinged arch, resting on stainless steel rocker bearings. The arch, in the form of a hollow steel box section, has a span of around 60m and a rise of 4.93m. Its cross-sectional width narrows from the crown to the impost foundations. Its cross-sectional height, however, increases in the same direction. The cross-sectional area thus remains constant over the full length of the arch.

This dimensional counterpoint generates a dynamic appearance as well as being structurally efficient.

AR

The superstructure is 6.75 m wide and is supported by slender, oblique struts rising from the arch. It is monolithically connected to each abutment via a vertically embedded, flexible steel plate about 1.15 m high, 3 m wide, and only 2 cm thick. A continuous steel sheet, 3 m wide and 30 mm thick, is mounted on the underside of the superstructure. It served to stiffen the steel arch and strut assemblies when the two segments of the arch were being lifted into place. In the finished state, the steel sheet acts as external reinforcement for the reinforced concrete deck. The width of the struts decreases from 280 mm to 30 mm corresponding to their decreasing lengths from the edges of the span to its middle. The arch is visually separated from the deck at its apex, expressing the principle that the forces are transferred from the deck to the steel arch via the oblique struts. This makes the way in which the arch works as a support clearly visible. The outer faces of the struts and the steel arch are defined by a single plane on each side of the bridge, each of which is angled downwards toward the other. This helps the steel sheet below the deck, the struts, and the arch to form a visual unit.

In order to assemble the structure, the steel components were transported to a nearby site and welded together into two large segments about 35 m long and weighing 120 t each. This phased construction process meant that the A8 only had to be closed completely for two nights when the segments were lifted into place. Once they had been welded together at the crown, the concrete deck slab could be cast—in five phases using a formwork carriage—without disrupting traffic on the highway below. Because the reinforced concrete composite structure was produced in phases, thorough deformation and camber analyses had to be performed for the assembly and construction work. It was worth the effort, though, because the elegant, low-maintenance steel arch bridge is an eye-catching sight with high recognition value. With both the design and the construction planning in the hands of the same practice, it was possible to ensure that the construction work progressed smoothly and the bridge was of a high aesthetic and technical quality.

Pencil and paper

When it comes to bridge construction, the relationship of the load-bearing structure to the appearance is closer than with any other type of structure, whether the design is linear or rather sculptural. It is therefore especially important to take a holistic view that considers every aspect during the design process. Ideally, *the structure that is built in the end reflects what was sketched out at the beginning.* ↘ 20

A load-bearing structure evolves from a process of conceptual abstraction that is nonetheless descriptive. So in order to communicate our thinking, we employ a wide variety of methods using the many technical aids now available, such as form-finding tools, 3-D visualizations, and parametric tools. However, for the people we work with—and maybe even for ourselves—the most reliable and easily understood method is to draw sketches. This is still the clearest way to demonstrate the thinking behind a particular structural concept or static system.

We explore many solutions before settling on a final design, trying out new options and discarding them again and again, but the precision offered by CAD tools is unnecessary and even a hindrance at the conceptual design stage. Freehand sketching, in contrast, does not restrict your geometrical visualization, so you have much greater creative freedom. The forms themselves can lead to new ideas. Sketching allows us to present our thinking in a form that can be understood by builders and laypeople, which arouses their curiosity about the design. The design process thus becomes a link to both architecture and Baukultur (culture of building and the building of culture).

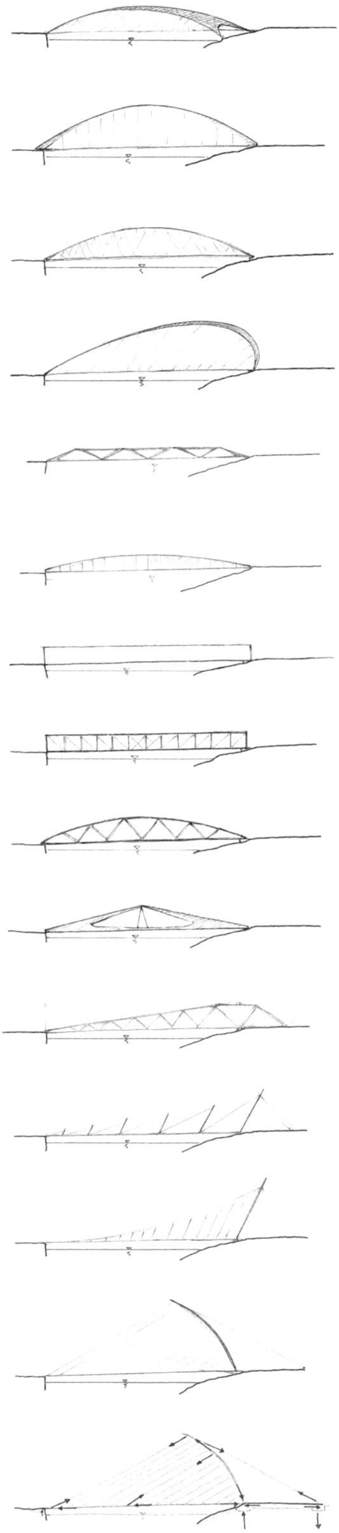

In designing, we strive to achieve concise simplicity and to reduce a bridge's structure to its essence. In the best cases, every single element is structurally necessary, appropriately shaped, and well-proportioned. At locations where the circumstances are rather complex, it is naturally more of a challenge to find a suitable solution. The **Bleichwiesensteg** (Dyers' Field Footbridge) demonstrates how a simple structural concept can produce a structure that takes very little time to build. Rudimentary as the sketch for the pedestrian

and cycle path connection over the Murr River may be, it nevertheless shows the essential aspects of the static system. Instead of a wooden walkway, a single-span steel girder connects the historic town center with the newly landscaped area of Bleichwiesenplatz. The link between the "old" and the "new" spans 27 m with a usable width of 2.5 m, resting on the original foundations, which have been repaired. The primary structure consists of two lateral box sections, which also form part of the railing. Spanning transversely between the box sections is an orthotropic deck, which makes the trough cross section into a frame and stabilizes the girders. These increase in depth from 30 cm at the abutments to 1.3 m towards the middle of the bridge. There they leave a triangular gap across which they are rigidly connected to each other by means of a hinged compression bar. With the compression bar acting as the top chord and the hinged connections left exposed, the maximum bending moment at the midspan is visibly divided into a force couple, making the flow of forces legible. The sturdy footbridge thus appears lightweight and dainty at the very point that is subject to the greatest bending moments. Not only is the central aperture an eye-catching design feature, it also made it possible to produce and

The delicate railings contrast with the sculptural form of the load-bearing components. The former consists of 4-mm horizontally prestressed stainless steel cables, which emphasize the structure's dynamic linearity. LED light strips set into the lower edges of the box sections illuminate the walkway in the dark without scattering light into the natural surroundings.

assemble the structure efficiently as two identical halves. These were connected on-site as a unified structural system.

Footbridges, more than other bridges, need not be solely—or even primarily—functional. They should also fit into their surroundings and offer a correspondingly attractive experience. Of course, they have to work statically and dynamically, but at the same time they have to be visually and physically appealing; after all, the users do come into direct contact with them. Since they are subject to fewer restrictive functional and static requirements than are road or railway bridges, there is greater leeway for devising solutions that respond to a particular location and use.

Drawing is the language of the engineer. It helps us to break down the problem and to contrast the possibilities or options at a fundamental level. It also allows us to consider variants and to think on a broad scale from the beginning, going ever deeper into the details as the design progresses. Andreas Keil

The **bridge over the Rhine-Herne Canal at Grimberg harbor** in Gelsenkirchen illustrates this in several respects. Functionally, it connects the Erzbahn cycle path—once a mining railway line—with the Emscher Park cycle path on the other side of the river; emotionally, it has given the place an identity of its own since its construction in 2009. It stands out for the way in which it traverses the canal in a sweeping arc rather than a straight line. The load-bearing structure, laid out as a crescent in plan, functions as a unilaterally suspended circular ring girder, as do others that we have constructed, such as the S-curved footbridge over **Gahlensche Strasse in Bochum** (2003) and the **footbridge in Sassnitz** (2007). The Rhine-Herne Canal bridge spans 141 m between the abutments. The suspension cable is 50 mm in diameter. It connects tangentially to the outer edge of the superstructure at points 24 m from the abutments, and is supported by a 45-m lateral mast, which is founded and guyed on the north bank.

The hangers are arranged radially at intervals of 3 m between these two connection points. They carry the torsion-resistant, steel box girder of the superstructure, which is asymmetrical and triangular in cross section. With a height of only 80 cm, it forms the backbone of the bridge's deck and carries the 12-cm concrete slab. The latter provides a durable surface for the cycle path while its mass and damping effect positively influences the dynamic behavior of the lightweight supporting structure. The bridge's delicacy is further emphasized by the transparency of the cable-mesh railings.

Built for Germany's Federal Garden Show in 2015, the **Weinberg Bridge** over the Havel River and its narrower side

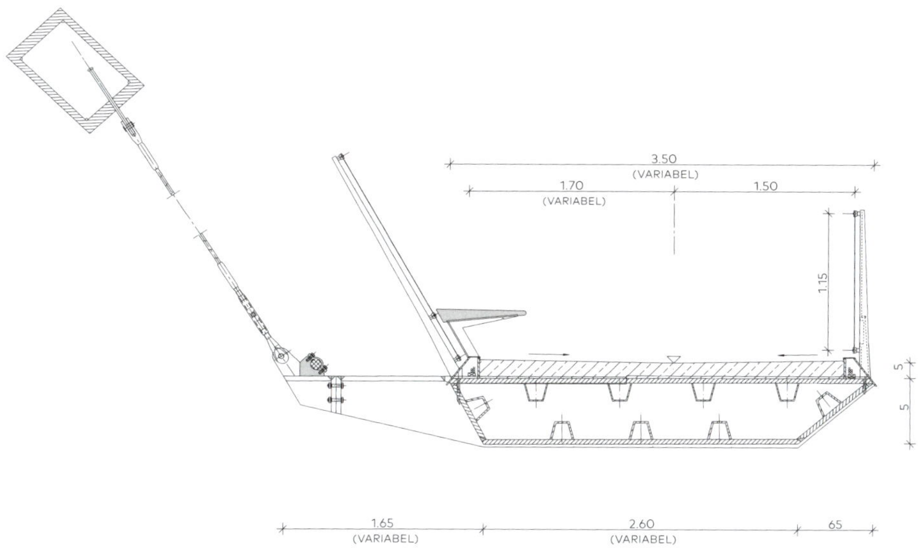

arm in Rathenow has become a veritable highway for pedestrians and cyclists. The flowing lines and striking silhouette of the bridge, which meanders for a distance of 350 m, announce that it is designed as an attractive place to spend some time. The deck rises gently to the arches across the water, where it broadens to accommodate integrated seating, while the unilateral suspension affords unobstructed views of the surrounding area. Appropriately for a bridge with the character of a treetop walkway, it links two recreational parks. The design originated in an entry by students at the HCU Hamburg in the 154th Schinkel Prize competition, which is held annually by the Architects and Engineers Association of Berlin. We were commissioned to take over the design development of this initial concept. The steel bridge is designed as an integral structure with a continuous beam comprising 15 spans. Its structure is defined by two asymmetrical arches, tightly curved in plan, consisting of square box sections. Hangers carry the longitudinal beams, which are curved in the opposite direction. The hangers are attached to cantilevered crossbeams that are joined to the longitudinal girders radially at intervals of 3 m, and extend inwards almost to the inclined plane of the respective arch. This refinement reduces the bending moments on the arch. The crossbeams also serve as fixing brackets for the tie cable that counteracts the outward thrust of the arch and thus establishes a static equilibrium. The arches are filled with self-consolidating concrete and incline outwards toward the apex, allowing them to function as counterweights to the deck.

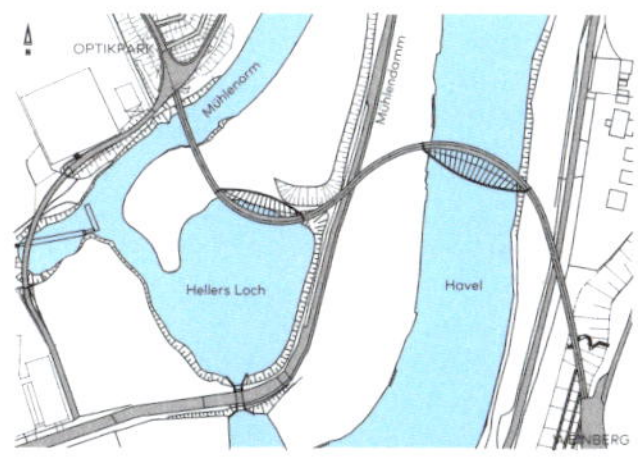

The routing is also the defining aspect of the **Passerelle de la Paix,** which we designed together with Dietmar Feichtinger Architectes. Erected in Lyon in 2014, this footbridge connects the 5-m-wide promenade of the Cité Internationale congress center with the suburb of Caluire-et-Cuire on the opposite bank of the Rhône. As well as providing a direct horizontal link at the embankment level, the steel bridge connects the riverside paths via a stairway alongside the arch. At the middle of the footbridge, the two routes meet to form an 8-m square, which transforms the structure into a public meeting place. The Peace Footbridge, as its name translates, is 220 m long altogether; it crosses the Rhône, which at this point is 160 m wide, in a single span consisting of an arch with an extremely low rise and no overhead supporting structure, in order to maximize transparency. Thick-walled, polygonal, welded steel tubes form a three-chord truss, the ends of which are restrained in foundations in the riverbanks. The three primary support elements are coupled at regular intervals by vertical triangular frames and are braced longitudinally by diagonal struts. The result is a spatial truss girder, which follows the rise of the arch and thus generates a dynamic geometrical form.

The slender bridge with a wooden-surfaced deck is designed without the need for movement joints, making it sturdy and reducing the required maintenance and repairs. However, the live load from pedestrian traffic is relatively high compared with the bridge's dead load, which makes the structure susceptible to vibration. Vibration absorbers at the third points and the midspan of the bridge dampen the torsional and vertical vibrations felt by the people walking across it.

The arch members and box sections were brought to the site after pre-assembly and welded together on-site. The entire central span of the three-chord trussed girder was raised on temporary pylons for assembly on one of the riverbanks. The structure was floated to its final position with the help of pontoons and then anchored in place. In order to stabilize it during the process, temporary guy wires were attached between the third points of the structure.

Although the Peace Footbridge pushes the limits of what is feasible with its extremely low rise, it achieves an elegant appearance and playfully demonstrates the spatial interaction of its supporting elements.

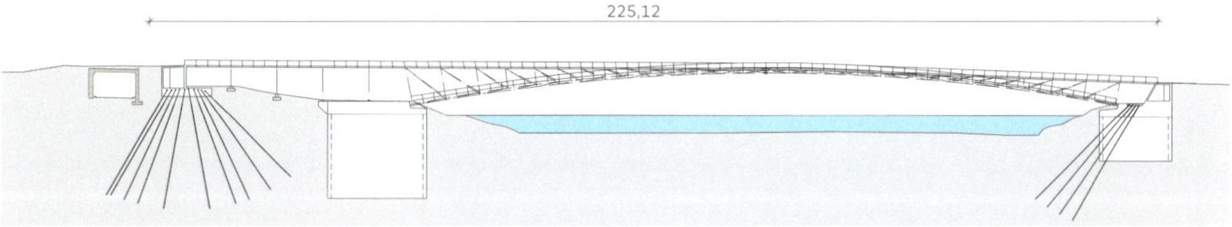
225,12

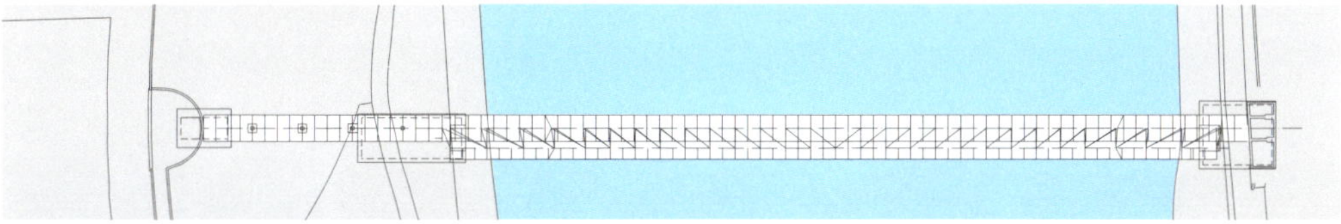

The supporting structure as a constitutive component

Many a famous bridge is remarkable for having an impressive location, or large spans, or perhaps an *extravagant supporting structure*. 50 ↙ Yet even a supposedly small and simple structure may boast of overcoming a variety of challenges relating to its materials, context, structure, appearance, and production. These inconspicuous objects often deserve the same degree of attention as major engineering works.

A creatively and properly designed structure can also be a crucial factor for bridges whose costs have to be kept low; in our view, it is really a prerequisite for them. Even what people consider to be rather insignificant construction briefs should lead to a high-quality result, however unspectacular the bridge may be. For example, roads for fast-moving traffic such as highways or dual carriageways, which often receive only uniform truss-and-plate bridges, can benefit from attractive infrastructure. The added value for motorists should not be underestimated, as such objects form landmarks for orientation and raise levels of attention on stretches that are otherwise monotonous.

People's perceptions and expectations of road, pedestrian, and railway bridges differ greatly within society. Most laypeople may be aware that the supporting structure of a footbridge is a designed element that contributes to the overall appearance. However, road—and especially rail—bridges tend to be seen as merely a means to an end. No matter what kind of bridge or structure we are working on, we always aim to make a worthy contribution to the tradition of building. Like our founding partners, we consider this the only acceptable *justification for altering nature by building on it*. 12 ↙

The **Josen Bridge** in Schwäbisch Gmünd, for example, has a modest span of 23.5 m. Carrying buses, cyclists, and pedestrians at a skew over the Josefsbach stream, it replaced two existing bridges in 2013. The bridge, with an arch and members supporting the deck, is a composite structure of steel and reinforced concrete. The choice of integral construction without structural bearings, at a design width of 7.7 m, has resulted in a simple, sturdy structure with low maintenance costs. The virtues of this bridge—its appropriate shape, its structural economy, and its long-term viability—only become evident upon closer inspection.

Another modest design that nevertheless significantly enhances the location is the **Bleichinsel Bridge** in Heilbronn. It connects the city center with an urban redevelopment area on the northern half of the Bleichinsel (Dyers' Island) in the river. Measuring 88 m long and 24 m wide, the road bridge over the Alt-Neckar is designed as a composite structure with a superimposed deck consisting of prefabricated concrete slabs supplemented with cast-in-place concrete. The steel structure beneath it consists of two slender longitudinal box girders and V-shaped struts that are inclined both longitudinally and transversely. Four of these struts meet at a single point on the pile foundations on each bank of the river. The struts and abutment walls are monolithically connected to the longitudinal girders and the superstructure. The bridge received a German Bridge Construction Award (Deutscher Brückenbaupreis) in 2018, in the category of Road and Railway Bridges. The jury was impressed by "its elegance and the ingenious node construction for bundling the columns." In addition, the jury emphasized that "with this design, the engineers have succeeded magnificently in fulfilling all of the requirements for a beautiful, low-maintenance, and inexpensive structure in a convincing manner."

AR

The idea that the load-bearing structure can also determine the interior of a bridge is illustrated by the **bridge at Seattle–Tacoma International Airport.** The overpass will connect two buildings at a height of approximately 24 m over a runway. Travelers entering the corridor will barely notice that they are high above the ground, similar to being in a large skyscraper. Only the striking diagonal stays will hint that the forces being transferred here are not the usual ones for a normal high-rise building. The passage belongs to a modernization program for the international arrivals area. Structurally, it is a large three-span girder on V-piers made of steel box sections, guyed at its ends to a pile foundation by cables of more than 140 mm in diameter. Escalators are installed in one leg of each V-pier; on one side of the bridge, a small, additional bridge branches off halfway up the escalator. The critical parameter for the design, which we have developed together with Skidmore, Owings & Merrill LLP, is the construction phase scheduling: it is only possible to close the runway once, and for no more than seven days. The middle span of the bridge will be prefabricated and lifted into place.

Another project by our office in New York is the construction of the **Arkansas River footbridge** in Tulsa. We developed The Gateway together with the architects of Michael Van Valkenburgh Associates as an entry in a design competition, from which it emerged as the winner. The new structure forms part of a park that is being created along the banks of the Arkansas River and is being planned by the same architectural practice. It will replace the badly dilapidated existing bridge connecting the east and west sides of the river and create a link between a park project called The Gathering Place and nearby neighborhoods. The bridge is designed exclusively for cyclists and pedestrians, and also aims to be a pleasant place to socialize. To this end, the deck broadens out at several places. These bays form separate areas from the walkway and are furnished with seating. As the design stands currently, the arch bridge will be constructed from a system of steel sheets, and would be the first of its kind in the United States.

Expertise plus endurance

In addition to creativity, a typical project by sbp requires expertise, courage, and patience. The story of the **Neckar Bridge in Bad Cannstatt** makes clear how much stamina may be needed for some processes. Carrying four tracks serving the local and national railway networks, as well as a suspended pedestrian walkway, the bridge is part of the Stuttgart 21 project. Its design is based on a proposal for a so-called steel-sail bridge, which won the design competition in 1998. Suspended from six slender masts by thick steel plates curved like sails, the composite steel structure forms a long, thin strip when seen from the side. The steel "sails" clearly illustrate the pattern of forces in the structure, resulting in a sculptural form.

The seven-span continuous beam is 345 m long, including two main spans of 77 m and 74 m. The bridge forms a central node in a dense transport network. Since it stands in Stuttgart's mineral spa protection zone, it is subject to tight restrictions on any disturbance of the subsoil. The "sails" that define its appearance are made of high-performance, micro-alloyed structural steel plates; this is the first time that thicknesses greater than 100 mm have been used

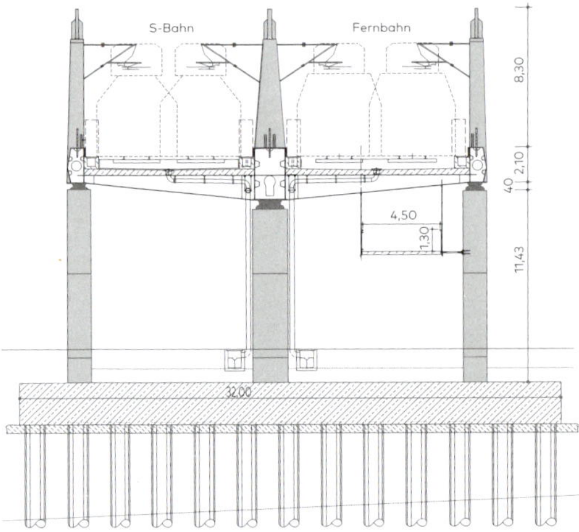

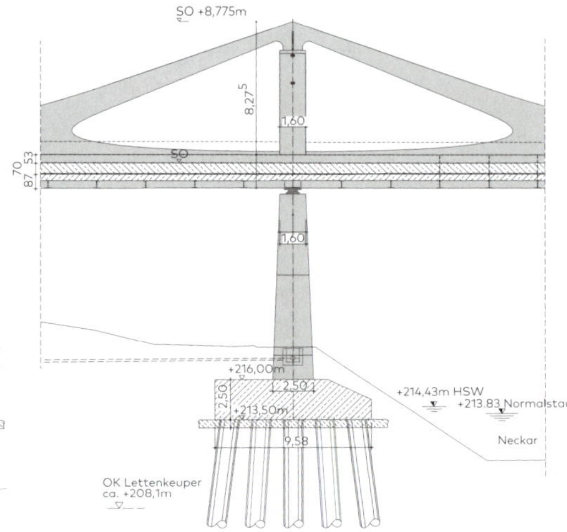

The bridge was launched across the Neckar River in twelve phases, spaced over a period of twelve months, using the incremental launching technique. The superstructure is suspended from the masts by steel "sails." In addition to their static function, they define the bridge's identity and serve as a sound barrier.

for a German railway bridge. This required not only special calculation methods in order to gain official approval of the designs, but also additional approval procedures.

The 24.5-m-wide superstructure is designed as a one-piece steel grid with one central and two lateral box girders running longitudinally. Steel girders at intervals of about 3m run transversely, acting in concert with the passively reinforced concrete deck. This construction results in a relatively light, sturdy, and durable superstructure with dynamic properties that are advantageous for railway bridges. The superstructure is suspended from the steel pylons by the steel "sails" and their "ties." Their geometry is derived from the principle of inverting structures subjected to compression or tension. Behaving structurally rather like membranes, they absorb the forces from the lateral girders and transfer them via extensions to the mastheads. The attachment to the mastheads is the critical point of the flow of forces between the "sails" and the masts. High-performance, fine-grained structural steel has therefore been used for these members. The loads concentrated at the mastheads are transferred via cap plates to the box sections that form the masts and then down these via reinforced concrete piers to the foundations. These have been constructed as deep foundations with bored piles under the main spans of the bridge and as shallow foundations for the abutments and approach bridges.

In designing the bridge, we had to resort to special calculation and dimensioning methods, beyond those provided for in the standards regulations. This meant that "approvals in individual cases" (ZiE) had to be obtained from the building control authority, which in this case was the Federal Railways Authority.

Thanks to our dedication and expertise, it was possible to use steel structures of a complexity and slenderness that had not yet been seen in railway bridge construction. The bridge thus sets an example for future structures of this type. In the best case, the format of the design documents submitted and accepted for the approval procedure will also serve as a basis for future amendments to the regulations.

Integral and semi-integral railway bridges, especially for high-speed rail transport, present a variety of technical challenges, so they are usually subject to additional approval procedures. Among these challenges are the verification of the stresses in the rail tracks for longer bridges, proofs of dynamic stability at 1.2 times the design speed, and proofs of the fatigue behavior of monolithic joints. We are constantly expanding our wealth of experience by planning such integral bridges. ↘ 331

Designing in context

Aesthetic sensitivity is a prerequisite for designing a good bridge, be it in the inner city or in an unspoiled natural landscape. Many of our bridges vividly demonstrate the importance of analyzing the functional requirements precisely in order to generate a robust basis for a tailor-made design. Probably the most memorable example of this is the **Boy Scouts Bridge** (together with Hatch Mott MacDonald) of 2013 in Glen Jean, West Virginia, built on the site where the Boy Scouts of America Jamboree is held every four years. The bridge occupies a prominent position in the topography, making it deservedly into a landmark. It is even possible to access the supporting structure itself. As well as crossing in the usual way, on the deck, the scouts can go from one end of the bridge to the other on steel catwalks attached to the two suspension cables. Starting from the abutments, the catwalks rise up to the heads of the oblique sets of masts, where they are connected transversely by a platform. After continuing over the saddle, the catwalks run underneath the bridge deck in the middle of the span, thus permitting a view of its underside, which would otherwise remain out of sight.

The **bridge to Mont Saint-Michel** in Normandy is another design that responds structurally and formally to its context. In this case, the value added is rather unusual, because in addition to providing a scenic approach to the island, the bridge's form is meant to prevent further sedimentation in the estuary. Mont Saint-Michel has been a UNESCO World Heritage Site since 1979 and is one of France's top tourist attractions; it now attracts more than three million visitors a year. Until 2014, a causeway built at the end of the nineteenth century led from the mouth of the river to the monastery and its mountain. Because of the causeway—and the tidal barrage built at Couesnon during the 1950s—sedimentation had increased because the natural outflow of water was no longer sufficient to flush sand deposits back into the sea. In order to prevent the estuary becoming choked, a new system of lock gates traps water from the river and the sea at high tide and lets it out at low tide so that it flushes sediment into the sea. A competition for a new crossing was held in 2001, which we won together with Dietmar Feichtinger Architectes. The resulting viaduct describes a sweeping curve across the estuary and terminates at an artificial platform located before the mountain. This area is periodically flooded by the tides, turning Mont Saint-Michel into an island on eighteen days each year. With a length of 756 m, the composite steel and concrete structure is designed as a semi-integral bridge.

The box girders of the superstructure combine with the crossbeams mounted every 3 m to form the backbone of the structure, a kind of steel grating. It is supplemented with prefabricated concrete slabs and concrete cast on-site to fill the joints between them. This causes the individual plates to act together statically as a panel.

Consisting of two welded box girders, the superstructure runs as a continuous beam over 134 steel columns, arranged in pairs every 12 m. The columns are restrained in pile foundations and connected rigidly to the superstructure. At the moment, these supports are still largely covered with sand, but the sediment is gradually being washed back out to sea. The columns will thus end up as stilts with an ever-greater buckling length of up to 6 m, which means that the structure as a whole will become less rigid and potentially susceptible to deformation. This predicted change in the static conditions had to be taken into account in our dimensioning. Taking a holistic approach allowed us to create a graceful bridge that will continue to fit unobtrusively into the landscape as its immediate surroundings change.

It is always a challenge to recognize how far I can go, how far I can manage the risk. We have the courage needed to do so, we understand the supporting structures, and we know what we are doing. Andreas Keil

Equally tailored to the local conditions, albeit radically different ones, the ***Bastia L'Aldilonda walkway*** on Corsica fits into its surroundings. The rough, steep rocks outside the fortifications were once intentionally left inaccessible, but times have changed. The zone is to be made accessible for residents and tourists by a promenade weaving its way 450 m along the cliffs from the bay of Ficaghjola to the beach at Arinella. A design competition was held, which we won together with Dietmar Feichtinger Architectes and Corsican architects Buzzo-Spinelli. The route responds to the topography in a variety of contexts, going down almost to the waterline or perching 5 m above the waves, and even passing through the cavernous ramparts. At the latter point, the 25-m gallery is illuminated by a light shaft and contains an internal staircase that allows access to the citadel. The material of the walkway has been chosen to reflect its natural surroundings. Locally sourced rock chippings will be added to the concrete aggregate. Where the path is cut into the cliffs, the deck of prefabricated concrete slabs will be anchored vertically in the rock. Where the promenade cantilevers out, it will be borne on brackets designed to withstand the enormous loads imposed by the surf. The railing is made of weathering steel, which is resistant to corrosion in saline climates. Its coloration also blends in perfectly with the rusty quartz tones found in the rock. When it has been completed, the promenade will be an attractive place to socialize and enjoy new perspectives of the picturesque city and the sea.

↘ 268

AR

A sensitive approach to design requires not only a carefully considered response to the context, but also a keen awareness of other aspects, such as statics, construction, manufacturing technology, and assembly methods. In the case of the **Flugfeld (airfield) bridge** in Böblingen/Sindelfingen, the context required a sophisticated planning strategy. Despite the comparatively small span, the assembly process, and thus the structure itself, had to be taken into account at the concept design stage. Normally, this is only necessary when building large bridges. The bridge is part of a project to redevelop the grounds of the former Württemberg state airport as a residential area and business park.

A long, straight lake, the Lange See, has been created at the heart of the neighborhood; its shape recalls a runway and thus the past use of the site. A direct link across the lake was needed for pedestrians and cyclists. The bridge also had to bestow a sense of identity as a local landmark. However, the scope for foundations on the northern side was limited, owing to the cofferdam serving as an embankment and the direct proximity of the promenade. Positioning supports in the lake itself was also out of the question, because the lake had already filled and any future intervention bore a risk of damaging the lake's waterproof lining. In these circumstances, the best solution was an asymmetrical, cable-stayed bridge. This allows almost the entire load to be transferred to the southern bank, where there is adequate space for foundations. Furthermore, the harp-like structure, with its intriguing double-curved pylon, generates the desired recognition value.

The railing is formed of stainless steel wire mesh, which offers the greatest possible transparency. The handrail is made of wood on a stainless steel bar with an inlaid LED light strip.

The special geometrical form naturally has structural advantages: the curvature reduces the bending moments created in the pylon legs by the stay cables, so that the cross-sectional dimensions can be minimized. The superstructure is designed as a composite construction. It consists of a superstructure deck plate only 15 mm thick, with lateral girders made from hollow sections, which also stiffen its edges. The steel trough thus created was conceived as lost formwork, serving as the bottom layer of reinforcement after the concrete had cured. The consequent reduction of weight and the phased assembly allowed the segments to be lifted into place with easily available, medium-sized, mobile cranes. The heavy composite slab offers better dynamic behavior than an all-steel solution would. The open spiral steel ropes that transfer the loads to the pylon are connected via turnbuckles to the lateral girders every 3 m.

The double-curved legs of the pylon are constructed of trapezoidal steel box sections of varying depths. At the head, they merge to form a single trapezoidal cross section, which is constructed as a flexurally and torsionally rigid element. Attached to the head are the two anchor cables, consisting of full-locked coil steel rope. An expansion joint is inserted at the northern abutment. Only lateral forces are transferred here, via two restraints. In the other direction, the superstructure gradually becomes thicker toward the southern abutment, where it merges with the abutment. The equilibrium of forces is accurately reflected in the static behavior of this small, but perfectly formed, bridge structure.

Big and bold

AR

Every design needs a good detailing, especially in the case of large structures, such as the **fourth Danube bridge** in Linz, another project that we are working on together with gmp · von Gerkan, Marg and Partners Architects. It is part of a major Austrian infrastructure development—the A26 highway, a four-lane western bypass for the city of Linz—and it crosses one of the busiest waterways in Europe, as well as rail tracks and a road. The crossing actually consists of two adjacent road bridges, designed as suspension bridges with a span of 305.55 m. Owing to the steep hillsides rising from the northern bank, they connect to the existing transport network there via tunnels.

The topography and geology of the Danube valley make it possible to anchor the bridges' suspension cables directly in the rock and to dispense with pylons within the structure gauge (minimum clearance outline).

Measuring nearly 22.5 m wide and 2.53 m high, the superstructure is planned as a composite steel construction, with a central steel box girder and haunched steel crossbeams spaced at the intervals of the hangers. The 145-mm-diameter suspension cable bundles are composed of 12 parallellay, fully locked coil ropes around 500 m long. The hangers too are coil ropes, but with a diameter of 95 mm. The cable clamps are cast-steel units. The required noise barrier with a height of 4 m is designed to be transparent, so that the bridge is perceived neither as an enclosing trough by its users nor as a bulky bar from the outside. The minimal, simple structure ensures that the bridge will blend into the landscape.

At 695.6 m long, the **Southern Elbe crossing** will inevitably be a striking landmark among the industrial areas and port facilities of Hamburg's Moorburg district, but it will be nonetheless graceful and transparent. The five-span road bridge is one of the construction works needed for the new A 26 highway link. The competition brief contained demanding technical and functional specifications, as well as aesthetic requirements, which were successfully met by our entry, designed jointly with WTM Engineers from Hamburg and DISSING+WEITLING architecture from Copenhagen. These requirements relate to the need to fit in with the location, which is primarily characterized by the existing Kattwyk bridges and the visually dominant port facilities.

The integral, cable-stayed bridge has a main span of 350 m and a two-bay sidespan at either end, measuring 88 m and 90 m. The bridge is notable for a technically advantageous and architecturally striking feature: its masts, around 140 m high, are split longitudinally both above and below the deck. The split section chosen for the mast piers lets them appear light and elegant, despite their size and the enormous loads. It was decided to place the masts centrally in the superstructure's cross section, which made it logical to divide the bridge deck in two and lighten its appearance by making the central gap continuous. The gap is continued in the viaducts on either side of the main bridge. The constant total width of 39.6 m is thus made up of two aerodynamically formed steel box sections, the transverse members extending to support the outer edges, and the central gap.

In the side spans, beyond the array of cable stays, the superstructure is designed as a robust steel composite structure for a length of about 71.5 m. The superstructure of the main bridge, however, is an all-steel construction with an orthotropic deck. The main transverse girders consist of steel box sections and are positioned at 12-m intervals. The cable anchorages are arranged alternately with these girders: in the main span at the same interval of 12 m, but in the side spans there are two anchorages between each of the main transverse girders.

The chosen structure is highly economical at spans of this length. In conjunction with the integral construction method, it creates a bridge that will become an unmistakable landmark, thus maintaining the tradition of innovative large-bridge construction in Hamburg.

The case of the **bridges for the A11 highway** near Bruges in Belgium illustrates how civil engineering of genuine quality can evolve from a conventional brief that, to begin with, is weighted in favor of financial considerations. Forming part of the 12-km-long infrastructure project are four integral and semi-integral viaducts up to 770 m in length, designed as prestressed solid superstructures. The sequence of bridges consists of separate structures for the northern and southern carriageways. Viaduct K032, with a total length of 770 m, was carried out as an integral construction for a length of 620 m, which is connected monolithically with the piers to the superstructure instead of via bearings. The superstructure, with a width of 19 m, is longitudinally prestressed. The prestressing tendons in the superstructure are laid in two layers, with the upper layer overlapping above the columns and the lower layer coupling to the construction joints, 6 m from the pier axis. The long, thin bridge forms a continuous beam with individual spans of 35 m, bearing on 24 slender pairs of piers. These vary in height up to 17 m, with a width of 2.5 m each and a thickness of only 50 cm in most cases. However, the seven pairs of piers in the central part of the bridge are 80 cm thick, so as to absorb vehicular braking forces and to stabilize the static system overall. The superstructure and the piers are made of high-strength concrete and are monolithically connected. Nevertheless, transverse and longitudinal bracing is ensured because the piers are so wide that they act as plates transversely, and so numerous that they distribute the longitudinal forces.

The piers are supported on displacement piles, an economical foundation with little tendency to settle, which is well-suited to the sand and gravel strata that are present here.

The bridge has an impressive length for the type of construction, which we were largely able to achieve thanks to decades of experience with integral bridges. This was significantly enhanced through very intensive and fruitful collaboration with the construction contractor, Jan De Nul. The company was not only able but willing to explore unconventional solutions—an attitude that deserves special praise given the fact that, after completion, it was contracted to take over the operation and maintenance for a period of twenty years. This project clearly demonstrates that designing a bridge well, both statically and aesthetically, can also be beneficial financially.

Long viaducts and a short construction period made a high degree of rationalization essential. Prefabricated concrete piers made of high-strength concrete together with a formwork carriage were the most economical variant, especially as the rather marshy ground would not have borne any falsework scaffolding without preparing the soil first. The piers were made in one segment with self-compacting, cast-in-place concrete.

The innovative, lightweight supporting structure of the bridge resembles a net, in fact, it is based on a very common one. The model shown in the photo used a net in which oranges are sold, which was pulled into the desired shape and thus acquired static rigidity. This ingenious idea led to an expressive form, which is sensitively highlighted by LED spotlights at night.

A walkable shell—tradition meets innovation

Some of our bridges illustrate more than others our affinity for creative design, our regular use of experimentation, and perhaps something of our playful approach. Since May 2018, the **Trumpf footbridge** in Ditzingen has linked two production sites of the TRUMPF company, allowing its employees to cross the road between them safely. This small footbridge is something of an engineering manifesto. It shows, firstly, that classic form finding and modern parameterized design and calculation methods can be combined; and, secondly, that new and old fabrication methods can complement one another perfectly, be they state-of-the-art laser cutting or traditional shipbuilding techniques.

The delicate, walkable stainless steel shell is around 28 m in length with a sheet thickness of 20 mm, making it proportionally six times thinner than an eggshell. It combines some of the principles that keep cropping up in our projects. Among them are the trick of using inversion to arrive at a form, the use of symbioses (such as transferring the advantages of double curvature from lightweight construction to bridge building), the exploitation of the physical properties of a material, and the development of details such as the spherical bearings at the abutments—a homage to Jörg Schlaich's concrete shell in Stuttgart of 1974.

In this case, it was a simple net for oranges that helped to establish the preferred form. Its square mesh clearly reproduces the pattern of forces when the net is stretched. That is because, in contrast to triangular mesh, it cannot transmit shear stresses and so, under load, it aligns itself with the main membrane forces. The wooden board in the model represents an inversion of the distributed pedestrian load in the area of the walkway, so that here it acts upwards, creating a purely tensile net. The geometry would remain the same if the loads were applied as they are in reality, which is to say, downwards. The forces in the system would merely change their (plus/minus) sign, resulting in a purely compressive lattice shell, whose elements would now need to be capable of resisting compression. The subsequent complex calculation of such a lattice shell and the comparison of many different hole sizes and distribution patterns would, however, be almost impossible without the software available to us today.

In order to avoid durability and corrosion problems, stainless steel was chosen as a shell material suitable for use in compression. The metal sheets and the oval perforations in them were cut by TRUMPF lasers. Like the stainless steel panels of the Porsche pavilion in Wolfsburg, the component parts were worked into their double-curved shapes by the skilled shipbuilders of a shipyard in Stralsund, using plastic deformation. In order to avoid stability problems, the edges of the shell subject to compression were folded back. These inverted upstands meet to form triangular feet in the area of the four spherical bearings. At the two abutments, the 2.2-m-wide walkway is stiffened with a transverse bulkhead and supported in a way that allows longitudinal displacement. Further bracing or bulkheads were not necessary.

For safety reasons, it was not permissible for the walkway area to have perforations cut in it as large as those in the rest of the shell, so corresponding groups of small holes were drilled instead. Their effect is almost as transparent as that of the large perforations, because small glass plugs have been glued into all 14,300 holes, transmitting daylight downwards and thus giving the bridge a bright, attractive underside. The mandatory 1.2-m-high railing could easily have been a visual burden on such a light, transparent structure. We therefore used antireflective safety glass so that the railing is hardly noticeable.

Everything came together favorably for this project: Berthold Leibinger as an adventurous client, Barkow Leibinger as a tactful architectural consultant, an enthusiastic construction company, and our dedicated teams in Berlin and Stuttgart, all of whom worked hard to make it a success.

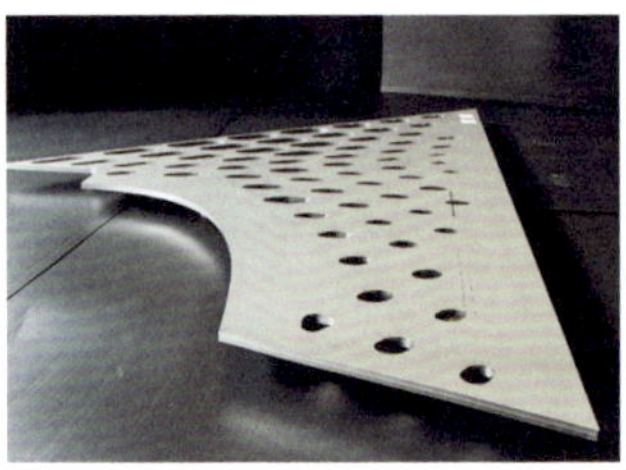

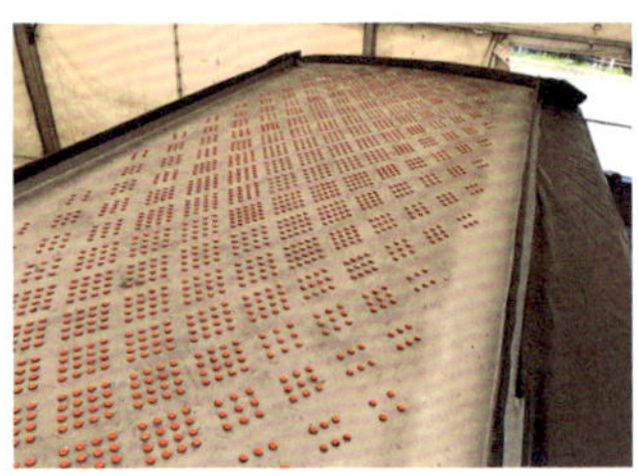

The shell was transported to the site in parts, which were welded together there. The whole structure was then lifted onto the bearings. The ropes carrying it were attached to a temporary framework underpinning the bridge.

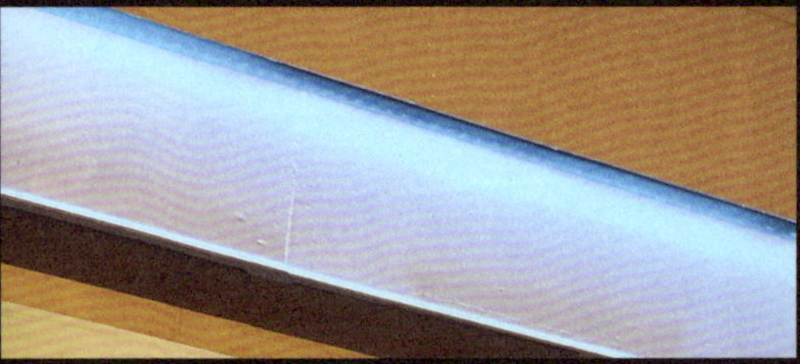

More about light and structure

Jörg Schlaich and Rudolf Bergermann are recognized worldwide as two structural engineers who have built innovative and unconventional engineering structures and, by virtue of their creative approach, have always been ahead of their time. Today, we are still inspired by elegant, resource-saving, lightweight structures and forward-looking ideas that are fit for the future of our industry. To keep pace with developments in this area, research—through the professorship of Jörg Schlaich at the University of Stuttgart—has always been an important aspect of our work. The ideas they developed frequently took the pair into new technical territory through which they navigated with the help of other specialists, including those from other disciplines.

Layer 04

Research

With Mike Schlaich as Chair of Conceptual and Structural Design at the Technical University of Berlin, we continue to link our practical activities with theory and research. In this way, our office has a direct connection to the latest knowledge and new research findings. This not only benefits our projects but feeds back current practice in our field to the university.

Our characteristic problem-solving skills shaped by curiosity are reflected in the areas of research we advise on, foster, or initiate. This research work benefits the projects arising from it and the clients involved.

Climate change, the energy revolution, and awareness of the need for sustainable behavior have led to a paradigm change in construction. An important example of this is our focus on *renewable energies*. After the oil crisis in 1973, we became involved with concepts and ideas for generating electricity from sunlight. Over the years, we found that this had opened a new field of activity for us. We gradually created an interdisciplinary team, which has now become an important part of us and has completed a long list of successful projects.

↘ 220

Climate covers—new spaces with reduced energy consumption

Sustainable building plays a large role in defining our value culture. It is forever throwing up new approaches in which we invest time and effort, in particular in the field of climate covers. Durable covers to buildings can, for example, make much more efficient use of the potential of difficult sites. They also greatly reduce the heating energy requirement and open new possibilities for leisure or work in spaces that can be used all year round. Glazed steel frames enveloping buildings subject to noise or other emissions or, in extreme climates, even enveloping whole commercial areas offer more flexible use of naturally lit spaces capable of being adjusted to changing requirements. The indoor temperature remains comfortable throughout the year. Passive solar energy prevents temperatures from falling below 5°C in winter, while in summer indoor temperatures are never higher than the ambient outdoor temperature, thanks to the variable solar shading and the use of water features and shade-giving plants.

Another advantage of a climate cover is that a conglomerate of individual buildings can take on the appearance of a single building with consistent architectural and urban design qualities. The protection of an external cover allows the buildings inside it to be much simpler in construction. The **Mont-Cenis Training Academy** on a 60-ha former industrial site in Herne was one of our first projects of this type and is exemplary of how to design a campus with short circulation and communication routes.

The project arose from a two-stage competition in 1991–92 in which the Jourda & Perraudin Studio, Lyon, emerged the winner with a forward-looking concept. Together with our project partners, Kassel-based architects Hegger Hegger Schleiff, and in cooperation with engineers from Ove Arup, we designed a timber construction and glass facade for the project. The load-bearing structure of the 180-m-long, 72-m-wide, and 16-m-high volume consists of truss girders supported on 130-year-old spruce trunks. The result is a light-flooded interior space containing the individual buildings. Completely protected from the weather, their building physics demands are rather rudimentary, offering new design and construction possibilities. The team recognized this potential, took an interdisciplinary approach, and purposefully realized the potential in the final design.

The **Children's Day Care Center** in Blankenfelde-Mahlow illustrates another advantage of climate covers. The project under the chair of Prof. Dr. Mike Schlaich at the Technical University of Berlin has been funded by the German Federal Environmental Foundation (DBU) as a prototype for a "moveable climate envelope for harvesting renewable energy" since 2014. It follows on from the research project "Climate Shells for Commercial Zones," which we managed and completed in 2006. The cover and the space it encloses actively harvest and store solar energy with the objective of further reducing heating costs and increasing the economic efficiency of the facility. The initially rather high capital costs have to be balanced against the savings in operating costs.

Together with the acoustic engineering consultants Moll, the climatic cover over the children's day care center was glazed in such a way that it also provided very efficient noise insulation. The children's day care center is located immediately north of one of the flight paths into and out of Berlin's nearby major airport. The potential of these sound-absorbing climatic covers is useful not only for buildings around airports but also, in particular, in heavily noise-polluted areas such as industrial and commercial zones, and alongside busy roads.

The cover in the case of the children's day care center is designed to be a moveable yet strong, durable, and robust steel frame structure. Retractable elements forming areas of the cover can open and close to adjust the artificial barrier to the outdoor surroundings to suit the use and requirements of the internal space. About 300 external solar protection sails, each 6.5 × 1.5 m in area and made from a PTFE membrane, are proposed for the glass roof and in front of the sidewalls. ↘ 263 *They open and close automatically, depending on the temperature and the amount of sunlight.* The moveable membrane elements have a light transparency of 25 percent and stay white because of the cleaning effect of the rain. The clever design succeeds in creating a transparent and moveable climatic cover that does not hermetically seal the 12,000-m^3 internal volume of the zero-energy building but connects the outside and inside environments with one another.

Cable-net facades with carbon tensile members

Many lightweight structures are possible only because they are prestressed. Cable and cable nets acquire the required stiffness by means of prestress. Without prestress activating "geometric stiffness," tightrope walkers could not perform their balancing acts nor a tennis racket rebound a ball.

Carbon structures that function on the same principle as a tennis racket look very promising. In order to investigate their potential, TU Berlin built a stressed ribbon bridge with a span of 13 m and a structural depth of only 1 mm in 2006. In 2013, using the carbon cables developed in that project, the university went on to design a spoked-wheel arrangement that could be used for stadium roofs. A prototype of a prestressed concrete bridge with carbon strands is currently being tested.

While steel cables were used for the first cable-net facade of its type

39 ↙

for the *Hotel Kempinski* at Munich Airport, our latest approach is to use slender carbon cables to produce extremely light facades that would make practically invisible load-bearing structures a reality. This is done by concealing thin, highly pre-stressed carbon strands in the horizontal and vertical silicone joints between glass panels. The result: the glass facade composed of many individual panels and an imperceivable load-bearing structure that appears elegant proportioned.

A practical implementation of this idea is currently being planned as a reasonably large cable-net facade for the project **Pavillon Albert Oehlen.** It was designed by architects Enguita & Lasso de la Vega from Madrid. Working with experts from the construction company Seele and the engineering company Carbo-Link, TU Berlin will carry testing for the necessary project-specific approval process required for construction methods not covered in building standards. There is no doubt that, when developing complex structural details designed to securely connect glass, silicone, and carbon, we are entering uncharted territory.

Academic freedom is a valuable asset. This freedom allows research without pressure for immediate economic benefit. The outcome is, however, beneficial to society and to "Baukultur." The knowledge gained spreads quickly among practitioners, just as their questions stimulate further research. Mike Schlaich

Load-bearing thermal insulation—infra-lightweight concrete

Not only glazing but also external walls in general will be the subject of continuous further development as increasingly more multifunctionality is demanded of them. Conventional wall systems with glued insulation layers are expensive to deal with during demolition, often cannot be separated for recycling, and have to be disposed of as special waste. Therefore, we are researching monolithic construction with a view to establishing its use in practice. Monolithic wall systems constructed in infra-lightweight concrete are an increasingly serious alternative, because here a single material not only acts as reinforcement but also performs other necessary functional roles: it carries loads, protects from weather, and insulates. Above all, it is durable. This unique combination of characteristics offers enormous potential and we wish to exploit it for the construction industry.

Infra-lightweight concrete is a high-performance concrete with an extremely low bulk density of less than 800 kg/m³. The aggregates are expanded glass or clay and are porous. Their porosity is responsible for their good thermal insulation properties. Although walls made out of infra-lightweight concrete are thicker, this offers new design freedom and unconventional shapes. Fair-faced facades in infra-lightweight concrete require less temporary and permanent support, and, without complex insulation details, simple building is once again possible. Another important aspect: porous infra-lightweight concrete carbonate absorbs so much CO_2 that it has a greatly reduced carbon footprint.

Practical applications reveal new knowledge, which in turn flows into research. We erected the first experimental house built using this type of construction in 2007. We entered the Smart Material House competition in 2012 in conjunction with Barkow Leibinger architects and Transsolar KlimaEngineering. In this competition, Mike Schlaich together with TU Berlin presented a further-developed infra-lightweight concrete with the high strength required for multistory buildings. Without additional thermal insulation, plaster, or other cladding, it would allow economical and ecological forms of fair-faced concrete structures in monolithic and single-skinned construction. The research work will be implemented in practice with a residential tower block in Berlin-Friedrichshain, also in conjunction with Barkow Leibinger and Transsolar. The tower will have twelve stories on a plan area of 18 × 26.5 m.

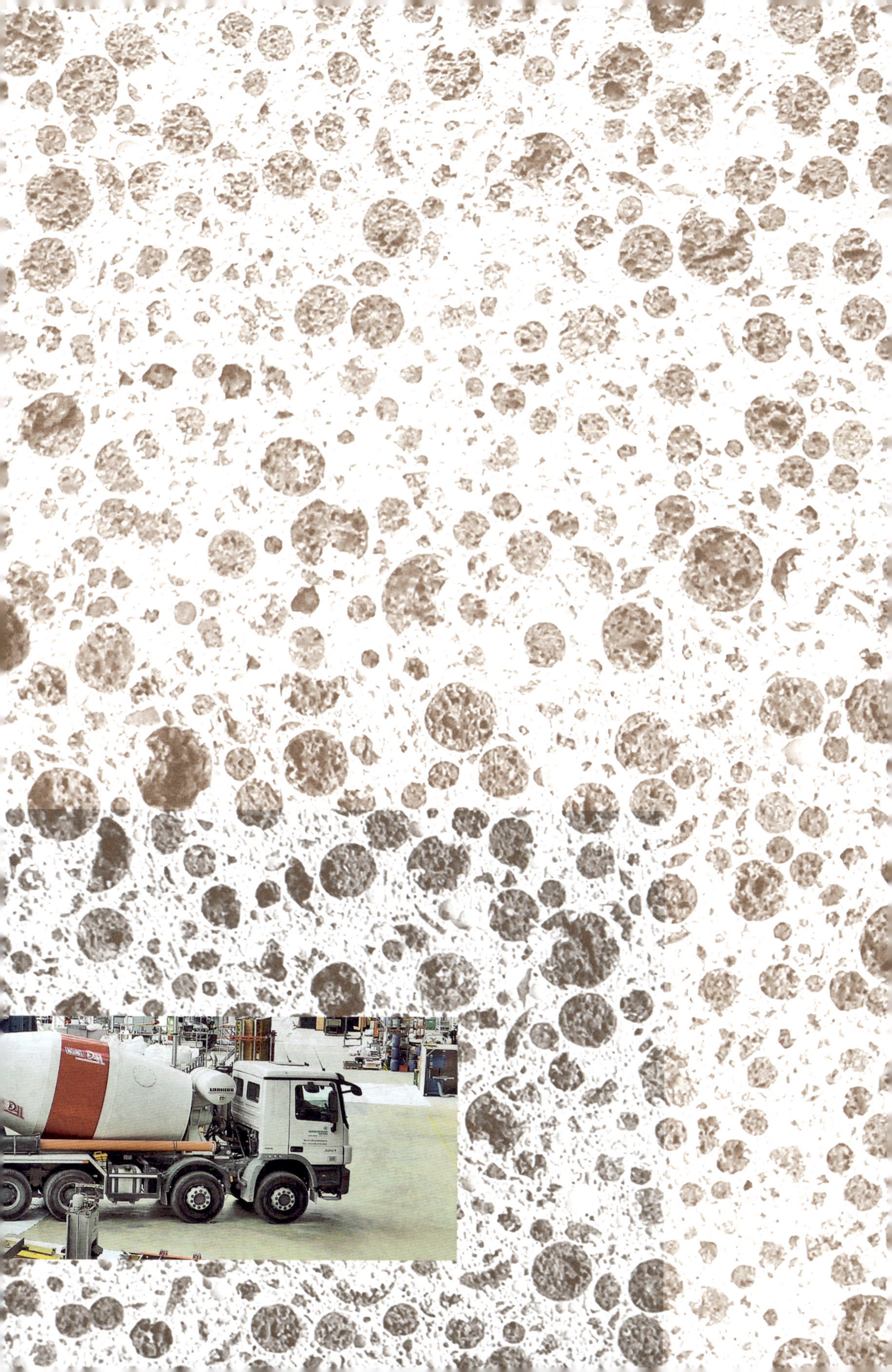
LIEBHERR

A further project in infra-lightweight concrete is the **Betonoase Youth Center** in the Lichtenberg district of Berlin. The building opened in 2018 and had to go through the project-specific approval process because the use of infra-lightweight concrete is not yet covered in the appropriate building standards. The necessary load tests were performed by Dr. Ing. Alexander Hückler at TU Berlin and verified by Prof. Manfred Curbach, TU Dresden. The certification engineer was Dr. Ing. Hartmut Kalleja.

Using the competition entry design from 2016, we worked with GRUBER + POPP ARCHITEKTEN—experts in school design and well-known for their sustainable building concepts—to complete the design of the single-story building. The 50-cm-thick external walls and 32-cm-thick canopy consist of infra-lightweight concrete with a bulk density of only 700 kg/m³ excluding the weight of the zinc-galvanized steel reinforcement. The building achieved passive house standard thanks to the good insulation properties of the concrete. This pilot project resulted in a single-skin, fair-faced concrete structure that will serve as a model for further applications.

AR

After more than ten years' research at the TU Berlin, countless bachelor's and master's degree projects, several doctorates, and many tests, we can say that infra-lightweight concrete is ready for use in practice. It is a true alternative. Mike Schlaich

Solar Energy

The greatest energy source available to man is the sun. Year after year, the earth's outer atmosphere is struck by 5,461,000 exajoules of radiant energy, which is roughly equivalent to 10,000 times the world's current primary energy consumption. Only if we are successful in using this free supply of energy economically through suitable technologies will the world be able to access this everlasting, resource-conserving, and environmentally friendly energy source. Markus Balz

1980

Gradual progress

With the objective of mastering interesting and demanding structural engineering challenges, we have been active in renewable energy since the company was founded in 1980. From this small niche field of operation, the intervening years have seen the development of a design team comprising various disciplines capable of tackling a wide range of projects. Engineers specializing in mechanical engineering, power generation, and aerospace, specialists in optical systems and thermodynamics, physicists, software experts, and, of course, last but not least, structural engineers work together in the team. This simplifies managing interfaces and allows systems to be optimized in a holistic way. Specialist knowledge of structural engineering alone, without a thorough understanding of thermodynamics, control and drive technology, without expertise in optics, is not enough to develop efficient and cost-effective systems.

Using the great potential of solar energy

The times when solar energy was almost only on the lips of scientists and idealistic environmental activists are long gone. Fortunately, renewable energy has become big business since then. Today's global investment in renewable energy systems is double that in power plants using fossil fuels because solar energy worldwide can make a cost-effective and considerable contribution to covering the world's requirement for electricity and heat. Two technical principles are available to make use of this potential: photovoltaics (PV) and Concentrating Solar Power (CSP).

Photovoltaic systems generate cost-effective electricity as soon as the sun shines. The required electrical energy storage that could be used with this technology is currently irrelevant to large-scale electricity generation because of its high capital and operation and maintenance cost. In the medium term, these systems will find use mainly in mobile applications or for stationary, short-term provision of high electric power.

Solar thermal power plants use large mirrored surfaces to concentrate sunlight. The light heats a heat-transfer fluid—for example, synthetic oil or molten salt. A heat exchanger is then used to generate steam, which drives a turbine with a generator. This "detour" through heat may appear at first to be a roundabout way of doing things, but it has the advantage that heat can be stored inexpensively, and that harvesting solar energy and electric power generation are decoupled from one another. For some years now, solar thermal power plants have been equipped with large thermal storage systems, enabling them to deliver firm and dispatchable power.

Both technologies, PV and CSP, are valid methods in their own right and have their own fields of application. The current trend is to combine them in large hybrid systems to make use of both sets of advantages. PV systems are combined with solar thermal power plants: the PV part supplies inexpensive electricity when the sun is shining, while in the early morning and evening or even at night, the solar thermal plant generates electric energy using solar energy collected and stored during the day. Because both systems operate on the same site, they can make joint use of one grid connection and other infrastructure, which further reduces costs.

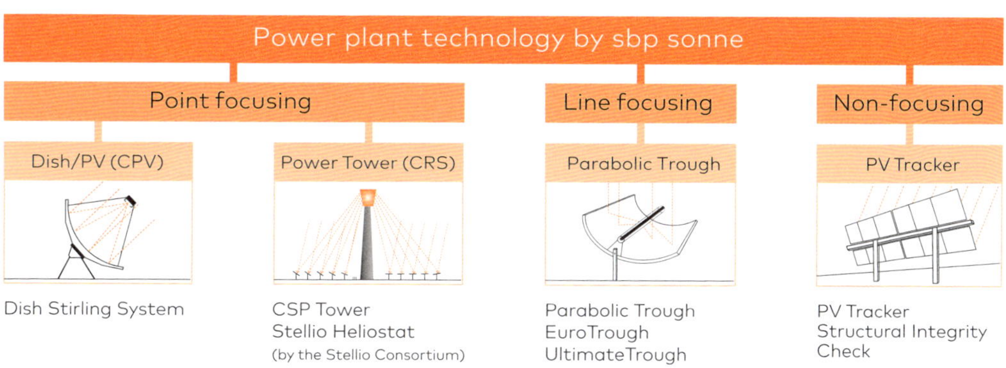

1990

The engineering know-how gained in many projects was then available to be successfully applied in other unusual projects, such as a 400 m² Fresnel concentrator (HelioFocus) and a telescope for observing gamma ray bursts (High Energy Stereoscopic System—HESS).

Thousands of identical components

Whether it's about heliostats, parabolic troughs or Fresnel collectors, structures for dish/Stirling systems, or concentrated PV systems, the task is fundamentally the same: to design a precise, moving optical instrument made up of components that are as simple as possible to make, and by these means to meet the high technical and economic requirements for manufacturing and assembly.

The solar fields consisting of individual collectors extend over square kilometers, with the fields often made up of 10,000 or more heliostats or parabolic trough collector elements as similar in construction to one another as possible. Unlike the usual situation in structural engineering, here the number of components is huge. There are no unique structures, but thousands of identical components. Thus we find ourselves, for example, designing a specific component for a heliostat field and this component may be manufactured and installed in more than 100,000 instances. Optimizing material requirements and the cost of material, logistics, and installation contributes greatly to the economic efficiency of the structure. Of course, this must not adversely affect the functioning of the system. A techno-economic optimization—efficiency versus cost—is thus a key task of each collector field development or design, always keeping in mind aspects of mass production. The concentrated attention paid to every detail is particularly crucial and can, in certain circumstances, require years of work following the desired objectives with perseverance.

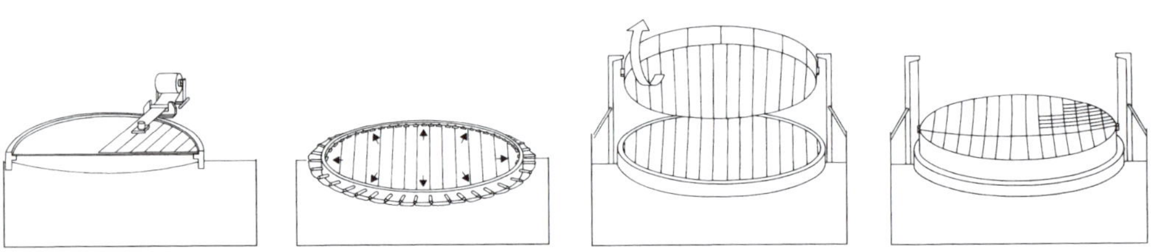

Manufacturing of the metal membrane concentrator

Further development is a recurring theme

The history of sbp sonne is one marked by continuous further development. Looking back, there was no single reason why Jörg Schlaich and Rudolf Bergermann got involved so early and so intensively in the field of solar energy use. In addition to an interest in the engineering challenges, such as membrane structures comprising thin metal sheets as part of the Collaborative Research Center (SFB) 64 at the University of Stuttgart's Jörg Schlaich Chair, there were certainly several contributory triggers—for example, the energy price crisis in the 1970s and other external stimuli—that led first to the development of solar updraft towers. The early focus was on this technology.

Metal membrane concentrators for dish/Stirling systems (top) and heliostats (middle and bottom).

The foundations for this technology were laid through detailed work on the aspects of supporting structures, wind loads, thermodynamics, energy storage, and turbines for a demonstration system in Spain and later for power plants with up to 200 MW nameplate capacity. Moreover, the development of concentrators using stretched membrane structures of metal sheets for shorter (dish/Stirling) and long focal lengths (heliostats) was an interesting field of activity because the metal membrane construction allowed high-precision, double-curvature surfaces to be constructed at a comparatively low cost—ideal for optical applications in the field of solar thermal power plants (see figure on page 224 bottom).

In addition to their links with the solar updraft tower, the names Schlaich and Bergermann are closely associated with dish/Stirling systems, which have been the second most important field of solar activity for many years. This is a mirror with a short focal length that can be rotated about two axes. A Stirling engine with a generator is driven by concentrated sunlight to produce electricity. The size of the concentrators corresponds to the size of heliostats, which we have been developing since the end of the 1980s. Dish/Stirling systems and, of course, the heliostats METHA and ASM150, developed on behalf of the German Aerospace Center (DLR) in the 1990s, provided a good starting point for new developments. After these came concentrators in the form of reinforced plastic composite shells (EnviroDish).

2000

Parabolic trough development

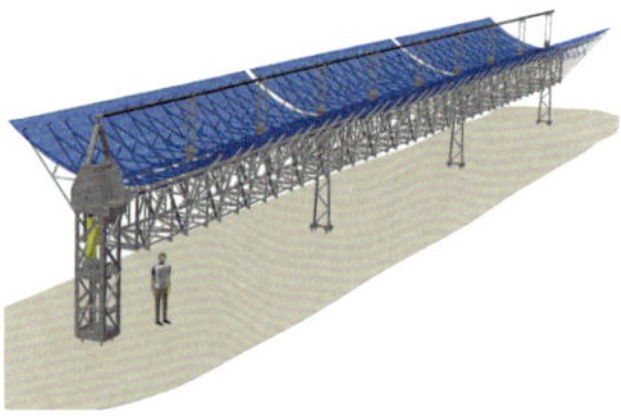

A European consortium began developing the EuroTrough parabolic trough collector as part of the European Commission's 7th Framework Program in 1999. Since then, this type of collector, a steel frame construction, has been used in a series of large power plant projects—and, to the surprise of most project stakeholders, has been and is still very successful, some twenty years later (see Table 1). Other types of collectors have been developed since then. First of all, the HelioTrough is a variant designed especially for the US market because of the country's high labor rates, particularly on construction sites; instead of the material-saving torque box normally used, a standard steel tube forms the main structural element, which is transported directly to site as a complete unit, whereas the torque box always requires intensive site work to join the subassemblies.
A further development of this idea, the UltimateTrough is a significantly larger-scale version of the EuroTrough that enables costs to be reduced. It is most suitable for systems using molten salt as the heat transfer fluid.

Name	Country	Nom. output	Collector aperture area
Andasol 1	Spain	50 MW	~510,000 m²
Andasol 2	Spain	50 MW	~510,000 m²
Andasol 3	Spain	50 MW	~500,000 m²
Kuraymat	Egypt	50 MW	392,400 m²
Morón	Spain	50 MW	380,000 m²
Godawari	India	50 MW	394,000 m²
Delingha	China	50 MW	621,300 m²
Shagaya	Kuwait	50 MW	673,620 m²
Duba	Saudi Arabia	40 MW	170,000 m²
Urat	China	100 MW	1,151,000 m²
Rotem	Israel	1.5 MW	20,000 m²

Table 1: Power plant projects with EuroTrough parabolic trough or UltimateTrough collectors (Duba, Saudi Arabia) in operation/under construction, respectively.

2010

Bundling of specialist knowledge

In 2012, we were commissioned by Sasol, a South African energy and chemical company, for a comprehensive study on the development of a heliostat for a power plant in South Africa. Working closely with the company, we devised and took forward concepts for a state-of-the-art, cost-efficient heliostat. The basis for the concept was an analysis of all known heliostat concepts and the identification of the most commercially efficient of the heliostats operating at that time that could be used as reference systems. Unfortunately, Sasol withdrew from the renewable energy business during the course of the project. However, the company transferred the rights to the new developments to us. At that point, we brought various European companies with the right sort of track record around a table to further develop the promising heliostat concept we had originally designed with Sasol. Together we conceived a research project and submitted an application for funding to the European Commission as part of the Horizon2020 Program. The application scored well but achieved only second place among the many competitors.

In spite of this setback, it was clear that the market was calling out for a new, high-quality, cost-efficient heliostat. It was therefore only a short time later that our friends from Ingemetal contacted us. The steel fabricator from Zaragoza, Spain, was already established in the CSP market and was known to us through its involvement in many joint parabolic-trough projects. The company had been asked to prepare an offer for the manufacture of a large number of heliostats, but recognized immediately that the heliostat in question was not efficient enough.

We formed the Stellio Consortium in order to be in the position to build a prototype based on the existing improved heliostat concept at short notice and offer a turnkey heliostat field. The consortium consisted of Ingemetal (structural steelwork, manufacturing, assembly, and installation), Masermic (mechatronics, heliostat control), and sbp sonne (consulting engineers). In view of the time constraints, we fell back on the drawings for the "Sasol heliostats." This concept was simplified because of the lack of time, which meant that the detailed design, fabrication, and final installation of the prototype at the Plataforma Solar de Almería (PSA) laboratory site in Spain were completed in only six months. Even with the prototype, which had been assembled outdoors under difficult conditions, we achieved outstanding values for optical quality and tracking accuracy, which were confirmed by independent third-party tests.

This was perfect preparation for winning the Redstone project in South Africa after intensive technical discussions with the general contractor. The Stellio Consortium received the order to erect a turnkey heliostat field consisting of over 20,000 heliostats near the town of Upington in mid-2016.

Beginning in the same summer and running in parallel with this, a research and development project was commissioned by the German Federal Ministry for Economic Affairs and Energy (BMWi). As part of this project, a pilot Stellio field was erected in Jülich (west of Cologne, Germany), which was tested with our partners DLR and CSP Services. Here we examined improvements to various details relating specifically to manufacturing, installation, and operation, the need for which had been highlighted during the construction and operation of the prototype in Spain. We benefited from working together with specialists in solar measurement technology (DLR and CSP Services) because it meant we could use state-of-the-art measuring equipment.

Because there had been frequent delays in the Redstone project due to political problems in South Africa, the focus at that time fell more strongly on the rapidly growing Chinese CSP market. With our partner Dongfang Boiler Company, the Stellio Consortium was awarded the contract for a heliostat field and the associated receiver for the 50 MW Hami/Kumul power plant, with around 14,500 heliostats. By October 2017, the project was in the detailed design stage. In July 2018, the assembly line was shipped off to China with the aim of assembling and erecting the first heliostats during the winter of 2018–19.

The successful contract represented the first major success for the innovative product of the consortium, but research still needs to be continually driven forward. An autonomous version of the heliostat is currently being developed.

The main characteristics of the autonomous variant are radio control and local power supply through photovoltaic modules and batteries instead of laying cables. Both features reduce the environmental impact because there is no need to excavate cable trenches. The levelized cost of electricity produced also falls. This variant is due to be used at a small power plant, and probably from 2019 in a European field with about 4,000 heliostats.

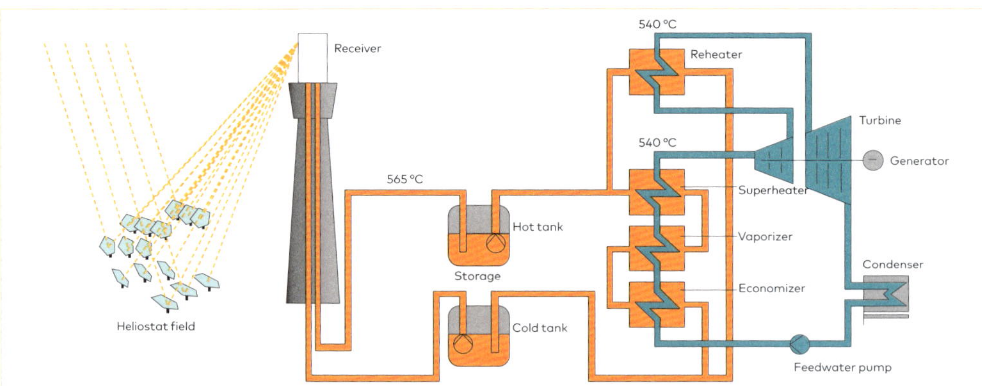

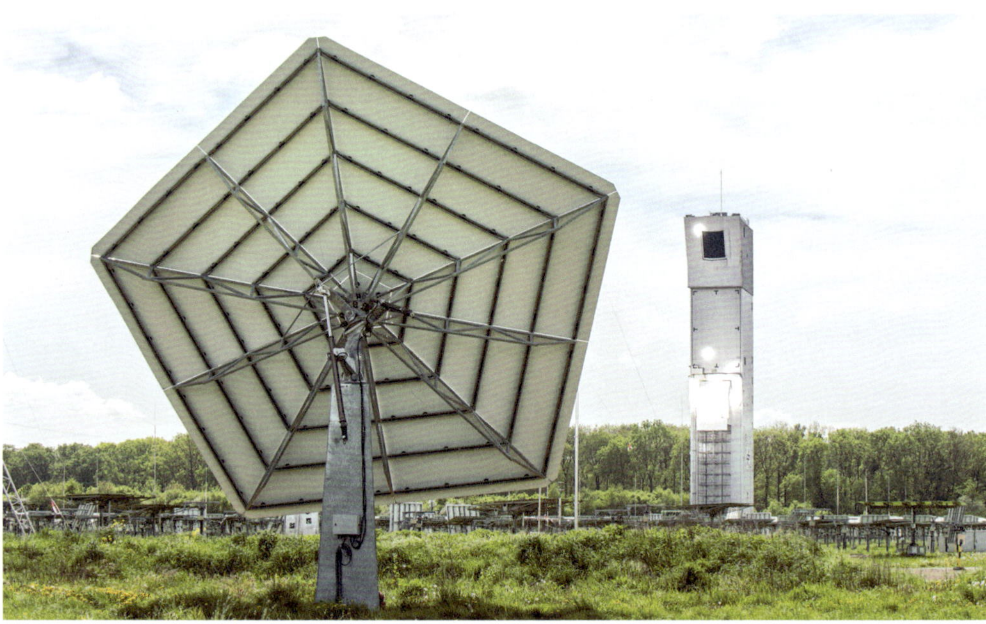

Development of sbpRAY

During the struggles with the Redstone project, it became clear that the Stellio Consortium had to be able to offer a heliostat-field layout design, and not just the heliostats alone. The heliostat-field layout defines the three-dimensional arrangement of heliostats on the power plant site. The following illustration shows an example.

Annual optical efficiency of a heliostat field. Each dot represents a heliostat. The heliostats are positioned up to one kilometer from the central tower (not shown).

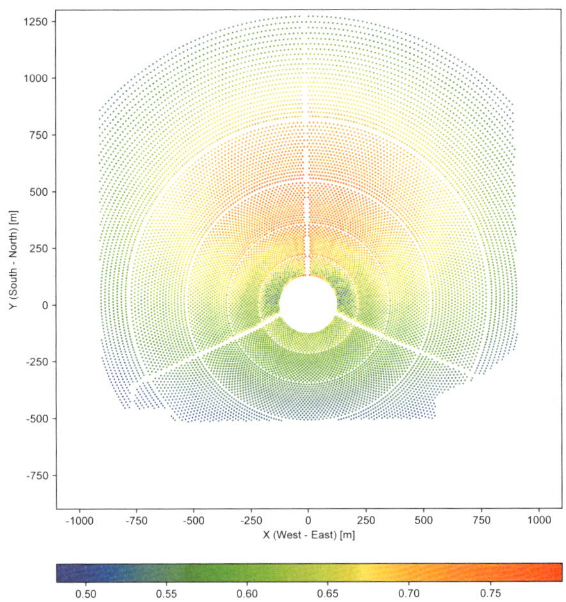

Optical Losses

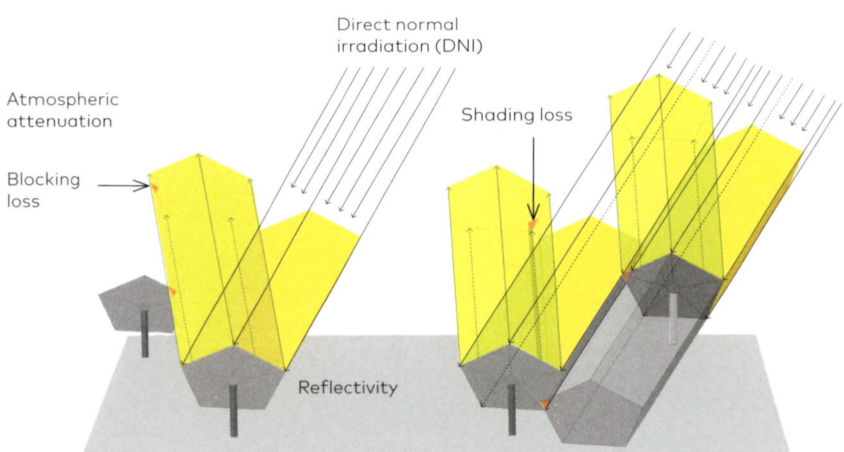

Therefore, the best commercially available software package for this task was initially licensed for the project. It soon became apparent that it failed to satisfy our team's flexibility requirements and did not offer enough linking options to other software packages. We then decided to develop suitable software ourselves. With a wealth of ideas and in close cooperation with our internal software specialists, for example in the area of form finding, we were able to produce the sbpRAY program—including many expansion modules—in a fairly short time. The program is continually updated in-house, notably with the addition of further features. We are now able to create our own optimized solar-field layouts to further improve solar tower power plants. All the possibilities of Stellio heliostats can be optimally implemented, which gives us a competitive advantage through higher solar-field efficiency.

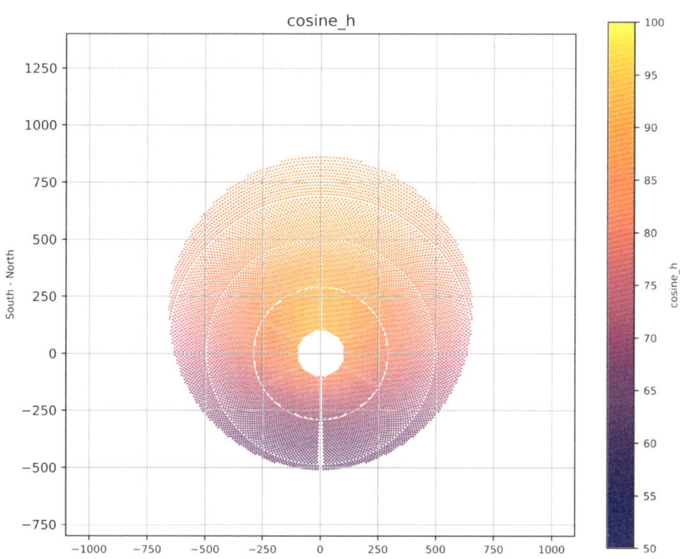

We developed our own in-house design tool to determine the optimum positioning of thousands of heliostats, because nothing suitable was available on the market. The software allows precise positioning of all heliostats in the field, with the result that losses, for example due to mutual shading, are minimized.

2020 +

Looking to the future

The proportion of fluctuating electricity feeds from photovoltaic and wind turbine systems will continue to increase, causing a higher demand for predictable, dispatchable, grid-stabilizing electrical energy, which can be covered in sunny countries by solar thermal power plants.

Increased efficiencies and lower costs will result in a clear reduction of the levelized cost of electricity. The effects of this optimization of technical and commercial aspects and the greater number of units are already apparent. While the 2007 Spanish feed-in tariff for electricity from CSP power plants was about 0.30 €/kWh, a very large system in Dubai—including large energy storage—won a tender in 2017 with a bid of 0.073 $/kWh. Our optimized collectors, such as UltimateTrough and Stellio, will make a considerable contribution to further cost reductions because the solar fields—whether parabolic troughs or heliostats—are an important power plant component regarding both cost and efficiency.

Further development in this area is therefore important and financially worthwhile. We are currently focusing on the following areas of development:

- ↘ Parabolic troughs using molten salt as the heat transfer medium to allow higher temperatures and make the heat exchanger between solar field and thermal heat storage superfluous.
- ↘ The use of small unpiloted aerial vehicles (drones) to calibrate the heliostat field in order to be independent of the progress of construction of the tower and calibration targets used today.
- ↘ Further development of Stellio heliostats: cost reductions and higher outputs may come about through the use of automobile manufacturing techniques and new kinds of glass-metal sandwich facets for concentrators.

Boosting Thermal Solar Energy into CCGT

Moveables

The role of the pioneer

AR

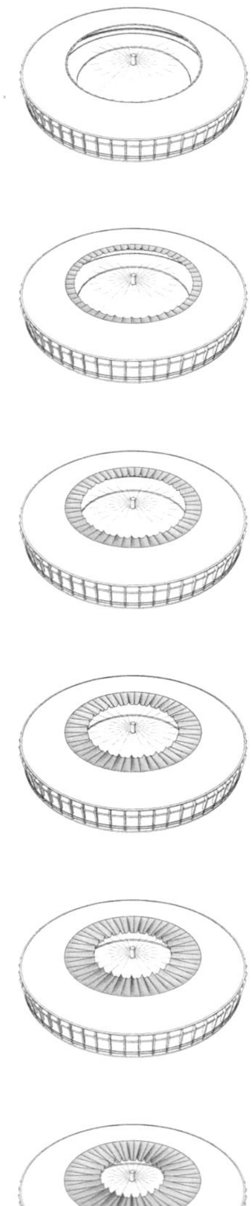

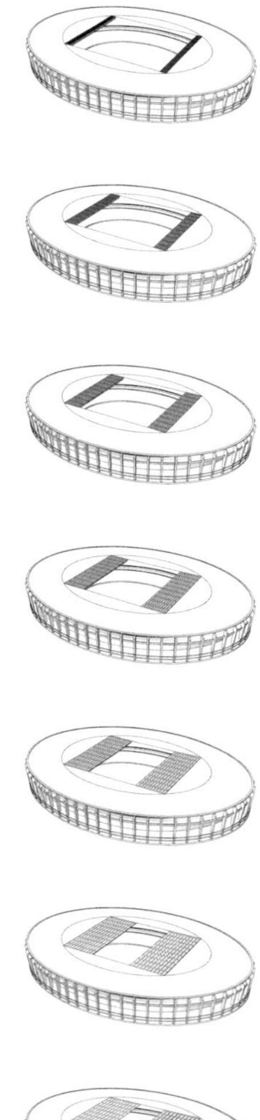

We live in a world of continuous change. Buildings and structures are therefore required to offer more flexibility; they need to be able to react to changing external influences and allow for flexible internal uses. Adaptive skins help to fulfill these additional requirements, and in doing so, they also contribute to sustainability because they allow different simultaneous uses and changes of use over time. Jörg Schlaich and Rudolf Bergermann have pursued this aspect of building with great interest since sbp was founded. Stadiums can be designed or redesigned to cater for a considerable range of different uses. Moveables—buildings with integrated retracting or moving building components such as roofs—are a perfect field of activity for us on two accounts: these types of structures require an intensive and interdisciplinary approach, and we have the full range of the required skills and know-how available in-house.

Prestressed cable-net facades and grid domes have been some of our exclusive products for a long time. Today there are many engineers who have acquired the specialist knowledge necessary for such structures; some of them are from the school of Jörg Schlaich. The competition this creates among these engineers enlivens the industry, inspiring us to evolve, further develop our ideas, and repeatedly exceed self-imposed boundaries.

Since those early days, we have established ourselves in another niche with moveables, a niche that demands specialist knowledge and a great deal of experience. Having building components that retract or move increases the number of unknowns, and hence the complexity of the design right from the start.

The various movement positions have to be taken into account and analyzed as variable load scenarios. They represent critical loading conditions, which must be considered carefully, even though they may be only temporary. Last but not least, the compatibility of the components must be ensured in every construction and operating phase. Variable loaded areas and variable wind loads act on the stationary and retracting parts of the load-bearing structure, resulting in not one but several states of equilibrium. The definitive factors are often not easy to identify immediately. The textile roof skin, for example, may become temporarily slack during movement and is only prestressed again in its final, deployed position, either mechanically or pneumatically. Overstressing due to unplanned deformations, wind actions, or accumulation of rainwater must be prevented. Using modern sensors, limit states can be monitored and, if necessary, the system can be adapted by adding automatic controls to keep the stresses or deformations within an acceptable range.

An efficient structural system reduces the overall dead load of the structure and as a consequence simplifies the driving technology required for its operation. Lightweight buildings with smart load-bearing structures and efficient structural principles using high-performance materials such as polyester and PTFE membranes are ideal in this situation. Key to achieving a reduced self-weight for the load-bearing structure is to design an efficient structural system with members that are predominantly in pure tension or compression. If disadvantageous bending moments can be avoided, the cross-section sizes will be smaller.

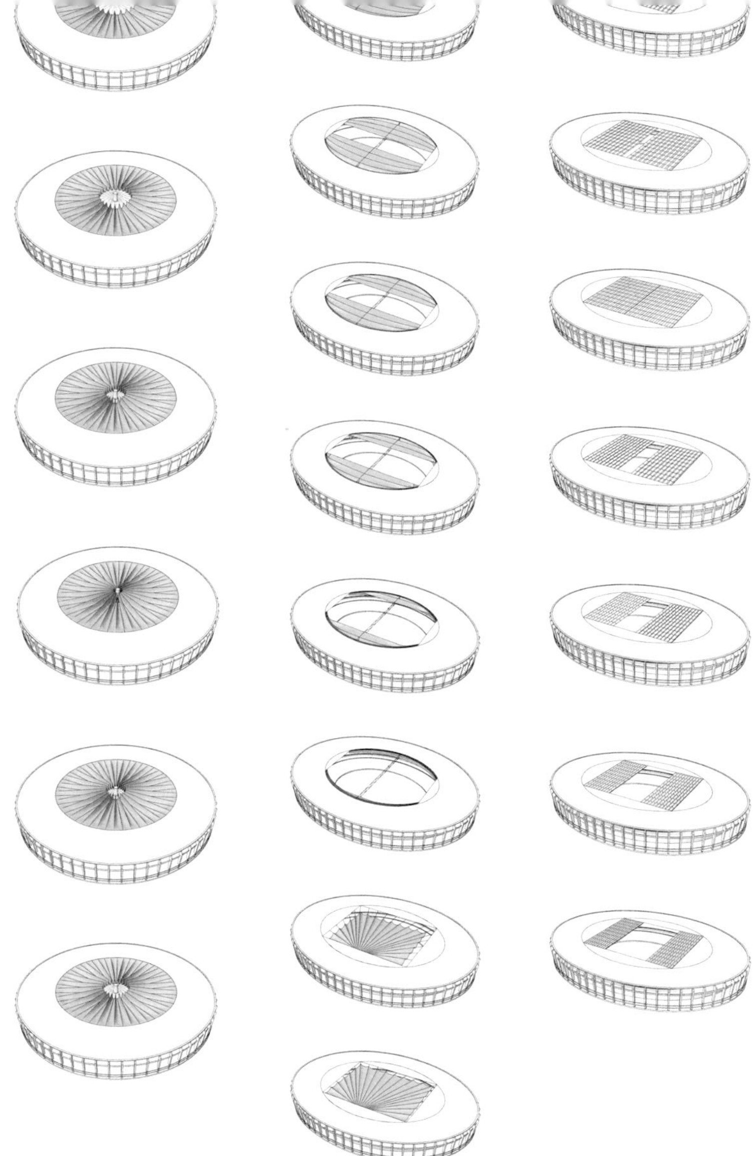

Embedded in the existing building

AR

The design for the mobile roof for the historic **Opera Arena di Verona** in northern Italy is a notable example of how a building can be given an extended scope of use by the installation of a retractable component, in this case a roof that would allow events to take place independently of the weather.

The amphitheater, which is almost 2,000 years old, could tell stories of gladiator contests with up to 30,000 spectators, of bullfights, and of legendary theater performances. Built around 30 AD in the reign of the Roman emperor Tiberius, the elliptically shaped arena originally measured 152 × 123 m. An earthquake in 1117 practically destroyed the complete outer ring. Only a three-story, four-arch-long relict is left of the original four-story outer ring, but the arena has retained its remarkable acoustics. The 24-m-high spectator area is divided into 45 terraced steps and has room for up to 22,000 people. The arena has been in regular use since 1913, and has acquired a reputation as a concert venue, mainly for classical opera.

The performances are limited to the months of June, July, and August because of the lack of protection against the elements. Even during the performance season, events may be canceled because of bad weather. The concert income is, however, urgently needed to maintain the arena. Therefore, the Verona municipality initiated a design competition in 2016 for concepts that would allow the arena to be used irrespective of the weather.

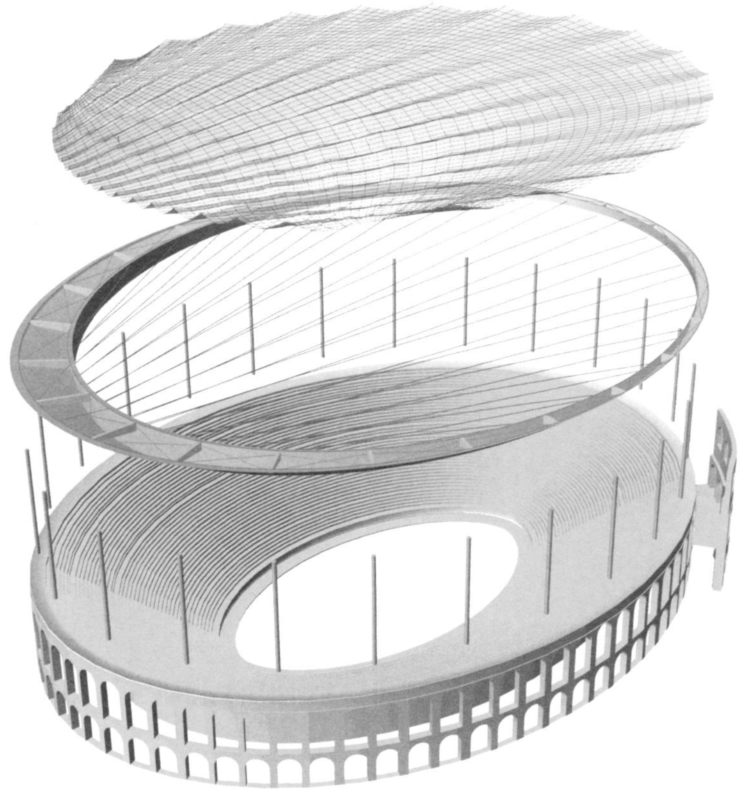

The design for Verona contains a piece of all our moveables. Knut Göppert

The compression ring is hardly visible at first glance because it is designed to match the shape of the top edge of the spectator stand. Although clearly offset with respect to the terraces, it does not project beyond the existing walls. Only at an appreciable distance from the building can the compression ring be seen, appearing like a halo floating over the arena.

The roof design has been developed not to adversely affect the arena optically or acoustically. The project, which we designed in cooperation with gmp · von Gerkan, Marg and Partners Architects, convinced the jury and was declared the winning project from among approximately eighty competition entries.

The proposed structure is ingenious: the cable system and membrane span the whole arena space without intermediate columns and can be completely retracted in only thirty minutes. Moreover, when the roof is open, not a single load-bearing element spoils the view of the sky. When the roof is closed, it provides reliable protection against sun and rain without inhibiting the view of the stage.

Like many similar projects designed by our office, the convertible membrane structure functions like a spoked wheel. The cables carrying the membrane span inside a continuous 800-t steel compression ring. In contrast to the existing symmetrical moveable cable systems, such as those for the conversion of the **Commerzbank-Arena Frankfurt** 2005 or the **National Stadium Warsaw** 2011, the cables are arranged asymmetrically in a fan shape within the oval compression ring, which is also asymmetrical. Its triangular cross section decreases gradually from where it is at a maximum to the opposite side of the oval.

When the roof is opened, the membrane and the supporting substructure retract automatically, one after the other, into the membrane garage in the ring, where they are sheltered. When the arena roof, which is more than 12,000 m^2 in area, is closed over again, the supporting cables inside the compression ring move out into position from both sides. Then the membrane skin is pulled in an elliptical shape in plan along the supporting cables over the whole arena area.

The cables are rolled out inside the compression ring on reels. Carriages take the cables out of the garage into their positions ready for closing. Each cable end is connected to its own cable carriage. Activated by individual and precisely synchronized electric winches, the thirty carriages are driven along a main channel-section guide rail. Each cable carriage is secured in the channel by captive heavy-duty rollers. As soon as the cables are in their final positions, hydraulic cylinders lock the carriages and cable winches. A precise amount of tension is applied to the cables during operation so that they form a substructure capable of providing adequate support under every loading situation. Then the PTFE membrane moves along the tensioned cables out of the garage. The folded panels open evenly into a fan shape to cover the roof opening. The roof deployment method we designed here is a completely new and unique approach, but we used well-established and proven technologies and components from our previous built projects that have been further developed.

The compression ring also carries the lighting and stage equipment. It is stiffened transversely with ribs and supported on slender steel columns. These penetrations of the existing terraces were minimally invasive and transfer all the resulting vertical forces from the compression ring via micro-piles into the ground. The clever design and structural system require the least possible interference with the existing structure and transport this technical masterpiece of a velarium into the present day—with the necessary respect shown to the historic existing building.

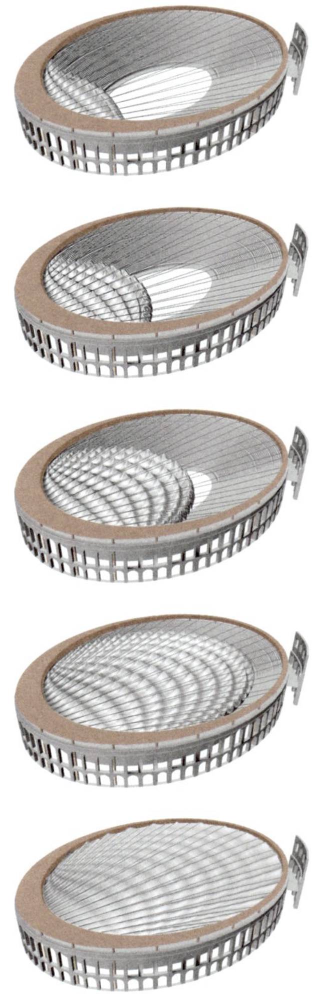

Specialist knowledge, pioneering spirit, and a never-ending flow of ideas are required to design this sort of special structure. Knut Stockhusen

As in the innovative design of Arena di Verona's roof, our wealth of experience and collective specialist knowledge are reflected in the design and realization of convertible roofs—whether the project is a new build or an extension to an existing structure. The roof of the **amphitheater in Zaragoza, Spain,** was the first retractable roof designed by our office and provided the inspiration for the asymmetrical roof in Verona.

Continuous further development

The retractable membrane inner roof of the Polish **National Stadium in Warsaw** is a milestone in the field of moveables for us. We designed the structure in conjunction with gmp International architects and engineers and J.S.K. Architekcki. It was the first cable-supported, all-weather membrane roof to permit all-year-round use—even with snow loads of up to 100 kg/m². The stadium, which was built for the UEFA European Football Championship 2012 in Poland and Ukraine, can be converted in just a few minutes into a multifunctional arena for 72,900 seated spectators. In autumn 2013, for example, the facility hosted the UN Climate Conference, for which the playing area was converted into a congress center and the existing boxes were used as small meeting rooms.

The stadium was erected to replace a completely open, earth-embankment stadium dating back to 1955. The lightweight design in steel, glass, and membrane creates a remarkable duality between the concrete plinth rising out of the previous rubble embankment and the new structure. The roof is an efficient structure with a winter-proof, retractable inner membrane. The facade is stationary; it does not move, but it changes its appearance. During the day, it looks like a patterned but solid surface with anodized aluminum expanded metal panels in silver and red, while at night, illuminated by LEDs, it changes into a light and transparent skin to reveal the load-bearing structure behind. The structural system combines various principles of the spoked wheel to form a single, complex, integrated structure. The self-contained structure floats, i.e., supported without horizontal restraints, on the plinth. This reduces the horizontal loads transferred from the superstructure onto the plinth, which therefore has to carry mainly vertical loads.

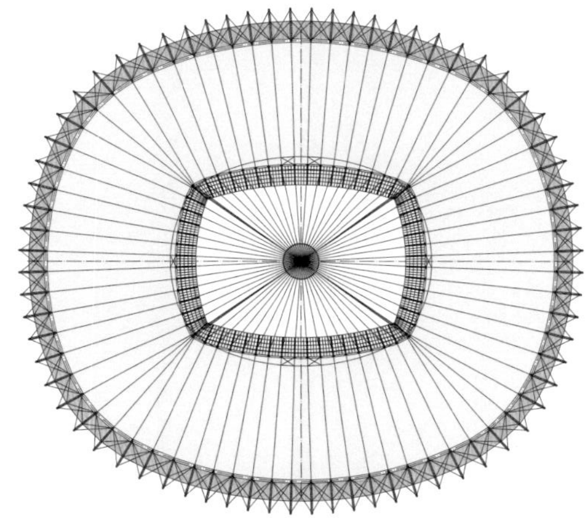

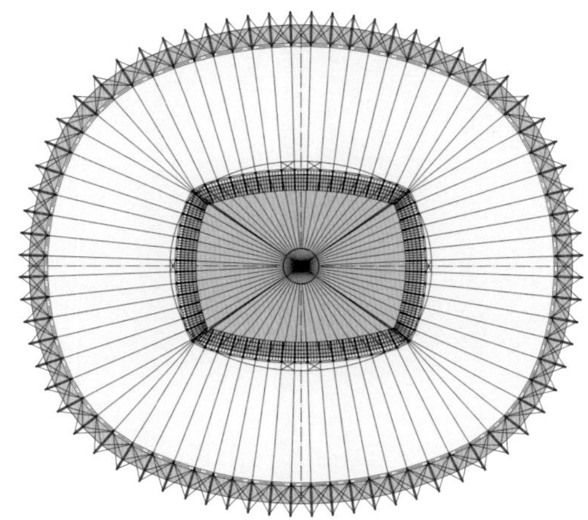

The outer roof over the spectator stands is designed as a cable-supported membrane arch roof projecting 91m into the space enclosed by the stadium. The structure supporting the outer area is designed as a spoked wheel with crossing bundles of cables as the spokes. The over 800-m-long lower compression ring defines the upper edge of the stadium. The usual upper compression ring was replaced by a stay system supported on 72 inclined struts off the lower compression ring. The struts project upwards to about 25m above the stadium bowl. The two tension rings of the inner roof act as a hub. This is also designed as a small spoked wheel, with the rims consisting of two tension rings that follow the shape of the edge of the playing area. A 10-m-wide glazed strip at the inner edge forms the transition from the outer (stationary) to the inner (retractable) roof. Flying masts act as spacers between the two tension rings to provide the necessary structural depth. The spokes are arranged in an upper and a lower plane. The lower radial cable group consisting of four bundles of three cables connect to the four kinked "corners" of the lower tension ring.

The upper cable group is clamped to the upper tension ring at regular intervals and attaches to the needle of the central hub at a rosette. The needle is 70 m high and its tip is around 100 m above the playing area. This key piece of the structure carries the membrane storage into which the retractable, 9,800 m², PVC-coated PES membrane parks. It also carries four large video screens. A lifting device with cable winches allows the video screens to be lowered to the ground, and the integrated, freely suspended lifting platform allows access to the hub for maintenance.

The structural system generates mainly vertical reaction forces; only the remaining resultant horizontal forces due to wind have to be transmitted into the foundations. In addition, the design is so efficient and flexible that the varying live loads, such as snow, can be accommodated without detriment to the structure's slender appearance.

Many modern stadiums with moveables can be converted into fully enclosed arenas within just a few minutes. The following maxim applies: the more flexibly an event venue can be used, the more successfully it can be operated. Knut Stockhusen

Pillows in the roof skin instead of a single-layer membrane

The inner retractable roof of the **BC Place Stadium** in Vancouver, Canada, which we completed in cooperation with Stantec and Geiger Engineers, has a similar structure to the National Stadium in Warsaw. The snow loads carried by the roof are far greater, and the approach used in Warsaw to keep the roof automatically free of snow would not have been practical. Therefore, the roof in Canada had to be designed for full snow load. At 175 kg/m² on the whole of the roof area and locally up to 350 kg/m², the snow loads in Vancouver are relatively high.

The roof covering the ranks of seats between the compression ring and the inner edge girder consists of a 34,000-m², single-layer membrane. It employs the proven double-curvature technique to span between the radial cables and the membrane arches, and accentuates the lightness and slender lines of this high-performance structure.

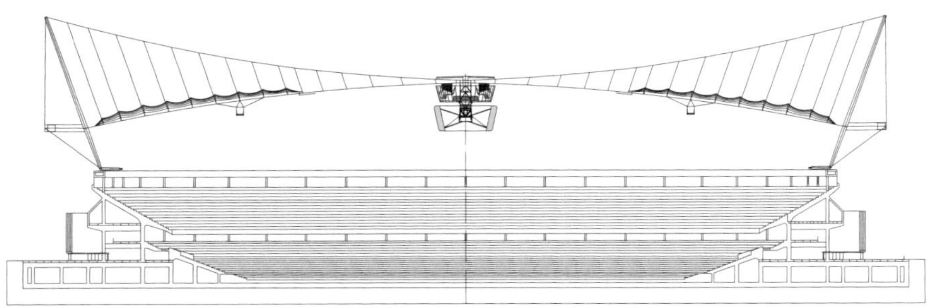

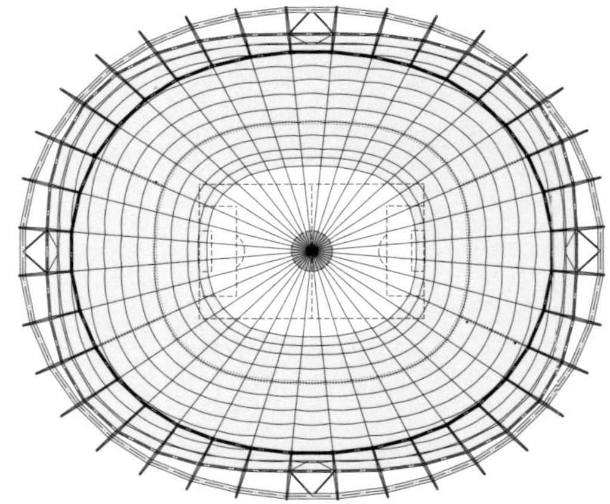

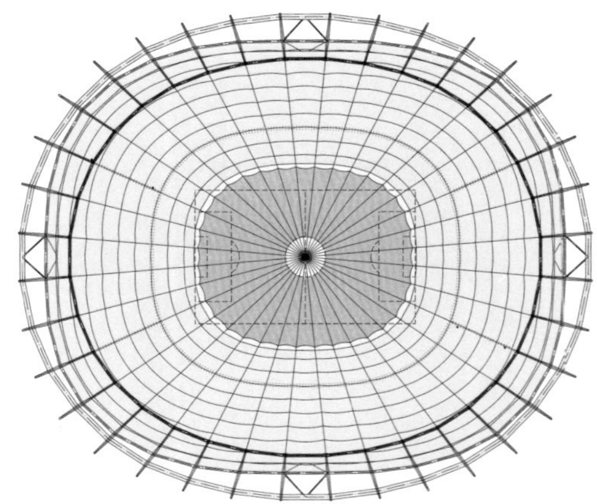

A single-layer membrane like the one used for the stadium in Warsaw would not have been adequate for the retractable inner roof in Vancouver. So instead, the roof was designed to have two-layer, pneumatically supported pillows. To achieve the desired translucency and remain true to the lightweight design concept, which is advantageous in the event of earthquakes and in terms of sustainability, a fluoropolymer-coated PTFE textile membrane was used for the pillows. This combines excellent folding properties while maximizing light transmittance at 40 percent. Once the membrane has been deployed and locked in position, the 36 inner roof pillows are inflated. The air handling units, which are located at the central node, create the required pressure inside the pillows and empty them again when the roof is about to be retracted. The internal pressure is set at the value required to resist the applied loads. The regular internal pressure within the pillows is 500 Pa, but this can be increased to 2,000 Pa based on the readings of the magnetic load sensors on the suspension cables and local climate data. This adaptability allows events to take place year-round, independent of environmental conditions. When closed, the new roof also improves sound insulation, which means less noise for the neighbors—an advantage that should not be overlooked with a stadium built in an urban context.

The stadium roof is a state-of-the-art structure that allows the covered space to be used in all weather conditions and at all times of the year. The roof structure with a retractable inner roof is supported on 36 masts that stand on the existing reinforced concrete structure.

Structural elegance despite seismic loadings

Similar to extraordinarily high snow loads, earthquake loads are an important aspect in the design and construction of buildings. They require well-conceived structures and sophisticated structural details. The **National Stadium Bucharest** lies in a high-risk seismic zone, a situation that has greatly influenced the design of the load-bearing structure of the Lia Manoliu stadium. From 2007 to 2011, working in a team comprising us, gmp · von Gerkan, Marg and Partners Architects, Krebs + Kiefer consulting engineers, and Iprolam Bucharest, we designed and completed a highly modern sports arena for 55,000 spectators and featuring a retractable roof that transforms the football stadium into a multipurpose arena. With its slender, 23.75-m-high columns, its external appearance suggests a coliseum. In spite of the design for severe earthquakes with a ground acceleration of 0.24 g, the resulting structure is a delicately proportioned reinforced concrete frame that supports the cable-ring roof.

Up to the upper level of the tiers, the supporting outer concrete columns are at 6-m centers. Above the tier, 16-m-high columns carry the roof. The extending columns have the same outer cross section as the ones below but are made out of structural steel. The roof structure is in the form of a cable-ring roof, which carries a fixed outer and a retractable inner membrane roof, with supports at 18-m centers. The outer roof structure consists of a box-section compression ring supported by the steel columns and an inner tension ring bundle. Between the compression ring, column base, and tension ring span upper and lower radial cables; the lower ables carry the roof membrane.

Eight vertical cable cross braces are arranged in pairs at the axes of symmetry of the roof. This intentional doubling of the tangential bracing was done to satisfy the earthquake loading calculations. They are a visible detail of the many other points where the structure has been strengthened in order to resist seismic effects.

In the area of the tension ring bundle, a planar polycarbonate roof forms the transition between the fixed outer and the retractable inner roof.

The inner roof structure carries the weight of the retractable, folding membrane roof over the field of play and the central video cube, which also the garage for the membrane in retracted configuration. The inner roof supporting structure is formed by a series of tubular-section flying masts that are supported on the lower tension ring nodes. The upper ends of the flying masts are tied by an upper tension ring. Upper and lower radial cables span between the upper and lower tension rings and form the direct support for the retractable membrane. The resulting force at the mast upper ends is end-anchored at the perimeter compression ring by a series of radial cables.

Moveables are seen by some as highly technical because the laws of mechanics dominate their design. More complicated analyses and calculations are involved in their design than is the case with structures having only static loads and systems. Despite this, lightweight structures such as our moveables offer a surprising degree of design freedom that can and should be used to good advantage on every project. Knut Göppert

Building on our heritage

The requirements placed on roofs vary according to the time of day and year but also depend on general changes associated with their use. This is reflected in the increased demand for roof designs that are flexible, adaptive, and multifunctional, which in turn demands pioneering developments in the field of transformable structures. Out of these new and further-developed ideas resulting from diverse engineering disciplines come innovative solutions that continue to expand the limits of what is thought feasible and practical. For moveables to be considered for everyday structures despite their highly complex construction depends on this process taking place, because it generates the essential prerequisites such as clever concepts, the development of high-performance materials, modern deployment mechanics, and sophisticated controls. These aspects play a role not only in large roofs but also in much smaller structures.

The curved roof in front of the former **casting house at the Landscape Park Duisburg-Nord** combines membrane, steel, and cable construction with mechanical engineering and complex computer controls. The resulting finely proportioned, lightweight structure, which can be reconfigured at the touch of a button, was completed in collaboration with architects planinghaus in 2003. The moveable roof is clearly differentiated from the heritage-listed foundry infrastructure, and shelters an open-air venue in inclement weather. The roof moves elegantly away from the casting hall as a 20-m-wide wave above some of the existing foundry pipework. The primary supporting structure comprises two curved rails running parallel to one another and connected by tubular sections.

The rails in turn are supported on two pairs of double V-shaped columns, which also resist horizontal forces. Inside the casting house, the rails are bolted to the building's roof beams in such a way that they can be removed if necessary. The transparent roof consisting of pneumatic foil pillows is moved along the rails by electric motors. If the roof is not required, it can be driven into its protected parked position inside the casting house. The roof is divided into nine segments connected by hinges. Each segment consists of a 20-×-3-m steel frame inside which is fixed the pillow made from 0.2-mm-thick ETFE foil. Stainless steel cables under- and over-span the frames to ensure they have the required stiffness. The pillows are inflated by an air handling unit to create the regular positive pressure, which can be adjusted in the event of strong wind or when the roof is not being used. Every second pillow frame has four wheels and the first pillow frame carries a motor on each side, an arrangement that makes the structure a machine.

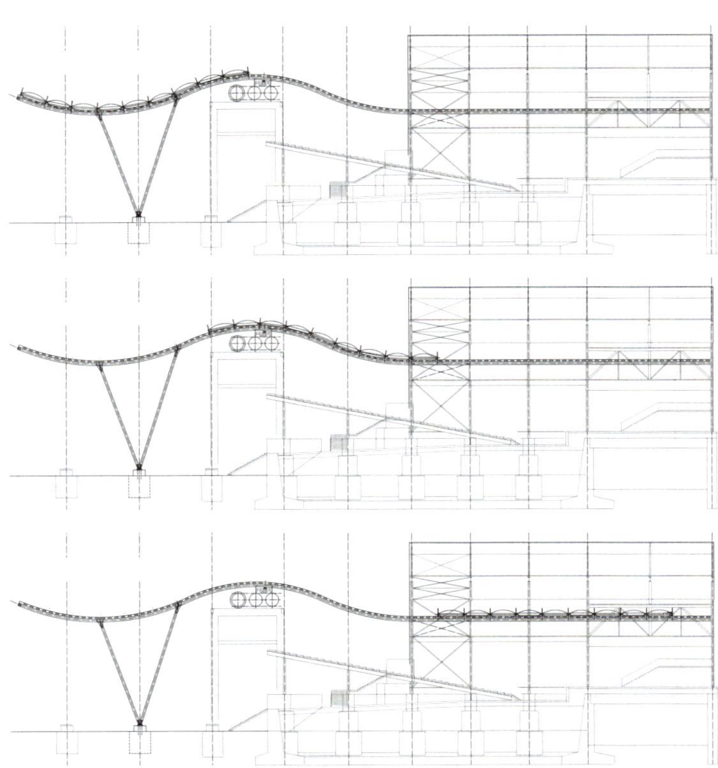

Giving shade

The **Heart of Doha**—an upmarket major project in Doha, Qatar, which we completed with Mossessian Architecture and Transsolar—is even more a machine than a mere structure. The folding membrane roof installed in 2018 covers the central Barahat Al-Nouq Square, which is approximately 90 × 35 m in size. The square is an important element of the city's urban renewal master plan. The development sets out to contribute to the creation of a mixed-use civic space between different residential quarters for communication and interaction. The intention is to draw the city's inhabitants together in the city center as was customary in the past. The square is therefore designed so that it can be used regardless of the weather. The lightweight, retractable roof will provide the necessary shade.

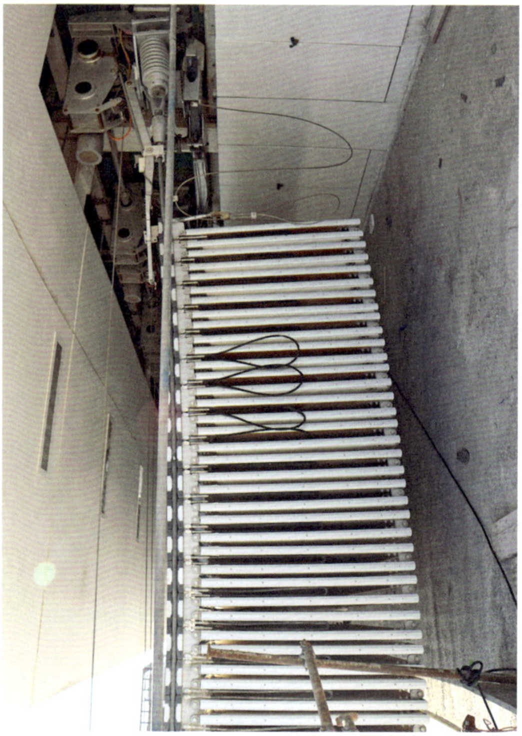

The shading structure suspended between two blocks of buildings consists of 30 axially folding and individually controlled membrane strips that can be drawn out and retracted again like a piano accordion over the public square. Each strip slides along a pair of cables spanning between the buildings. If shade is not required, the strips park in a sheltered storage on one side.

Each strip comprises 36 hinged panels consisting of a PTFE-coated glass-fiber membrane wrapped around 3-x-1.5-m lightweight aluminum frames. These framed panels are paired to form a V-shaped folding element, of which there are 18 in each strip. A clever deployment system adjusts the position and folding angle of each series of frames to suit the direction and intensity of the solar radiation. The folding roof is also part of an automated but nevertheless natural cooling and ventilation system. Barahat Al-Nouq Square's shading system, combined with the paving used on the ground, accomplishes the delicate task of converting the large square into a manageable and pleasant zone for people to use at all times during the summer months in the desert climate.

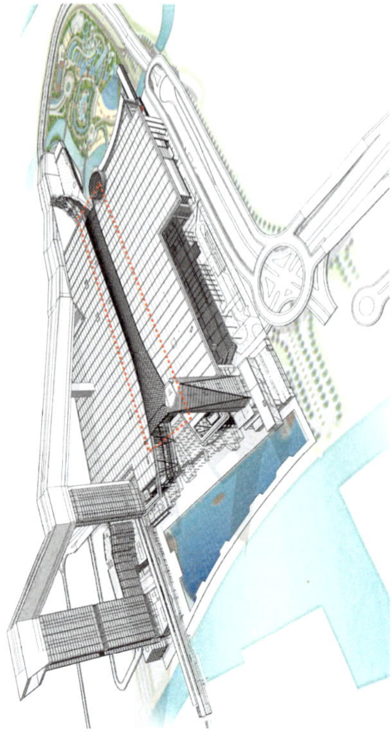

Creating amenity value

The shopping and entertainment complex **Meydan One** in the center of Mohammed Bin Rashid City includes, in addition to the shopping center, four hotels, a water park, and the world's longest indoor ski piste and highest residential tower. The shopping center designed by AE7 architects extends over an area of 6.7 km^2. High-end luxury brands are sold in a 37,000-m^2 Central Canyon. To provide a suitable setting around this 450-m-long, five-story shopping experience, an impressive skylight roof is set over a space with a tapering, funnel-shaped layout in plan. The spectacular steel-glass roof will be one of the largest in the world.

The glazed roof construction consists of a slender steel grid frame supporting the glazing. Five moveable glazed strips open the roof over a spectacular area of 90 × 80 m when weather conditions permit. Visitors are then free to enjoy the plaza in the open air. The facades at the north and south ends of the plaza can also be opened. These facades are edged by a large post-and-rail construction and allow visitors a clear view of the attractions in the surrounding area. The way they open to the sides like a curtain creates an attractive interplay between internal and external space.

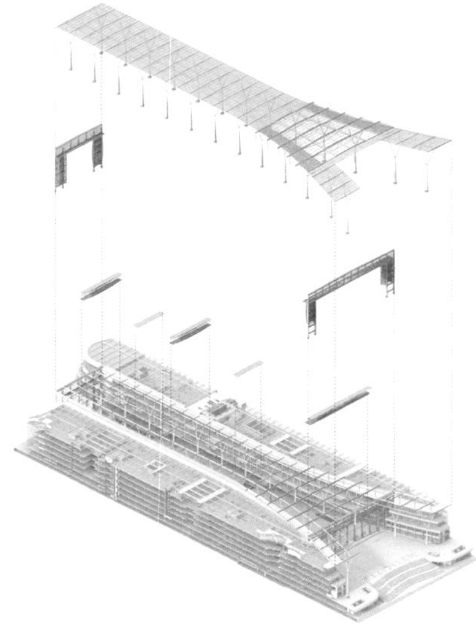

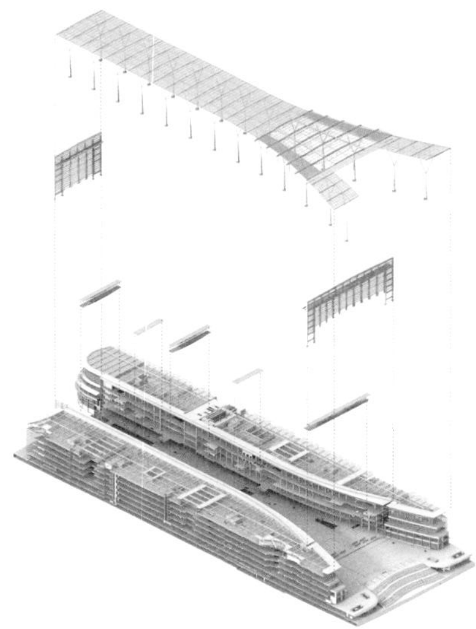

Great potential

A roof acts as a technical and architectural fifth facade and determines the functionality of the whole building. It protects against the weather, controls room climate, and influences the building's appearance. To accomplish this complex design task and achieve a holistic and intelligent solution is at once exciting and challenging. The necessary cross-disciplinary work requires a meaningful interdisciplinary dialogue from the very beginning. This type of successful cooperation is always evident in the completed structure.

The design of the cable-net roof over the **Frost Amphitheater at Stanford University** was never realized, but it is a perfect example of a particularly lightweight roof construction that appears to hover over the venue.

The open-air stage has space for an audience of around 6,900. Built in 1937, the stage stands in an 8-ha, gently sloping green space and is surrounded by trees. The role of the roof is to protect the spectators from sun and rain without adversely affecting the aura of the place. Together with James Carpenter Design Associates, we developed an axially symmetrical, fan-shaped, double-curved, and extremely slender cable-net structure. It is suspended from six points: at the two ends near the stage by a lightweight, rear-stayed, steel-truss arch; at each of the two high points at the back of the spectator terrace by a stayed mast; and at the longitudinal sides near the middle of the net by a single cable stay.

AR

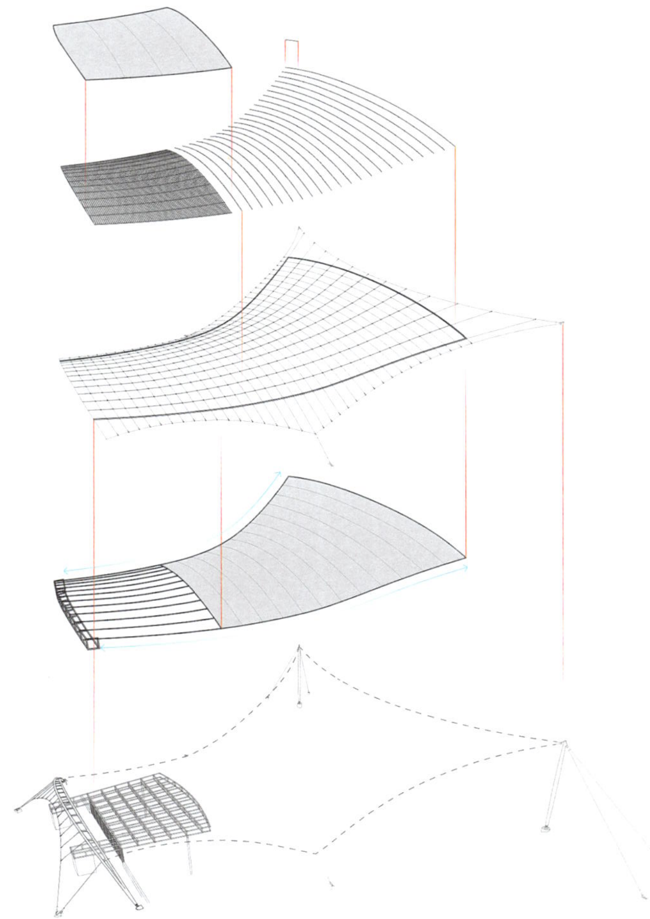

The stage equipment is attached to a self-supporting steel grillage above the stage and below the sail. The retractable solar sail made from water-repellent and UV-resistant textile is suspended below the cable net and can be drawn back into the storage on the steel-truss arch. The shape of the cable-net construction ensures a pleasant climate for the stage and the seating area: the lowest part of the structure at the stage collects cool air, which is then sucked through below the sail by the heating effects of solar radiation on the upper end of the spectator terrace and by thermal convection.

Our capabilities also grow through competitions and projects that we do not win. They often generate new ideas that we can use in future projects. Knut Stockhusen

We also designed a retractable skin for the **Black Sea Arena Batumi** (working with DREI ARCHITEKTEN), which has a capacity of 9,000 spectators and is located in Batumi, Georgia. According to our proposals, the stage and spectator seating for the oval auditorium would have been covered by a unique roof construction with a peripheral compression ring. A fixed, anchored metal construction roof was proposed for the stage area, while the spectator seating would have had a retractable membrane roof. To emphasize the open-air atmosphere, the facade was finally designed to have 168 rotatable lamellae that could be adjusted to the requirements of the performance space. While all the non-moveable parts were realized, in the end the facade was the only moveable component built. As the relict of our solution package, it illustrates the potential of convertible structures: exhibition venues that can be put to various purposes, even under different weather conditions, at all times of day, in all seasons, and create an adaptable ambience.

L4
U
L3
L2
L4
V2
L3
L2
W
L4
L3
L2
X

Completely modular construction AR

Another project with much potential is the **Ras Abu Aboud Stadium** planned for the FIFA Footfall World Cup 2022 in Qatar. This consists of a completely modular system that allows the stadium to be reused in a way that has never been proposed before. The whole stadium can be dismantled into its separate modules and re-erected to provide a stadium for 40,000 spectators at a different location or divided and rebuilt as several smaller stadiums. Thus the structure, the seats, the roof, and the other components can be reused in other projects to give lasting and sustainable benefit for years or even decades to come. The area on which the stadium is built can be returned to its original use or be redesigned to give a more balanced cost-benefit ratio.

The construction of the temporary stadium consists of a steel frame structure reminiscent of a high-rack store. The steel frame carries modified shipping containers that incorporate all the necessary functions. They can be installed and taken out again very quickly. The floor slabs and spectator-seating steps are stackable and therefore easy to transport. These temporary overall concepts considerably improve the carbon footprint during construction and operation. Moreover, construction costs are reduced because less material is required. Large, lightweight stadiums are therefore more sustainable and more economic structures.

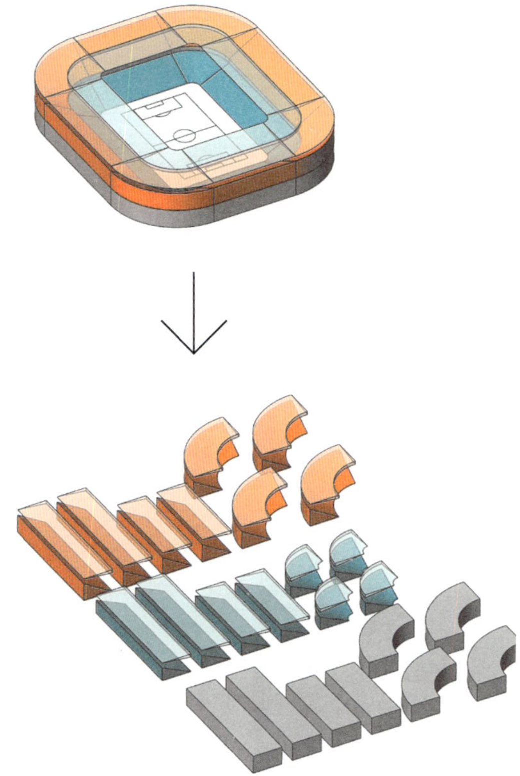

The concept, which we realized with Fenwick Iribarren Architects and Hilson Moran, has already received a four-star certification in accordance with GSAS (Global Sustainability Assessment System). Thus the modular system represents a true alternative to traditionally constructed venues for mega-events and is not only a significant development for world championships but also a pertinent stimulus for future building. The temporary character of event venues and the clever modular construction are an inspiration for all stadium designers who are searching for intelligent solutions. Although temporary and designed to be dismantled, the stadium has a pleasing appearance. The stadium will be an unmistakable, colorful, modern, and unique arena predestined by design for regular future use.

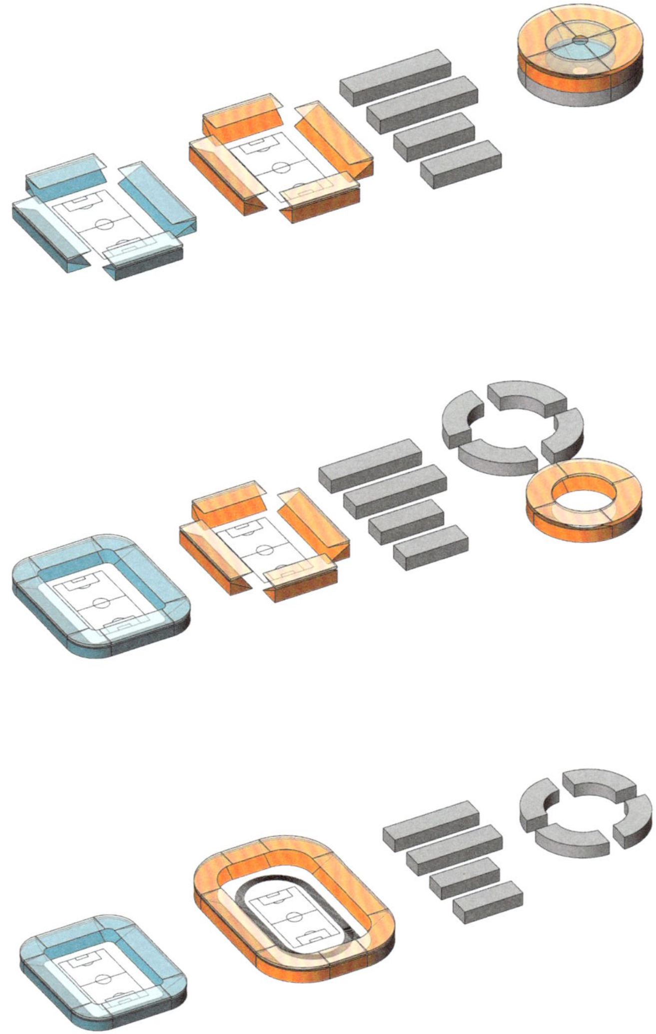

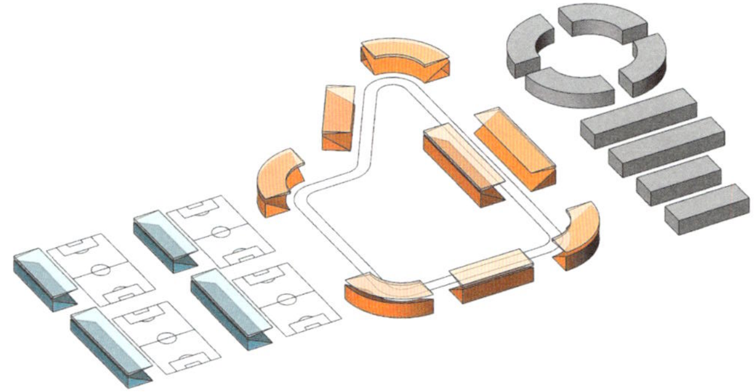

This stadium underlines our most important principles, which we apply to all our projects: reproducibility of construction, material efficiency, interdisciplinary cooperation, and teamwork. Knut Stockhusen

Unique structures

With unusual projects—which moveables tend to be—there is a close working relationship between all project stakeholders and the greatest possible participation from the client before and during the entire planning, design, and construction process. This approach and way of communicating gives reassurance and promotes trust. Mock-ups or partial prototypes have a role to play in the field of moveables, where they do not necessarily model the structural requirements for the final condition, but rather the mechanical, dynamic, and electrical movement processes.

The refurbishment of the Real Madrid football stadium is a fine example of an efficient solution developed by an interdisciplinary team. Design, analysis, detailing, and drawing up tender specifications for electromechanical and hydraulic drives are just as much part of our activities as traditional structural engineering. Work on drive technology for retractable roofs has interdisciplinary benefits: the solar energy team gains from the traditional building team, and vice versa.

Real Madrid's Santiago Bernabéu Stadium was constructed between 1944 and 1947 and is located in the city center. The football stadium, which has been modified and redesigned many times before, is planned to be radically upgraded over the next few years and will retain its capacity of 81,000 spectators.

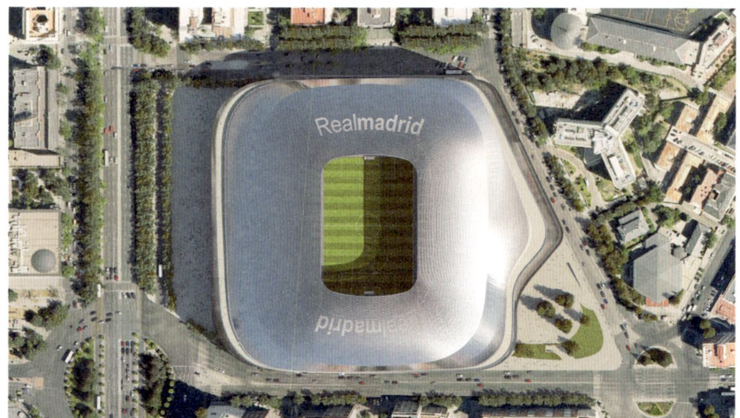

The design team is made up of architects gmp · von Gerkan, Marg and Partners Architects, L35, and us. The facade will be a megascreen based on LED technology and incorporating noise mitigation measures. Inside the stadium, there will be a 360-degree video wall, an integrated retractable roof over the pitch, and covered spectator stands.

The main roof has dimensions of 220 × 240 m and is based on the spoked-wheel principle. It consists of an inner tension ring connected to an outer compression ring by 44 radial cables. The cable system carries the steel structure of radial girders and V-columns. The compression ring is supported off the steel frame structure of the existing bowl. The retractable roof is oval in plan with dimensions of 75 × 110 m, has a textile membrane made of a fluoropolymer-coated PTFE fabric, and allows multiple types of use, not only sporting activities, at all times of the year.

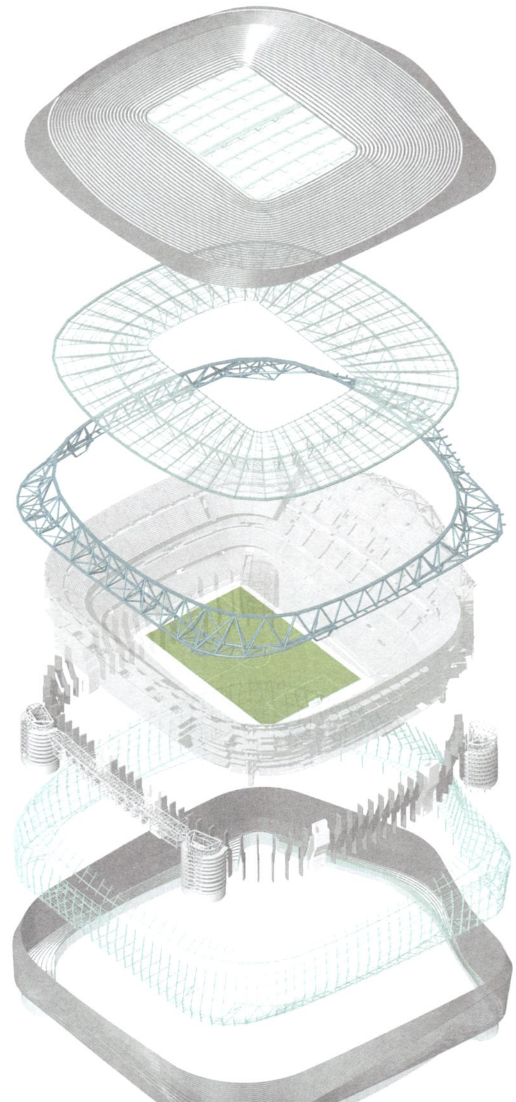

Moveables are given roles to play as unconventional projects for rather conventional uses. Although still special, they are therefore becoming more commonplace. Knut Göppert

ESTADIO SANTIAGO BERNABEU
EstadioSantiagoBernabeu

Building Construction

Stadiums

The goal is to make something new every time, even on a small scale—with due regard to the cultural sphere in which we are working, and in proportion to the freedoms that the process allows us. Knut Göppert

Family tree of cable-net nodes (selection)

1970 2010

Olympic Stadium Munich
1972

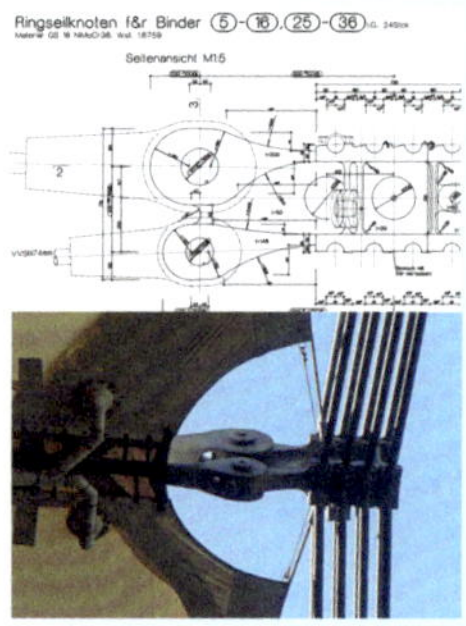

Gottlieb Daimler Stadium
1993

King Fahd International Stadium 1984

Cape Town Stadium
2009

National Sports Complex Olimpiyskiy
2011

Moses Mabhida Stadium
2009

Stadium Maracanã
2013

Cast

AR

2015 2020

Welded

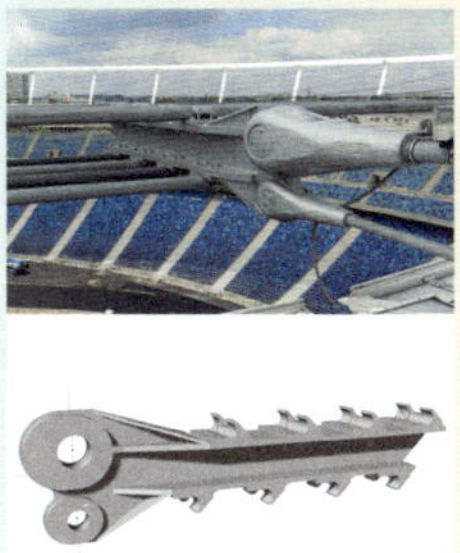

Stadium Slaski
2016

Stadium Wanda Metropolitano 2017

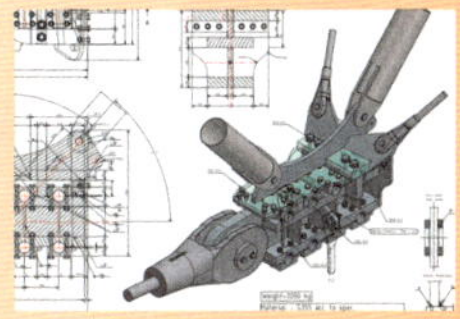

Al Thumama Stadium
2019

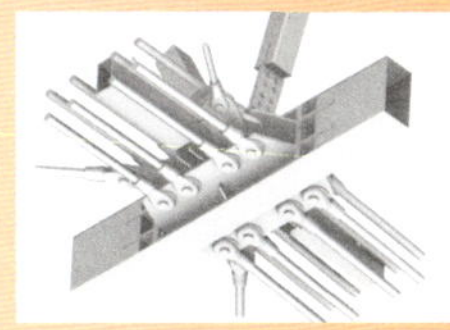

Al Rayyan Stadium
2019

Hybrid

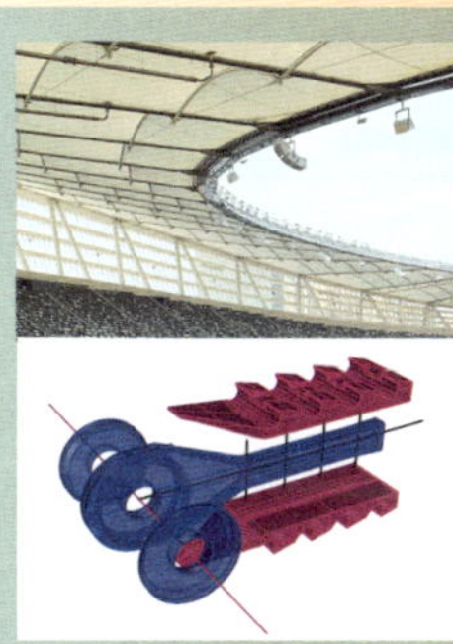

Suzhou Sports Center
2018

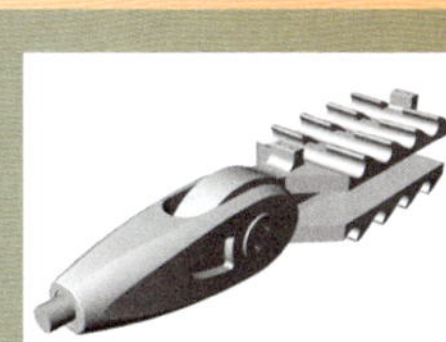

Pudong Stadium
2021

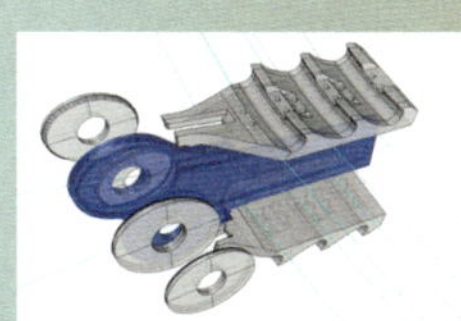

Wuyuanhe Stadium
2018

Cast

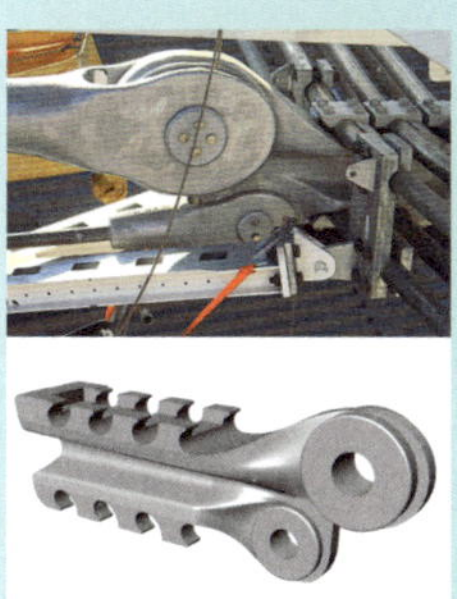

FK Krasnodar Stadium
2015

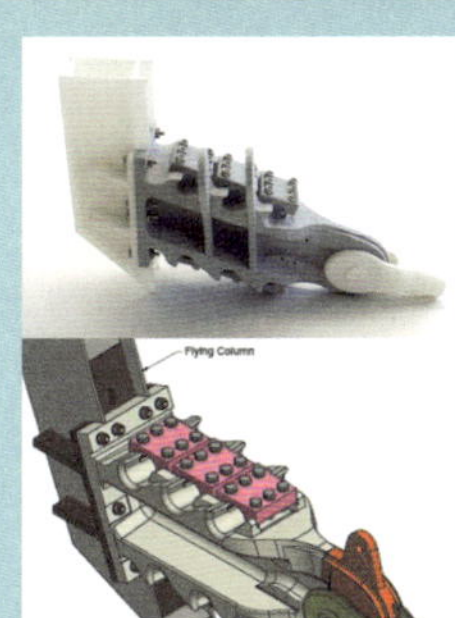

Tottenham Hotspur Stadium 2019

Our practice is known, probably more than any other, for lightweight construction—the efficient use of materials, the legibility of the pattern of forces, simplicity (in the sense of keeping to essentials), and, last but not least, the honesty to design and produce structures whose appearance reflects the way in which they actually work. In our designs, we *try to* 328 ↙ *design the details* so as to show what they do, and to make them an integral part of the structure as a whole rather than serving as merely ornamental accessories, or purely to conceal things. Ultimately, this aspiration lays the foundation for efficient and perennially durable—and therefore sustainable—supporting structures, and it is clearly evident in every field that we work in, especially in stadium construction, where very large spans are involved. We can certainly look back on a wide repertoire of such buildings. Each one has left us richer in experience and able to make a more valuable contribution to architectural brainstorming sessions.

All around the world, every day, new stadia are being built and existing ones altered. We have been involved in projects like these since our early years. In addition to radical changes in the functions expected of a stadium over the decades, significant advances have been made on the structural side as well. For the 1974 World Cup, stadium roofs were still being designed as cantilevers with radial axes and a structural system that did not have a spatial character, but nowadays the majority of designs are lightweight and translucent, transferring loads spatially. The use of novel materials makes it possible to exploit the potential of efficient structural systems to the full.

For me, elegance means effortless beauty.
Basically, of course, every process is strenuous to begin with.
But if all this effort is no longer visible in the result,
then we have achieved our goal. Mike Schlaich

The spoked wheel in lightweight construction

Many of our stadium roofs exploit the spoked wheel as a structural principle. It is one of the most efficient systems, so it is not surprising that it has been applied to the construction of wide-span roofs.

Together with gmp · von Gerkan, Marg and Partners Architects, we designed a canopy using the spoked-wheel principle for the **FK Krasnodar Stadium,** which was used as a training facility during the 2018 FIFA World Cup in Russia. Despite the need to allow for heavy earthquake and snow loads in southern Russia, between the Black Sea and the Caspian Sea, this new stadium—the first of its kind in Russia—has a lightweight roof, contributing to its elegant, classical aura.

In principle, the structure here works with two uncoupled, concentric outer rings as the wheel's rims in the facade plane, and one inner ring as its hub (tension ring) over the pitch. Tension cables spanning between the rings serve as the spokes, and prestressing the cables turns the rim into a compression ring. The internal tensile and compressive forces were fine-tuned with great precision during assembly in order to distribute them evenly and optimally in the rings, thus producing a stable system. Additionally, the upper compression ring has a sliding pendulum bearing, which can compensate for large horizontal displacement in the event of an earthquake. Finally, the construction of the roof in two layers creates an intermediate space that accommodates all of the technical equipment, including gas heating for the comfort of the spectators. This cable-ring roof, covered with a membrane, is a highly stable structure that can withstand very high wind and snow loads, as can any other roof created according to this principle. For example, in 1993, our practice devised a lightweight cable-ring structure of this type for the Gottlieb Daimler Stadium in Stuttgart (now the Mercedes-Benz Arena). It was the first of its kind.

AR

In 2017, the existing **Wanda Metropolitano Stadium** was given a roof on the spoked-wheel principle. It was being upgraded as the new home of Atlético de Madrid football club. Originally an athletics stadium, it was built in 1994 to a design by Cruz y Ortiz architects. Beginning in 2011, the same architects had converted it for sole use as a football stadium with a covered seating capacity of more than 67,700.

The entire new roof—the steel structure, the cable structure, and the membrane structure—were completed within a short construction period of about one year. It is notable for the use of two tension and two compression rings with a pleated membrane between them and it is unique in the geometric arrangement of the tensioning cables. They cross in the vertical plane towards the center of the membrane, creating an eye-catching, folded surface.

On the outside of the stadium, a third chord complements the two compression rings to form a triangular truss, bearing on the columns of the vertical facade, which extends outwards over the existing main grandstand and supports the cantilevered exterior canopy. This canopy is constructed of radial truss girders, with membranes spanning between the chords. Seen from the stadium approaches, they give the impression of a lightweight blanket, flowing over the existing structure and the grandstands of various heights. As an extra touch, the 46,000-m² PTFE/glass membrane surface can be backlit in various colors in response to the action on the pitch.

On this project, the reduction in weight offered by a spoked-wheel, lightweight structure played an important role. The big advantage of the cable-ring roof is that it is a self-contained structural system. The structure balances the forces internally and transfers almost exclusively vertical bearing forces to the substructure. This was the only solution that would enable the existing building to absorb the additional loads from a roof, thanks to its weight of only 6,300 t. The more dead load a roof imposes, the less loading capacity remains for the other loads that must be allowed for.

The courage, proficiency, and confidence that we are able to invest in such roof structures, thanks to our experience, ultimately benefits everybody involved in the construction work. The stadium upgrade owes much to the principle of lightweight construction, which is the key to this wide-span roof above the 248-×-286-m stadium bowl.

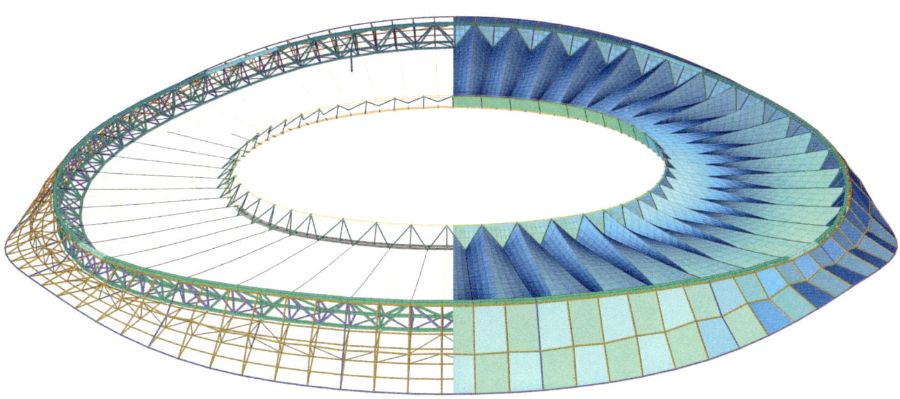

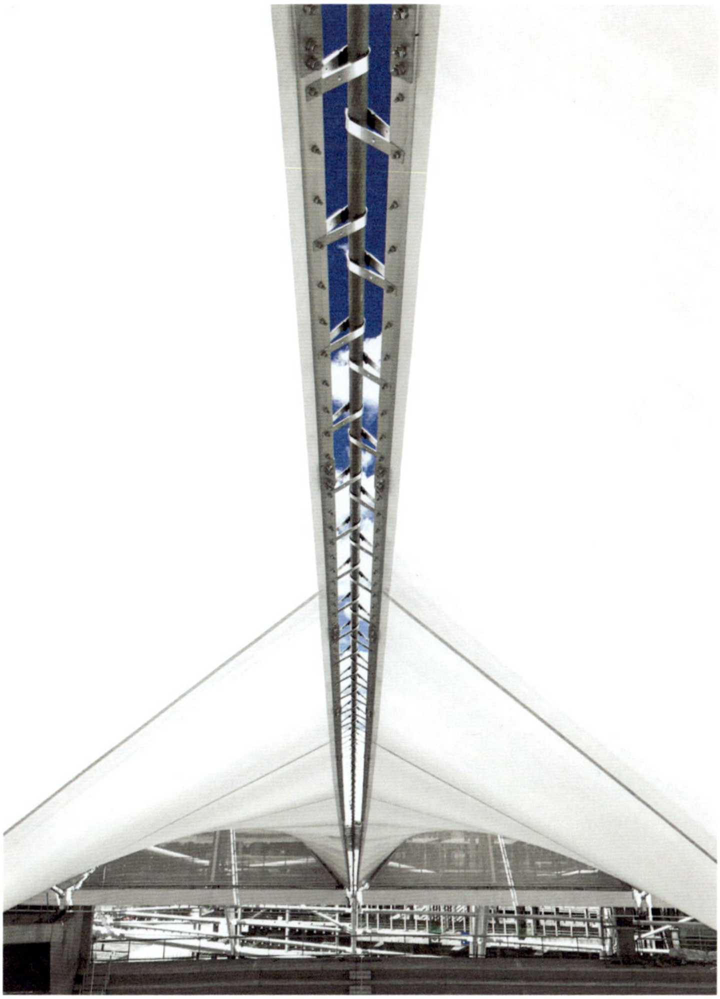

MADRID
HAZTE SOCIO NO ABONADO POR TAN SÓLO 50€
atleticodemadrid.com
CONTAMOS CONTIGO
万达WANDA
bwin
Mahou
Plus500
renfe

HAZTE SOCIO NO ABONADO POR TAN SÓLO 50€

Metro
Estadio Metropolitano
Metro

ATLÉTICO DE MADRID
1903

The cable-ring roof for the **Tottenham Hotspur Stadium,** which we designed together with POPULOUS and BuroHappold, is a unique project with a novel cable-ring roof. These sophisticated structures are more efficient and more economical than conventional cantilevered canopies of comparable dimensions, because the ratio of dead load to imposed and environmental loads is more favorable than it is with other systems.

Here too, the cable-ring roof is a transformation of the spoked wheel, which typically is stressed within its plane for transferring loads perpendicular to the spoked-wheel plane. Between the two (in this case) tension rings and the compression ring, there is a wide-meshed, radial cable structure with steel sandwich cassettes as a secondary structure. These cassettes prevent the potential instability of the paired tensioning cables acting as prestressed beams.

The outer compression ring, supported by the primary columns of the grandstand structure, is connected to the tension rings by pairs of radial cables; the upper radial cables connect with the upper tension ring, the lower ones with the lower tension ring. Attached to a point on the compression ring, each pair of cables diverges as it approaches the tension ring, with the cables being connected and kept apart by five flying columns. The tension rings, which are likewise connected to each other via flying columns and are cross-braced, also serve as a rigid bearing for the glass roof, which is cantilevered for up to 20 m. This shelters the foremost seats while allowing enough daylight to fall onto the pitch and the surrounding areas. It is float-mounted on steel girders, which in turn are supported by steel struts. This translucent inner ring promotes turf growth and visually enlarges the central aperture above the pitch, making the entire space feel more open.

In addition, the pair of tension rings supports a spectacular event space: the Sky Bridge on the north side. This is a steel structure with floor-to-ceiling glazing where it faces the pitch, offering both a close-up view of the roof and a bird's-eye view of the game. A similarly spectacular experience can be had above the roof on the south side. The Sky Walk, which spectators can walk along during the stadium tour, loops over the tension cables as far as the inner edge of the glass roof, allowing them to gaze out over London and peer down into "the cathedral of football."

In most places, the supporting structure transfers the loads in the facade area directly via primary columns into the subsoil, but on the southern side of the stadium a special buttressing structure has been added. Here, the loads from the stand and the roof are transferred down two visually striking columns, branched like a tree. The result is an expansive, welcoming entrance area. This arrangement reflects a skillful channeling of the play of forces and deformation that spoked-wheel structures are capable of handling. Such structures are characterized by the fact that they are able to react to loads by deforming. Changing temperatures and wind loads may cause the roof structure to move horizontally by a number of decimeters; vertically, the deformation at the center of the roof may be as much as a meter, or even more in exceptional cases. Deformation can be initiated by large wind or hail loads pushing the structure down, or wind uplift forces acting in the opposite direction. Potential deformations of the structure must be carefully considered and allowed for with careful detailing.

Cast-steel cable-net nodes

1 Concept Sketches

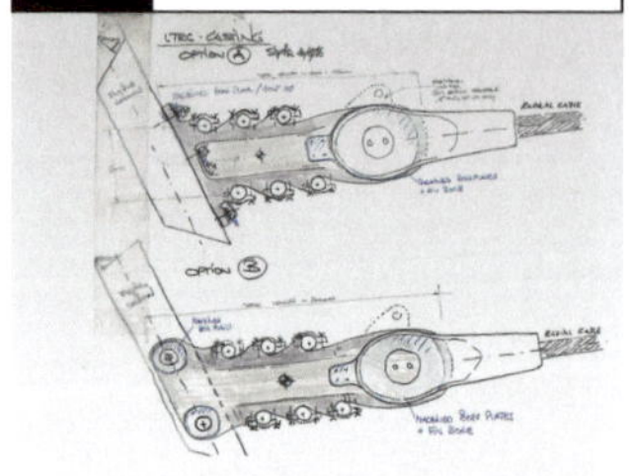

- First drafts regarding dimensions, numbers, and intervals of cables as well as the spacing of the cable-net bundles; connection of flying struts and other adjoining structural components; dimensions and spacing of the radial cables
- Hand sketching and dimensioning

2 Structural Analysis

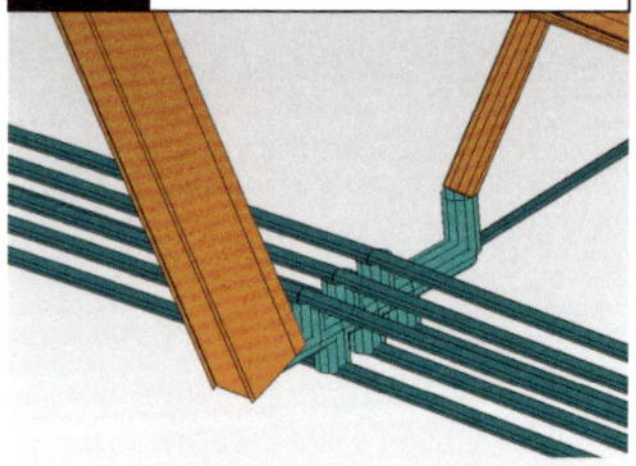

- Determination of loads on the cable nodes via a global computer model, considering eccentricities and the position of the system line

3 Geometrical Parameters

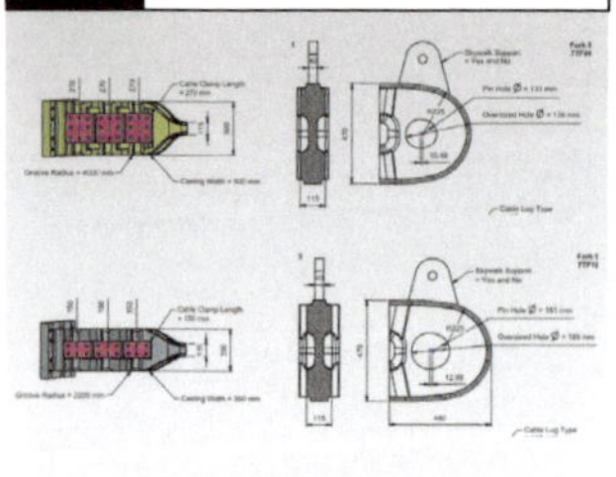

- Grouping of the nodes regarding similar geometric constraints and, corresponding to the occurring loads, deviation angles and tangential forces
- Specification of required numbers of different grooves and rope lugs

4 System Design

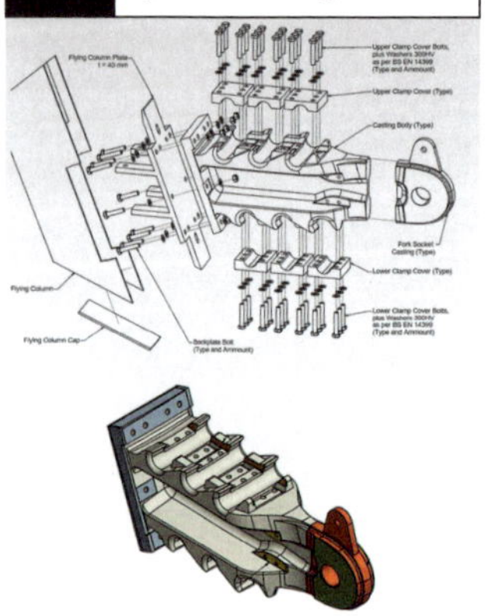

- Determination of system and load-bearing principle of the individual components of the node as well as of the connections to adjoining structural components
- System of production and assembly

5 Modeling

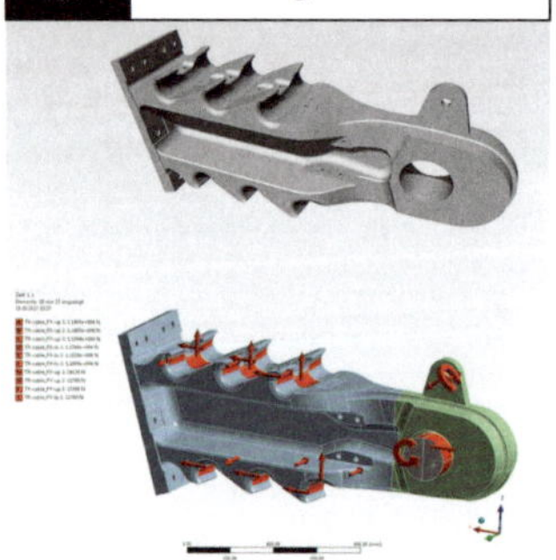

- Parametric modeling, forming optimization for minimal notches and a form suitable for casting
- Material distribution and wall thicknesses suitable for casting

6 Detail Design

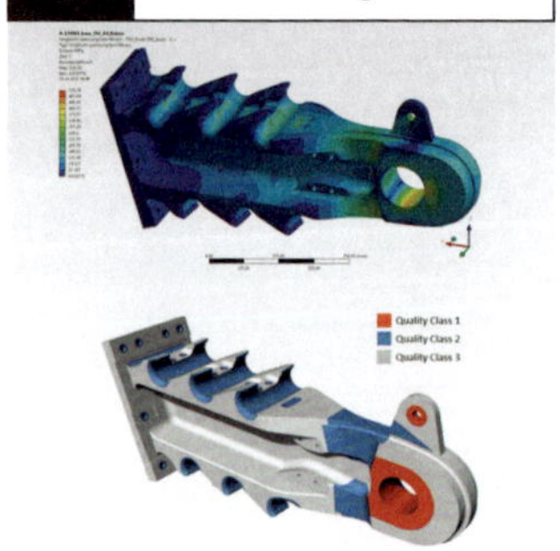

- Determining of the utilization, optimization of the distribution of stress, verification of the load-bearing capacity
- Specification of the required material quality levels

12 Serial Production

- Serial production of cast bodies (top) and mechanical finishing (bottom)

11 Quality of Materials

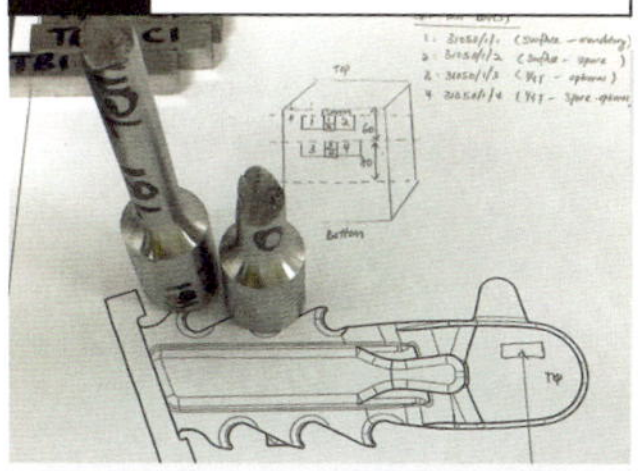

- Destructive testing of a structural component, removal of specimens at locations of high stress and at locations with assumed discontinuities
- Determination of strength and toughness of samples

10 Geometry

- Checking the dimensional accuracy of the casting; uniformity and shape of the cable grooves, spacing of the system points

7 Solidification Analysis

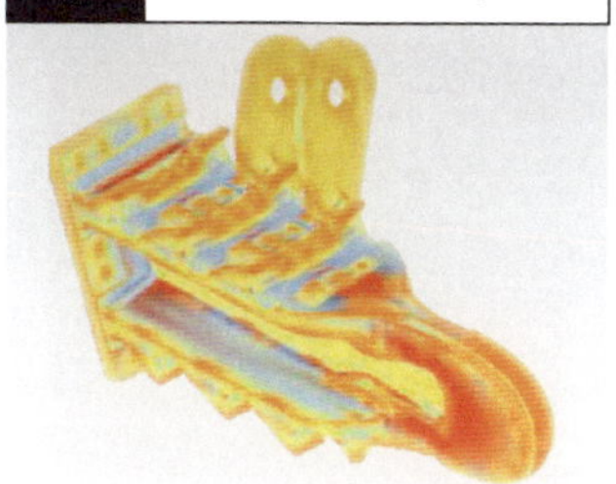

- Analysis of the casting process of the flow velocities during the filling of the mold
- Analysis of the solidification process with prediction of the expected quality levels
- Planning of quenching and tempering as well as heat treatment

8 Casting Mold

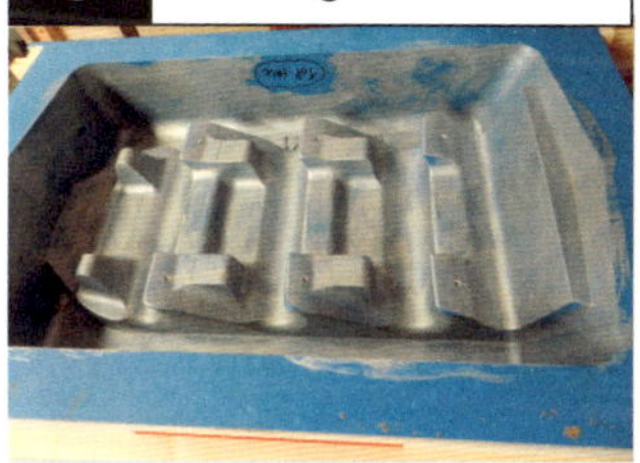

- Production of the positive mold from wood
- Making of the mold from molding sand

9 Manufacture

- Casting, cooling, removal of risers and gates, heat treatment

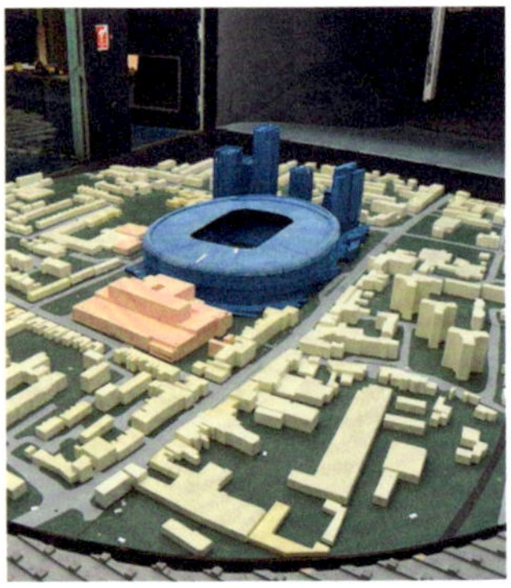

Suzhou is known throughout China for its parks and gardens, some of which have had the status of a UNESCO World Heritage Site since 1997. This tradition of Chinese gardening is continued in the master plan for **Suzhou Sports Center,** which stands among generous green spaces that are freely accessible to the public. With countless residential developments nearby, the park is naturally popular as a recreational area. The complex, which we planned jointly with gmp · von Gerkan, Marg and Partners Architects, was completed in 2018. It consists of three separate buildings: a multipurpose stadium with an integrated athletics track, able to hold up to 45,000 spectators; an indoor pool for 3,000 spectators; and a multipurpose hall for up to 15,000 spectators. The complex also includes a shopping center and numerous outdoor playing fields. In addition to the competition and training pools, the swimming pool building contains a spa area and a leisure pool complex. The plinths of the stadium and the swimming pool building accommodate additional areas for recreational sports such as tennis, table tennis, billiards, basketball, volleyball, and bouldering, among others. They are supplemented by shops on the ground floors opening onto the park.

All three oval buildings have flowing, curved contours, alluding to traditional Chinese pavilion architecture. The open roof of the sports stadium is constructed as a single-layer cable-net structure with a membrane covering and axial diameters of 260 m and 230 m.

The inner tension ring of the roof comprises eight cables. Forty separate radial cables connect it to the outer compression ring. This rises and falls through a vertical range of 25 m as it follows the outer contour of the stadium bowl, thus creating a structurally effective saddle surface, which allows the cable-ring roof to be constructed as a single layer. The system as a whole rests on paired diagonal columns, which also incline outwards at up to 35° from the vertical as they follow the dynamic sweep of the roof.

The roof of the swimming pool, which has a nearly circular floor plan about 107 m in diameter, is designed as a single-layer, double-curved cable net. This undulating roof rests likewise on inclined columns. The prestressed cable net, consisting of pairs of cables arranged at right angles to each other, has a mesh size of about 3,300 mm. The mesh panels are covered with trapezoidal sheet metal cassettes.

The multipurpose hall has a similar geometric form, but the roof structure is a grid of steel trussed girders. Here too, paired diagonal columns support the roof—both structurally and formally. On the outside, the facades are clad with continuous horizontal louvers in a sweeping arrangement that follows the undulations. These strips also clad the facades at plinth level, thus giving all of the buildings a degree of visual unity.

3

240

These three roofs in China show that our repertoire of geometric shapes and structural forms is far from exhausted. The same applies to other roof structures, be they classic cantilevers, membrane shells, or (curved) grids.

The extensive redevelopment of **Camp Nou,** the home of FC Barcelona, was the subject of an architectural competition, won by the Japanese firm Nikken Sekkei. The stadium itself, with a huge seating capacity of 105,000, is due for completion in 2022. The unusual aspect of this competition was that we had analyzed different structural variants for the stadium roof beforehand, on behalf of the organizers. The competition entrants were allowed to use these as given in their own designs, or to take them as a basis for their own ideas. The architectural concept chosen by the jury was

based on one of our variants. Consequently, a membrane and cable-ring roof with a transparent inner roof will soon grace the existing building, which dates from 1957. As specialists for such structures, we were commissioned with the further planning and realization of the roof structure.

In fact, the stadium has been altered three times before: a third tier of grandstand seating was added for the 1982 World Cup, the club's museum was built in 1984, and the first tier was renovated in 1994. The current proposed alterations, including the roof, will be the building's most extensive makeover so far. The roof's supporting structure, with main spans of 280 m and 240 m, consists of a cable net in a two-layer variant with three tension rings and a compression ring, which is supported eccentrically on columns.

The two-layer configuration permits a relatively flat construction, despite a large horizontal roof depth of almost 80 m. This makes it possible to stay below the maximum building height specified by the city's planning authority and yet to maximize the field of view for the spectators inside.

The various loads that need to be allowed for are transferred from the roof into the subsoil via slender pier walls. These are restrained at their one-third points by the floor slabs. Each level opens to the outdoors; as a tourist attraction situated in a hot Mediterranean climate, the stadium features circulation spaces with a character like Barcelona's famous "Ramblas". Visitors are greeted not by a forbidding, high-walled block but by an inviting series of open spaces full of activity.

Having designed and completed more than fifty stadia, we have developed considerable structural expertise and specialized construction experience. It is from this reservoir that we draw our drive to innovate for minimal weight and high energy efficiency on future projects. Knut Göppert

Like the spoked wheel at the new Camp Nou, the classic spatial girder grid was the original source of inspiration for the new **Palau Blaugrana** sports complex. Designed by HOK with a local practice, TAC Arquitecte, this multipurpose arena will hold 12,000 spectators. Taking shape on the plot adjoining the new Camp Nou, the trussed girders of the roof are laid out on a square grid of 8 × 8 m. This bidirectional load transfer was the only real solution for achieving the two desired cantilevers: the rising roof above the main entrance, spanning 56 m; and the 14-m overhang above the terraces on the opposite side of the oval roof.

Diversity in uniformity

The spectacular roofs of the stadia—be they part of a sophisticated modernization or a challenging new build—combine the highest standards of structural safety, durability, urban integration, functionality, fire safety, and, of course, sustainability with regard to the construction. When a structure successfully meets these specific requirements, it is not only engineers and architects who take notice. These qualities are also perceived by laypeople, especially in the field of stadium construction, if the structures become part of the overall design and the architectural genius loci.

Notwithstanding the diversity of people, projects, and cultures that we encounter and come together with in the course of our work, we live our values in a way that creates unity. The engineering structures that we develop may well be carried out in different contexts, but they live up to our standards nevertheless. In that sense, the design for Chelsea FC's home **Stamford Bridge Stadium,** although currently on hold as a scheme, represents a continuation of the many and varied stadia that we completed before it. Chelsea FC intends to replace the old stadium at Stamford Bridge, in Fulham in southwest London, with a new one, designed by HERZOG & DE MEURON ARCHITECTS, which would increase seating capacity to 60,000. The exterior contours are generated on all sides by a rhythmic array of radial masonry ribs: 264 brick-faced pillars, alternating in width. They support a ring-beam roof that covers the grandstands.

Also unbuilt as yet is the **Forest Green Rovers stadium.** The design is the result of an international design competition, which we entered and won together with Zaha Hadid Architects. The stadium is to be built as part of the Eco Park Development Project, a 40-ha, sustainable sports-and-technology park planned near Stroud in southwest England. Forest Green Rovers is a regional club, playing only in the fourth league in England, but its owner is a green-energy entrepreneur who follows sustainable principles. The brief naturally stipulated that the structure should be eco-friendly. The design has an organic aesthetic generated by a rhythmic *wooden frame,* which is covered by a transparent, prestressed membrane on the roof and the upper parts of the facade. The glulam beams are dimensioned with large cross sections and produced with a taper where it makes sense statically and aesthetically. Regardless of the fact that it has not yet been implemented—like the stadium at Stamford Bridge—the two projects have already been seen as an enrichment of architectural tradition and a source of inspiration for other projects, especially, in Forest Green Rovers' case, when it comes to the use of wood in sports facilities.

↘ 24

From detour to destination

Over the years, we have learned to take an optimistic view of whether the designs that we are commissioned to work on can be built. Even if it is not clear how to do so at the start of the engineering planning, we don't question whether it can be done. Any doubts ought to be dispelled by our many successfully completed projects, which give us reason to believe that if we keep moving forward and are not afraid to explore detours, we will arrive at a place that becomes our destination.

Many a first idea—be it ours, the builder's, or the architect's—is discarded to begin with, or is modified again and again. Planning loops of this kind are in fact of great value because they hone the reasoning and thereby consolidate the concept. Another reason to be optimistic about mastering the ever-growing variety of challenges is the broad international base that we enjoy, *with employees from many countries.* We encounter different cultures, approaches, specialisms, and characters daily. We see all this as a great opportunity to create a working atmosphere that promotes our values. After all, that's how we can best ensure that project ideas are actually realized.

↘ 346

For that, you need courage—the courage of your convictions, which we try to preserve on every project and which we consciously promote in our teamwork.

The development or improvement of novel membrane materials for stadia is one area that needs the kinds of iterative design process mentioned above. Textile membranes, for example, usually consist of a conventional fabric. In order to protect them against environmental influences and to make them watertight, a surface layer is applied to them. As a result of this coating, however, they often lose their visual and tactile character as textiles. If you explicitly want to preserve this character, you need innovative approaches. We have tackled this challenge because the visual and tactile qualities of a woven texture, combined, for example, with a traditional pattern and colors that evoke a particular identity, may sometimes be a key design parameter for buildings that use membranes.

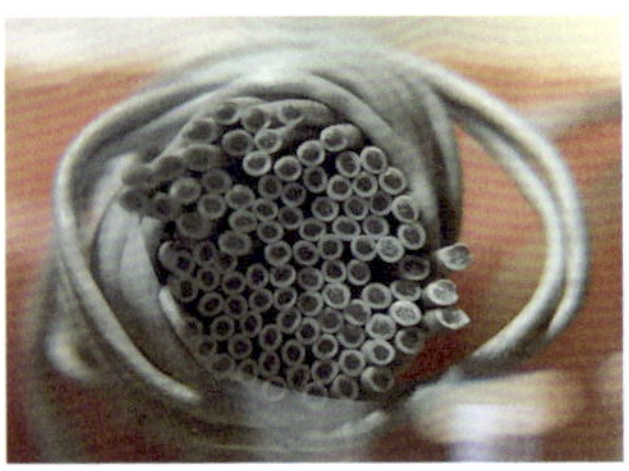

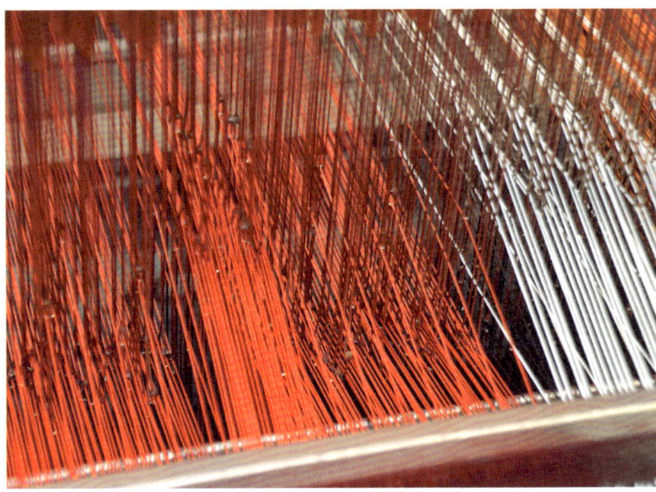

Together with Serge Ferrari, we have developed a membrane in which every single polyester thread is directly coated in the desired color with a PVC extrusion that shields it from UV radiation, and then used to create fabric woven on a Jacquard loom. The actual task was to develop a material whose appearance is reminiscent of traditional Bedouin tent fabrics, while satisfying the requirements for the durability and robustness of a membrane for use on a large scale.

Capable of many different patterns, this new fabric opens up completely new possibilities for designers. The membrane retains a recognizably textile character while promising high durability and color stability, unlike the printed alternatives. Furthermore, the material and surface properties lend the membrane good acoustic properties, so that the reverberation time limits specified for the design of a stadium, for example, can be observed without taking additional measures. In order to stabilize the fabric, which after weaving is still loose and thus cannot be cut accurately to the desired size and shape, the warp and weft threads are heat-set in a separate process, without melting and losing the fabric structure. In these specially woven, patterned membranes, the mechanical properties of the material may differ between the warp and the weft as well as varying at different places in one direction. This creates local variations in stiffness and uneven stress distribution within the fabric, making exceptional demands of the dimensioning and tailoring. In addition, the membranes have to be robust and durable in order to withstand extreme climatic conditions, including temperatures of over 50 °C. Since the material strength and weld strength of PVC-coated polyester membranes declines at high temperatures, this factor had to be taken into account when choosing a suitable material and during the technical development.

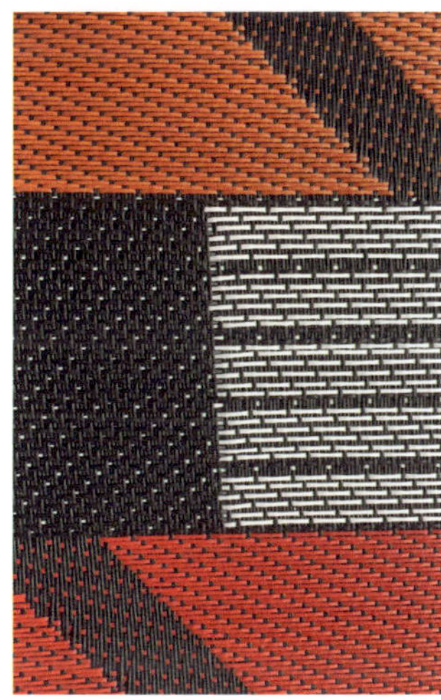

In order to quantify the respective influences, we performed both uniaxial and biaxial tensile tests. In addition to this, experiments took place to determine behavior in fires. These membranes are meant to satisfy specific fire safety and acoustic performance requirements so that they can be installed, for example, as a sub-membrane, without failing to get fire department approval or making reverberation times unacceptably long. Attached to the bottom chords of a roof's supporting structure, they could also conceal the often-numerous installations located within it.

We spent a great deal of time trying out various manufacturing processes and testing different materials before getting the finished prototype into production. Our efforts have unlocked new design potential. Due in no small part to their open working method, the interdisciplinary team of engineers, architects, and manufacturer's specialists that was entrusted with the task managed to create a membrane that met all of the necessary requirements. This demonstrates that innovative thinking, together with third-party expertise, can even lead to the development of wholly new materials, which in this case will eventually generate a variety of new applications in roofing and facade construction.

In keeping with the idea that the art of building cannot be divided into various parts, we do not split the process of building—which extends from concept to construction—into an architectural part, a structural engineering part, and a construction part. The same applies to the disciplines of architecture and engineering: they should work with one another from an early stage in the project and as equals. Only through this kind of interwoven cooperation can the creative potential required for good buildings be achieved.

One example of such cooperation is our relationship with gmp · von Gerkan, Marg and Partners Architects, which is very much a dialogue between equal partners. It all began with a project in the 1980s—the *roofing-over of an internal courtyard at the Museum for Hamburg History*—and has continued over 150 joint, often prize-winning, projects, including many in China.

26 ↙

Layer 05

Partnerships

Long-term partnerships like this, be it multidisciplinary commissions from clients or intensive cooperation with companies such as the rope-and-lifting-technology manufacturer Pfeifer, provide ample evidence that our way of working is greatly valued. In the case of Pfeifer, with whom we have been cooperating successfully since the 1980s, we have completed over forty projects, including many prestigious stadiums in Germany and abroad. These partnerships exemplify the quality of the cooperative work we look for from both parties. They highlight the special mutual appreciation the parties show for the work of the other. Appreciation means respect and interest for that which we can all produce together. Getting this kind of relationship to work is not always easy, because our partner must have the confidence to trust us.

There are no well-trodden paths to follow in our business. We work logically and doggedly toward the goal of a unique solution. Architects and clients can sometimes see this as complicated and involving a lot of work, but many examples show that it pays off for both sides. For instance, we were engaged as a long-term partner of Deutsche Messe AG to design a continuous series of projects for the **Hanover Fairground,** including many exhibition halls and visitor-access bridges on the Expo 2000 site. More than ten structures have been built there since the early 1990s.

Because our office has such a long history on which to reflect, there are a number of projects in which we have participated in more than one intervention over time, as the client for a building or bridge project has recommissioned us for later conversions or extensions. The **Mercedes-Benz Arena** in Stuttgart provides a good example of this type of commission. Over the last twenty-five years, we have been involved five times in various redesigns of parts of the stadium. We were called upon for the first time when the original 1933 stadium required a modernization for the World Athletics Championships in 1993. For this project, the spectator stands around the arena, which continued to be used for live sports events in the meantime, were covered with one of the first cable-ring-and-membrane roofs for modern sports facilities. Seven years later, we were again in the design team when the 1960s-era main spectator stand was rebuilt and extended, and a reception building, a bridge over the adjoining road, and a parking garage were erected. We designed the stand on the opposite side of the pitch for the FIFA World Cup 2006, hosted by Germany. Just three years later, the stadium—again while continuing to operate—was converted into a dedicated football stadium with an integrated sports hall. In 2015, about twenty-five years after our first involvement, we were part of a scheduled project to upgrade the roof.

Our role was the design of the roof-membrane renewal, including a new corrosion protection system, improvements to the drainage, and modification of the lighting for the roof and the compression ring. These multiple commissions make us proud, and we take from them that clients appreciate our way of working.

Sometimes with these projects our own history catches up with us. This was the case with the **Olympic Stadium Roof** in Munich. Intimately woven into our company history, the lightweight cable-net structure has a special significance for us, as, almost fifty years ago, the progenitor of all lightweight structures in Germany was built here. The roof is one of the first large construction projects undertaken jointly by our two founders. In 2019, the condition of the whole roof and supporting elements had to be assessed in order to be able to continue maintenance of the listed structure. Working with the team from Feix Ingenieure, Munich, we were commissioned by the Munich municipal works organization to reanalyze and assess the condition of the whole roof construction and the anchorages.

We have also successfully renovated two more of Munich's membrane roofs with which Jörg Schlaich and Rudolf Bergermann were greatly involved as designers at the start of the 1970s: **the Olympic Hall** and **the Olympic Swimming Pool.** In both cases, we were able to maintain the balance between retaining and improving the structure: the existing fabric with its structural system was retained and its construction upgraded with modern materials and design methods.

Projects of this type allow the designers to reflect on their own work. This was the case with the **National Sports Complex Swimming Stadium** in Kuala Lumpur. Although the roof is now getting on in years, it is still in good structural condition. The stadium is part of several buildings that comprise the NSC, built for the 1998 Commonwealth Games. The swimming stadium's delicately proportioned membrane roof with an area of 7,500 m^2 protects spectators and athletes from solar radiation and tropical rainstorms. The striking 100-m-high mast, together with the edge supports and the suspension cables, forms the fixed point for the one-piece membrane skin. Suspended at twelve high points, the roof forms areas with opposing directions of principle curvature, which gives the roof its stiffness and characteristic shape. The nodes transferring the forces from the membrane to the suspension cables reflect the flow of forces and look like flowers. Here, as the membrane has to transfer higher forces, it is made up of radial sections incorporating higher-strength materials.

The swimming stadium, which was designed jointly with Weidleplan in 1997, was selected in 2017 as the venue for the Southeast Asian Games (SEA Games) and had to be refurbished. Nineteen years after the stadium was first brought into operation, we were commissioned with the renovation of the membrane. In addition to the replacement of the membrane, the client also required slight modifications, but in general the structural principle of the roofing concept was confirmed fit for purpose. New developments in the field of membrane modeling and precision-cutting techniques allowed the roof skin and details to be further optimized. The flower petals characterizing the design were retained; they structure and enrich the roof skin over the swimming pools. The close working relationships with the client and the contractor—then, like today—were crucial for the success of the project.

Continued involvement during the life cycle of a project increases our wealth of experience, and the synergies from the continual new knowledge gained on other projects lead to a steady accumulation of information about the behavior of our structures over the long term. All this effort is therefore not without self-interest, because we transfer experiences and new knowledge from planning, design, construction, and operation to existing structures and other ones yet to be built. The object is to create something new by further developing a tried-and-tested solution, a strategy from which all stakeholders in the construction of the project benefit and from which a client who commissions us multiple times on the same project profits.

Deutsche Bahn is another client for whom we have completed several challenging bridge projects. From this fruitful relationship, we were able to realize a set of general guidelines for the design of railway bridges with the Deutsche Bahn's Bridge Advisory Council in 2008. The **Aller Bridge** near Verden, built in 2015, is just one such successful structure designed in accordance with these guidelines. As the designers intended, the result unites several aesthetic and practical features in one bridge structure.

The bridge is notable for its appropriate use of materials and a design that represents the flow of forces. This structure, which has been designed to be durable and not susceptible to fatigue, not only has load-bearing and sound-dampening webs, but it also fits into the sensitive landscape of the Aller valley. The replacement structure is a continuous girder with a main span of 80 m and headroom of 4.5 m. The positions of the new piers and abutments correspond with those of the previous bridge, albeit reduced in number from 18 to 7. This diffuses the solid-wall effect of the bridge against the background of the landscape. Plate girders connect to both sides of the steel deck plate, and their variable depth reflects the undulating shape of the bending moment envelope. The dimensions of the main girder webs and flanges, which act as the top and bottom chords, are also variable. The width and number of steel plate lamellae forming the top and bottom chords vary according to the span length.

A similar symbol for this fusion of technical and aesthetic qualities is the Grubental Bridge. It was built in 2013 on the new Ebensfeld–Erfurt high-speed rail link and is one of the first semi-integral prestressed concrete railway bridges in Germany. The 215-m-long bridge has a robust, double-webbed prestressed concrete beam superstructure, which is monolithically connected to the slender reinforced concrete piers over the 25-m-long approach spans. The bridge girder is furthermore monolithically connected—"merged"—to the crest of the strut-framed concrete arch, which is bridging the 90-m main span. The piers and the strut-framed arch are monolithically connected to the superstructure, which allows a minimal structural depth of 2.4 m to be adopted for the eight-span continuous beam deck. Sliding bearings support the deck at the abutments. The lower segments of the strut-framed arch, which is designed as a two-pinned arch with a pronounced apex, spread slightly as they approach the springing at the base of the pier. The apex of the arch is the fixed bearing point for the whole superstructure.

The main advantage of the semi-integral design is its low maintenance cost: there are fewer components at the abutments, inspection is made much easier, and construction costs are lower because there is no need for bearings. This form of construction also gives more design freedom: in spite of the low-deformation design necessary for a high-speed railway link, the bridge itself is quite slender. This more than justifies the higher design and detailing costs resulting from the integral construction, the additional approval processes, and the static and dynamic analyses.

The range of ideas—even those that are never built—is extremely broad thanks to the many and varied types of projects dealt with in our office over time. We bring all that we have learned with us into the design process; none of the potential of this knowledge is left to stagnate. Architects, clients, and employers who know how to use this potential and engage in this creative dialogue with us receive the best possible input for themselves and their project.

Through lively internal discussions between our experts, we also ensure the consistency of our collective knowledge across our many offices and the creative potential out of which the individual projects develop. The choice to retain our services over many years and projects requires long-term trust and confidence from our clients, which is of invaluable benefit to engineers and their work.

How do I design a structure so that I can identify with it? The structure must represent your personal objectives and values so that you feel you would want to connect with it. Andreas Keil

Our Offices and Projects Worldwide

Shanghai

Further Projects and Outlook

Transbay Transit Center, San Francisco (US)

The five-story bus-and-railway terminal is topped by a public landscaped park and enclosed in a double-curvature, glass-grid-shell skin. The grid shell is based on a quadrilateral mesh and is covered with flat glass panels.

Architect Pelli Clarke Pelli Architects, New Haven | **Client** Transbay Joint Powers Authority (TJPA), San Francisco | **Completion** 2017

Kunsthalle Mannheim, Mannheim (DE)

The extension building consists of stacked cubes. The cubes surround a glass-covered, 22-m-high marketplace and connect to one another by bridges. A fabric facade covers the building, and the rehabilitated, heritage-listed Athenetrakt building wing links the old with the new.

Architect gmp · von Gerkan, Marg and Partners Architects, Hamburg | **Client** Stiftung Kunsthalle Mannheim | **Completion** 2017

Xinzhou Mansion, Shanghai (CN)

The 170-m-long and up to 33-m-wide office building stands close to a major traffic junction. It is a four-story glass volume with a reinforced concrete load-bearing structure resting like a bridge on two massive concrete piers. The building represents a gateway in terms of urban design and allows use of the space below.

Architect gmp · von Gerkan, Marg and Partners Architects, Shanghai; SIMEE | **Client** Caohejing Hi-Tech Park Development Corp., Shanghai | **Completion** 2017

Louisiana Museum of Modern Art, Humlebæk (DK)

The ELEMENTAL architectural practice of the Pritzker Prize winner Alejandro Aravena portrayed their working methods and work philosophy in an exhibition in Humlebæk, Denmark. The studio curated and presented a collection of their most significant projects. We assisted with the structural engineering aspects of the extraordinary exhibition content.

Architect ELEMENTAL, Santiago de Chile, for the Louisiana Museum of Modern Art, Humlebæk | **Completion** 2019

Al Janoub Stadium, Al Wakrah (QA)

The stadium was built for the FIFA World Cup 2022 in Qatar and has a retractable membrane roof. The roof runs on 50 cables that connect alternately to the top and bottom chords of the main three-chord truss girder. The inner roof continues the folding pattern of the outer facade.

Architect Zaha Hadid Architects, London; AECOM, Los Angeles | **Client** Supreme Committee for Delivery and Legacy, Doha | **Completion** 2019

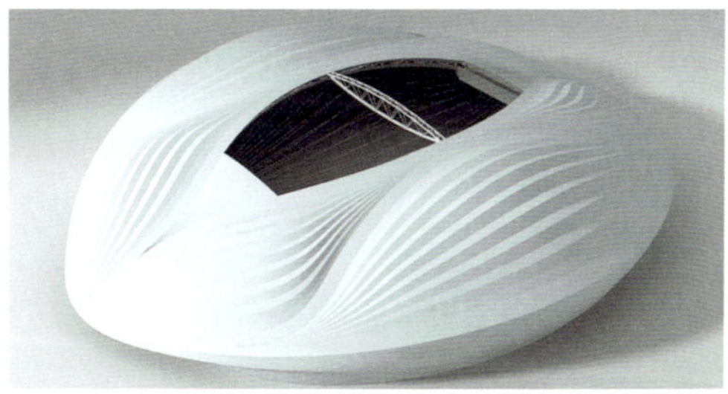

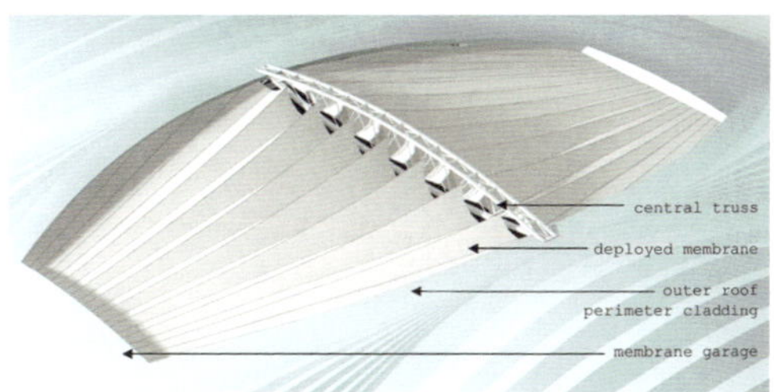

Waste-to-Energy Power Plant, Shenzhen (CN)

On an area of about 44,000 m^2, which makes up about two-thirds of the whole surface, the roof of the Waste-to-Energy Power Plant is covered with photovoltaic panels. The roof's supporting structure is based on 4-m-deep steel trusses spanning up to 60 m. Inclined trusses form a cost-efficient supporting substructure for the facade.

Architect Schmidt Hammer Lassen Architects, Aarhus | **Client** Shenzhen Energy Environmental Co. Ltd. (SEE) | **Completion** 2019

LGS Bridge, Ingolstadt (DE)

The 150-m-long pedestrian-and-cycle bridge is a semi-integral steel structure designed to act as a continuous girder. The legs of the slender Y-piers resolve into four steel plates on each side. Lighting units at the branching point of the Y make a feature of this detail at night.

Architect sbp | **Client** Landesgartenschau 2020 GmbH, Ingolstadt | **Completion** 2019

Kampmann Bridge, Essen (DE)

The Kampmann Bridge is a 173-m-long cable-stayed bridge with a single pair of pylons; a composite deck, which also forms the highway surface; and an integral reinforced concrete foreland bridge. Erecting the new bridge on a scaffold supported off the existing bearings of the old bridge did away with the need for a complex balanced-cantilever approach. The bridge is therefore not only elegant but also cost-effective.

Architect sbp; Breinlinger Ingenieure, Tuttlingen; eberhardt—die ingenieure gbr, Tecklenburg | **Client** Roads and Traffic Authority, Essen | **Completion** 2019

Asian Infrastructure Investment Bank (AIIB), Beijing (CN)

The AIIB was established to strengthen infrastructure provision along the Silk Road. The 300,000-m^2 building occupies a prominent position on the approach to the Beijing Olympic Park. The building, which was designed as a steel/steel composite structure, has very few columns. Generously sized rooms, terraces, and internal courtyards reinforce the spacious atmosphere of the offices.

Architect gmp · von Gerkan, Marg and Partners Architects, Beijing | **Client** AIIB, Beijing | **Completion** 2019

Parabolic Trough Power Plant, Urat, Inner Mongolia (CN)

The Parabolic Trough Power Plant is a 100-MW solar thermal power plant based on the EuroTrough collector. It consists of 352 loops, or 16,896 individual solar collector elements. The design was adapted to take into account the very high wind loads and the requirements of Chinese technical standards. In addition to the EuroTrough technology, we were also responsible for providing support, checking, and inspection during manufacture, assembly, and erection of the collector field.

Employer Royal Tech CSP Limited, China | **Engineering design partners** Walter, Remshalden (drawings), Wacker-Ingenieure, Birkenfeld (wind design certification) | **Client** China Shipbuilding New Power (CSNP), China | **Completion** 2020

German Pavilion Expo 2020, Dubai (AE)

The campus is an ensemble of steel frame boxes surrounded in a double-curvature grid shell. Three reinforced concrete cores stiffen the complex and pick up all the applied forces—completely in accordance with the Expo motto "Connecting Minds, Creating the Futur."

Architect LAVA Laboratory for Visionary Architecture | **Client** Bundesministerium für Wirtschaft und Energie (BMWi), Management: Kölnmesse | **Contractor** ARGE Deutscher Pavilion facts and fiction GmbH/NUSSLI Adunic AG | **Completion** 2020

Inter-American Development Bank, Buenos Aires (AR)

The new headquarters is a building, bridge, and park. A three-span, room-height box girder consisting of longitudinal frames crosses railway tracks and a freeway to connect the formal with the informal city. It stands on four concrete towers, has a total length of 240 m, and offers 3,800 m² of office space and a linear park on the roof.

Architect ELEMENTAL, Santiago de Chile (Design); FJA, Buenos Aires (Execution)| **Client** Inter-American Development Bank, Washington DC | **Completion** 2020

Promenade Deck Erfurt, Erfurt (DE)

The pedestrian-and-cycle bridge is part of a planned extension of Erfurt's city center. The box-girder superstructure fans out in response to structural and traffic engineering objectives and other boundary conditions relating to this particular structure. The new bridge seeks to emphasize the quality of the urban space.

Architect DKFS Architects, London | **Client** Tiefbauamt Erfurt | **Completion** 2021

Nou Mestalla Valencia, Valencia (ES)

The existing reinforced concrete bowl with seating for 55,000 spectators is to have a suspended roof. Columns fabricated from concave hollow steel sections support the outer compression ring, from which steel girders cantilever inwards toward the playing area. The design was based on the spoked-wheel principle.

Architect Fenwick Iribarren Architekten, Madrid | **Client** Valencia Club de Fútbol | **Completion** 2021

DFB Academy, Frankfurt am Main (DE)

The elongated sports boulevard is a glazed, reinforced concrete structure. The folded roof consists of steel truss girders incorporating areas of transparent ETFE pillows.

Architect kadawittfeldarchitektur, Aachen | **Client** Deutscher Fussball-Bund e. V. (DFB) | **Completion** 2021

Road bridge on the A8 freeway, Stuttgart (DE)

An urban light-railway line with a bridge over the most heavily trafficked road in southern Germany is to be built to connect the airport, the trade fair center, and the new national-network railway station. An integral lattice-arch bridge with carbon suspenders and a free-standing steel arch with a main span of 105 m crosses all of the carriageways without any intermediate supports. To minimize disruption of traffic on the freeway, the arch was erected to one side of the road and launched longitudinally during an overnight closure.

Architect sbp | **Client** Stuttgarter Strassenbahnen AG (SSB AG) | **Completion** 2021

Quzhou Sports Center, Quzhou (CN)

The 700,000-m² sports campus has facilities for numerous sports and a science-and-technology museum, a hotel, and retail stores. The various attractions are integrated into a landscaped park with a range of artificial hills. The largest sports facility on the campus is a crater-shaped stadium with a translucent circular roof in the form of a steel structure.

Architect MAD Architects, Beijing | **Client** Quzhou West District Development Committee | **Completion** 2021

Instituto do Futuro, Sesi e Senai, Brazil (BR)

The Instituto do Futuro is a building complex designed to house the Brazilian industry association's innovation center. The main building consists of five connected cubes and has its own power plant. The steel composite structure allows long cantilevers and large areas of glass. All the roofs are capable of supporting foot traffic.

Architect Gustavo Penna, Belo Horizonte | **Client** CNI Confederação Nacional da Indústria, Brasília | **Completion** 2021

Pudong Stadium, Shanghai (CN)

The design of the stadium took its inspiration from a traditional Chinese porcelain bowl. This idea has been realized with a white, shimmering metal facade and a slightly domed roof. A special cable-ring roof with an internal compression ring and a tension ring below it was developed for the stadium. As a consequence, the roof geometry is not determined by the compression or the tension ring. Instead, its form tends much more to follow the flow of forces and is independent of the outer and inner edges of the roof.

Architect HPP, Shanghai | **Client** Shanghai Sports Bureau | **Completion** 2021

Institut de recherches Servier, Paris-Saclay (FR)

The science and technology campus of the pharmaceutical company Servier brings together all its internal research facilities. Six rectangular wings are arranged around a circular central building. The types of facade, which were developed specially for this building, include the first closed-cavity facade with an integrated mashrabiya in timber built in France and a double curtain wall facade extending over three stories manufactured out of thermally formed, laminated safety glass units.

Architect Wilmotte & Associés, Paris | **Client** Laboratoires Servier | **Completion** 2021

Wildpark Stadium Karlsruhe, Karlsruhe (DE)

The Y-shaped column facade surrounding the stadium gives the structure its striking appearance. The impressive 17-m-high columns are constructed from two precast concrete units. A centrally positioned shadow gap ensures the required plasticity. In the design, they act as ties to anchor the cantilever moment from the roof, while their high self-weight reduces the tensile force transmitted into and the balancing force required from the foundations.

Architect sbp together with agn Architekten, Ludwigsburg | **Client** City of Karlsruhe | **Completion** 2022

AR

Frankenwald Bridge, Landkreis Hof (DE)

Two suspension footbridges are to be built in the former border zone between Thuringia and Bavaria. The Lohbach Bridge, with its walkway suspended from a single pylon at one end only and curving in plan, spans 380 m from the Lichtenberg ruin (photo) to the ridge of the Drehkreuz Wildnis, from where the similarly curving Höllental Bridge crosses the wild, romantic Höllen valley in a single, world-record span of 1,000 m.

Architect Walch und Partner, Reutte | **Client** Landratsamt Hof | **Completion** 2022

Mendizorrotza Stadium, Vitoria-Gasteiz (ES)

Coincident with the plans to expand the seating capacity of the stadium from 20,000 to 32,000, it is to be given a 19,000-m² translucent membrane roof over the spectator stands. The structure supporting the roof was designed for the undulating spectator stand geometry and uses the spoked-wheel principle with one external compression ring and two tension rings.

Architect L35 Architects, Barcelona | **Client** Deportivo Alavés | **Completion** 2022

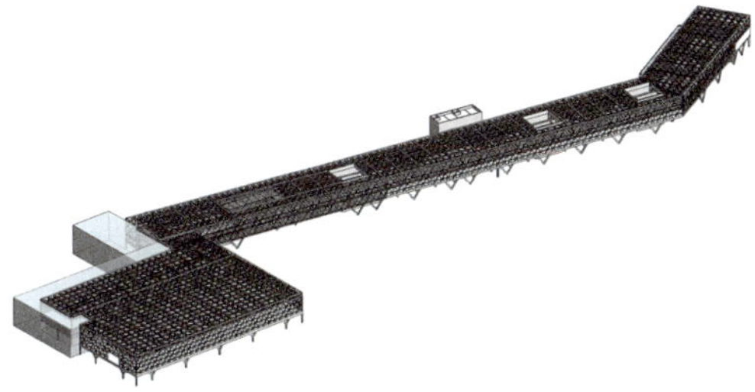

Nice Airport Extension, Nice (FR)

The extension divides into a large check-in hall and an elongated two-story building through which passengers walk directly before departure and immediately after arrival. Both buildings are of steel-timber construction with concrete cores designed to withstand high earthquake forces. The new extension is structurally independent of the existing buildings.

Architect Stéphane Aurel Architecture | **Airport planning** AMD Sigma | **Concrete structure, MEP, acoustics** TPFi | **Baggage handling system** Egis Avia | **Client** Aéroport de la Côte d'Azur | **Completion** 2022

Königsstuhl Footbridge, Sassnitz (DE)

Proposals for a new walkway access to the chalk cliff Königsstuhl (King's Chair) on the island of Rügen are based on a looped footbridge with an elliptical shape in plan. The bridge, a single-pylon suspension bridge, crosses the Königsgrab (King's Grave) in one 80-m span. The structure is designed to have minimal impact on the delicate natural environment of the national park.

Architect sbp | **Client** Nationalpark-Zentrum KÖNIGSSTUHL Sassnitz gGmbH | **Completion** 2022

AR

Kai Tak Sports Park, Hong Kong (CN)

The Kai Tak Sports Park is planned to be constructed on a 28-ha former airport site. The park will contain various sports and leisure facilities. When it is completed, it will be the largest sports park in Hong Kong. The main stadium, with a seating capacity of 50,000, will have a retractable roof and be suitable for all kinds of sports and major events.

Architect Populous | **Client** Home Affairs Bureau | **Design Build & Operate** Consortium Kai Tak Sports Park Limited | **Completion** 2023

Shanghai Grand Opera House, Shanghai (CN)

Working with Snøhetta and ECADI, we are planning the new Shanghai Grand Opera House. The shape of the building is intended to resemble a traditional Chinese fan. An important aspect of the design is the connection between the building and the surrounding park, which is emphasized by spacious entrance stairs leading onto the public roof. For the interior, the design envisages three halls—the largest being a 2,000-seat auditorium.

Architect Snøhetta, ECADI | **Client** People's Government of Shanghai Pudong New Area | **Completion** 2023

New lightweight roof on the Montreal Olympic Stadium, Montreal (CA)

AR

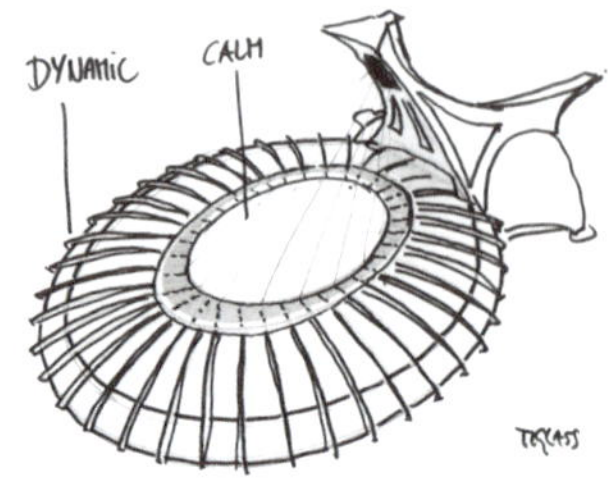

Since its opening in 1976, the Olympic Stadium has been a symbol of the city of Montreal. In addition to its function as a sports arena, the stadium is also used as a high-profile stage for concerts or state visits. The existing lightweight roof, however, had reached the end of its useful life and is now to be replaced by a new roof that not only will allow events all year round in the harsh climate conditions in Montreal, but will integrate itself completely into the unique architecture of the stadium.

Architect gmp · von Gerkan, Marg and Partners Architects, Berlin, Drawings Martin Glass | **Client** Parc Olympique Montréal | **Completion** 2024

Vast Project, Jemalong (AU)

The small faceted heliostat is based on an existing Vast design. The Vast Project involves the implementation and testing of a small pilot plant with a specially developed sodium receiver on a site at Jemalong, Australia. Following successful verification of the new design, it is intended to be used in a 30-MW multitower power plant in Charleville.

Project partner and project developer Vast Solar, Sydney

Grand Dome Villebon, Villebon (FR)

Le Grand Dome sports center is to be brought back into use for the Olympic Games 2024 in Paris. The existing dome with a diameter of 80 m is to be enlarged and renovated. The venue will also be surrounded by a new, prestigious glazed facade supported by a timber diagrid frame.

Architect D&A, ATSP associate architect, ALTERNATIVE acoustician, INEX MEP, CYPRIUM économiste, SCENE EVOLUTION scenography, and ALTO STEP landscape design | **Client** Fédération Française de Judo | **Completion** 2024

Credits

↘ Page	↘ Copyright
Front cover	Andreas Deffner/Kris Provoost/ sbp/sbp/Knut Stockhusen/ Ingolf Pompe

Layer 01—Working Methods

11	Andreas Martin.com
13, bottom	sbp
13,16, background	Andreas Martin.com
16	Drawings: sbp employees

Building Construction—Cultural Buildings —Glass

26, 30, 40, 41, 43	Graphics/drawings: sbp
18	Sketches: sbp/Sven Plieninger
20, top left	sbp
20, top middle, bottom	Gabriele Glöckler Architektur
21, left	experimenta gGmbh
21, top right	sbp
21, bottom right	Roland Halbe
23, top	BIG – Bjarke Ingels Group
23, bottom	ELEMENTAL
24, left	sbp/David Sommer
24, right	Beauty & the Bit/Schmidt Hammer Lassen Architects
25	bloomimages
26, top left	Klaus Frahm
27	Jan Bitter
29	sbp
30, top	authorized by the company 苏州恒泰控股集团有限公司
30, left, 32, 35	sbp
34, 36	authorized by the company 苏州恒泰控股集团有限公司
38	Christian Gahl
39	Jürgen Schmidt
40	sbp/Stephan Hollinger
41, top left	Michael Young
41, top right, bottom	sbp/Eoin Casserly
42, top left	sbp
42, top middle	Nordstrom Inc.
43, top	sbp

Layer 02—Internationality

50, 51	Graphics/drawings: sbp
46, 49	sbp
48	Roland Halbe
52–63	Andreas Deffner

Building Construction—Infrastructure —Special Purpose Structures

64, 68, 69, 79, 80	Graphics/drawings: sbp
66, 67	sbp
68, 70–73	Marcus Bredt
74, top left	Skidmore, Owings & Merril
74, middle left, bottom left, top right, bottom middle	sbp
76	Auer Weber Architekten
77	Marcus Bredt
78	Hanns Joosten
79	Tobias Hein
80	Michael Moser Images
81, top	Atelier LOIDL
81, bottom, 88	sbp
82–87	Michael Moser Images

Art

98, 121	Graphics/drawings: sbp
90	sbp/PrePost/Edward M. Segal/ Max Dowd
92–95	Antony Gormley/Photo Henning Rogge
96–99	Roman Mensing
100	Grit Schwerdtfeger, Lux Fotografen
102	sbp
102, bottom left	Grit Schwerdtfeger, Lux Fotografen
104–107	sbp/PrePost/Edward M. Segal/ Max Dowd
108	Estudio FAM
110–113	sbp
114–117	Enrico Fiorese
118	Photo: André Grossmann, © 2013 Christo
120, 122, 123	sbp

Building Construction—Towers

124, 127, 139	Graphics/drawings: sbp
126, top	sbp
126, bottom	Roland Halbe
127–129	sbp
130–134	Conné van d'Grachten
135	sbp
136	LAVA Berlin
137	Sketches: sbp/Knut Stockhusen
138	sbp/Knut Stockhusen
141, top	sbp
141, bottom right	Gerhard Spangenberg Architekt
142	Michael Wolff
143	DIE WOHNKOMPANIE, Berlin

Layer 03—Checking

146	E2A Piet Eckert and Wim Eckert
149	BIG – Bjarke Ingels Group
151	sbp
153	Jakob Schoof

Bridges

157, 173, 175, 182	Graphics/drawings: sbp
154	Drawing: Andreas Keil
156, left	Graphical overview: Moniteurs
157–161	Conné van d'Grachten
159, bottom right	sbp
162	Graphical overview: Moniteurs
162, 163	sbp/David Sommer
164	Kris Provoost
165, top, 166	sbp
165, bottom	David Hannes Bumann
167	Ingolf Pompe
168	Burkhard Walther
169	Drawing: Andreas Keil
170	sbp/Michael Zimmermann
171	Drawing: sbp/Christiane Sander
172	sbp/Michael Zimmermann
173, bottom right	Stephan Falk/baubild
175–177	sbp/Michael Zimmermann
179, top right	sbp/Michael Zimmermann
179, bottom	Ingolf Pompe
180, top	Skidmore, Owings & Merril
180, middle left	sbp
180, bottom left	Michael Van Valkenburgh Associates
181, 182, 194	sbp
183	Christian von Holst

185–186	sbp/Michael Zimmermann
187	Ilulissa
187, bottom	Dietmar Feichtinger Architectes/Buzzo Spinelli Architecture
188	Ingolf Pompe
189, top left	sbp
189, top right	Ingolf Pompe
190	gmp · von Gerkan, Marg and Partners Architects
191	Dissing+Weitling architecture
193–197	Kris Provoost
198, top	sbp/Andreas Schnubel
198, left	sbp
199–205	wilfried-dechau.de
206, 207	sbp/Andreas Schnubel
208	sbp/David Sommer

Layer 04—Research

212, bottom	TU Berlin Fachgebiet Entwerfen und Konstruieren – Massivbau Prof. Mike Schlaich, Dirk Peissl
212	Thomas Robbin
215	sbp
216, 218, bottom	TU Berlin/Alexander Hückler
217, 218	Alexander-Blumhoff.com

Solar Energy

220, 223, 224, 228, 238, 239	Graphics: sbp sonne
222–225	sbp sonne
225, middle, bottom	sbp sonne/Gerhard Weinrebe
226	Infinia Corporation
228–231	sbp sonne
230	Timo Richert
233, top right	Filmfabrik Schwaben
233, middle right	sbp sonne
234	Graphic: Moniteurs
234, bottom	DLR Fotomedien
235	sbp sonne
236	Filmfabrik Schwaben
241	sbp sonne
241, bottom left	sbp sonne/Gerhard Weinrebe

Moveables

242–244, 247–248, 251, 254, 262, 266–268, 271–273, 276	Graphics/drawings: sbp
245, 250	gmp/a-promise
249, 246	sbp
252, top left	sbp
252	Marcus Bredt
253, top right	sbp
253	Section: National Stadium Planning Consortium Warsaw
255–257, 259	sbp
258, 260	Marcus Bredt
261, 262	planinghaus architekten bda/ Photo: Thomas Eicken
263, left	Transsolar
264, 265	sbp
266	AE7
268	James Carpenter Design Associates
269, top left	Drei Architekten
269, bottom left	Zooey Braun
270, 272, 273	Fia
274, 275, 277	gmp/L35/Ribas

Building Construction—Stadiums

285, 295, 296, 317	Graphics/drawings: sbp
278	sbp/Knut Stockhusen
280, 281	sbp
283	Marcus Bredt
284	FCC
286, 287, 290	sbp/Knut Stockhusen
288, 291	Luis Asin
292	sbp/Knut Stockhusen
294–301	sbp
302, 303	Kris Provoost
304–309	sbp/David Sommer
315, middle	FC Barcelona Santiago Garcés Villanueva
315	Model images: sbp
316	FC Barcelona Santiago Garcés Villanueva
317	HOK I TAK ARQUITECTES
318	Herzog & de Meuron
319	Zaha Hadid Architects
320–323	sbp

Layer 05—Partnerships

326, top	Swen Carlin
326, 329	sbp
329, middle	Erich Schwinge
330	sbp/David Sommer

Appendix

332	Moniteurs
334, top	Jason O'Rear
334, middle	HGEsch Photography
334, bottom	sbp/David Sommer
335, top	Kim Hansen/Lousiana Museum of Modern Art
335, middle	Zaha Hadid Architects
335, bottom	SHL Architects
336, top	sbp
336, middle	Andreas Kordt/City of Essen
336, bottom	sbp/David Sommer
337, top	sbp
337, middle top	LAVA
337, middle bottom	ELEMENTAL
337, bottom	DKFS Architects
338, top	sbp
338, middle	kadawittfeldarchitektur
338, bottom	GmasP Engineering & Architecture
339, top	MAD architects
339, middle	GPAA
339, bottom	HPP Architekten
340, top	Wilmotte & Associés
340, middle left	agnNiederberghaus & Partner GmbH
340, middle right	Landkreis Hof/sbp
340, bottom	L35 Arquitectos
341, top	Rendering: Stéphane Aurel Architecture, image: 3d Fabrique
341, middle right	sbp
341, middle left	KTSPL and Populous
341, bottom	MIR and Snøhetta
341, top	Martin Glass, gmp
342, middle	Vast Solar
342, bottom	D&A - BY - ENCORE
346	Andreas Martin.com
348	Annette Diehl
348, top left	Zooey Braun
348, top middle	Annette Diehl
348, top right	Zooey Braun
348, bottom left	Zooey Braun
348, bottom middle	Andreas Martin.com
348, bottom right	Annette Diehl
349–362	Andreas Martin.com

Our Worldwide Staff

Povilas Ambrasas
Jérémie Amsler
Sarah Arbes
Anna Lena Assel
Nada Babin
Melanie Bagi
Eden Bales
Markus Balz
Ron-Marten Behnke
Tilo Behrmann
Rudolf Bergermann
Dan Bergsagel
Horst Binz
Luiza Boechat
Evgeniya Borovleva
Nicolas Bouchet
Sam Bouten
Andreas Brodbeck
Camillo Bueno
Stephanie Büsch
Anne Burghartz
Uwe Burkhardt
Xu Cao
Juliana Carvalho Martins
Eoin Casserly
Andre Castro
Cui Chen
Wei Chen
Jorge Chenevey
Alexandra Cheng
Stefano Corciolani
Miriam Cuypers
Birgit Dephoff
Ria Dierichen
Hao Ding
Matteo Dini
Powell Draper
Simon Durand
Stefan Dziewas
Jannika Erichsen
Fernando Escamilla
Thomas Fackler
Lars Feller
Frauke Fluhr
Martin Frank
Konrad Freymann
Hansmartin Fritz
Manuel Fröhlich
Dmitrii Garin
Daniel Gebreiter
Enrique Goberna
Verena Göcke
Knut Göppert
Birgit Graupner
Carolin Groß
Fabian Gross
Sebastian Grotz
Jochen Gugeler
Sabrina Gutlederer
Dagmar Häfele
Sandra Hagenmayer
Lorenz Haspel
Matthias Heidt
Nadine Held
Robert Hellyer
Lukas Hennings
Michael Herrick
Stephan Hollinger
Gustavo Jacomini
Patrick Jagiella
Monika Jocher
Shawn Johnson
Stefan Justiz
Brinda Kakkad
Stefan Kammerer
Nikola Kardzhiev
Thomas Keck
Andreas Keil
Thomas Kemmler
Susanne Klauser
Bernd Klostermann
Andras Kovacs
Amal Kraiyem
Burkhard Krenn
Gustav Krieg
Christine Kritzer
Sebastian Krooß
Jens Kuhn
Anna Kulzer
Katharina Kunz
Matthias Längle
Willem Landman
Camille Lauras
Jack Lehrecke
Sebastian Linden
Dongyuan Liu
Ana Llinares
Giovanni Lunelli
Andrea Mangold
Cesar Mauricio Mantilla
Florian Markert
Brigitte Marquardt
Ludwig Meese
Moritz Meiselbach
Milton Méndez
Herminie Metzger
Tingjun Miao
Tim Michiels
Thomas Moschner
Jörg Mühlberger
Andreas Nägele
Sandra Niebling
Daniel Nieffer
Mathias Nier
Johanna Niescken
Pedro Nobrega
Martina Nunold
Christoph Paech
Matthias Peltz
Samo Pergarec
Andreas Pfadler
Roberto Piñol
Denis Piron
Sven Plieninger
Ulrike Plieninger
Jiangchang Qiao
Lisa Ramsburg
Martin Rettinger
Boris Reyher
Klaus-Jürgen Riffelmann
Bernd Ruhnke
Nicholas Rumsey-Hill
Alberto Sánchez Gómez
Christiane Sander
Miriam Sayeg
Frank Schaechner
Jürgen Schilling
Nicole Schillo
Jörg Schlaich
Mike Schlaich
Laura Schmidt
Andreas Schnubel
Vanessa Schönfelder
Thomas Schoknecht
Dieter Schorr
Julia Schuler
Axel Schweitzer
Miguel Serrano
Jiahua Shang
Frank Simon
Christine Smith
David Sollner
David Sommer
Michael Stein
Daniel Stiegler
Knut Stockhusen
Klaus Straub
Cornelia Striegan
Eva Sundermann
Stephanie Thurath
Benjamin Touraine
Daniel Tröndle
Chih-Bin Tseng
Rebecca Veit
Olga Wagner
Tobias Waldraff
Irena Walter
Jakob Weber
Gerhard Weinrebe
Monica Weisheit
Rüdiger Weitzmann
Philipp Wenger
Michael Werwigk
Mathias Widmayer
Philipp Wölm
Werner Wolfangel
Minya Xu
Wen Yin
Zengzhi Yu
Isabella Zerbe
Michael Zimmermann
Bernd Zwingmann

As of 08/2019

Partners

Knut Göppert
Dipl.-Ing.

Born in Triberg/Black Forest in 1961
Graduated from the University of Stuttgart
Joined schlaich bergermann partner in 1989

Partner since 1998
Managing Director

Andreas Keil
Dipl.-Ing.

Born in Stuttgart in 1958
Graduated from the University of Stuttgart
Joined schlaich bergermann partner in 1985

Partner since 1994
Managing Director

Sven Plieninger
Dipl.-Ing.

Born in Heilbronn in 1964
Graduated from the University of Stuttgart
Joined schlaich bergermann partner in 1991

Partner since 2000
Managing Director

Mike Schlaich
Prof. Dr. sc. techn.

Born in Cleveland, Ohio, USA, in 1960
Graduated and received doctorate from ETH Zurich
Joined schlaich bergermann partner in 1993
Professor at TU Berlin, Chair of Conceptual and Structural Design
Certified checking engineer for structural analysis

Partner since 1999
Managing Director

Knut Stockhusen
Dipl.-Ing.

Born in Waiblingen in 1974
Graduated from the University of Stuttgart
Joined schlaich bergermann partner in 2000

Partner since 2015
Managing Director

Michael Stein
Dipl.-Ing., Dipl.-Wirtsch.-Ing. (FH), P.E.

Born in Stuttgart in 1968
Graduated from University of Stuttgart (Civil Engineering) and AKAD University of Applied Sciences, Stuttgart (Industrial Engineering)
Joined schlaich bergermann partner in 1996

Managing Director of schlaich bergermann and partner lp, New York, since 2009

Making-of

#multilayered

AR

Talking to the author

#understand

Discussing the book's contents

#brainstorming

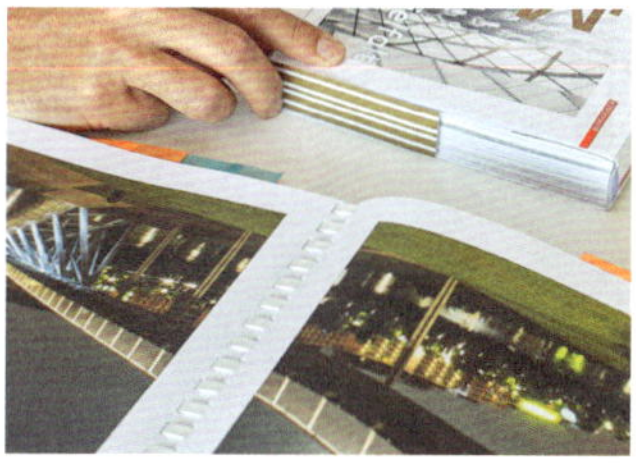

#implementing

Discussing possible layouts

#insidesbp